TAKEOVERS, ACQUISITIONS AND MERGERS

TAKEOVERS, ACQUISITIONS AND MERGERS

Strategies for Rescuing Companies in Distress

E A STALLWORTHY and **O P KHARBANDA**

KOGAN PAGE

First published in Great Britain in 1988
by Kogan Page Limited
120 Pentonville Road, London N1 9JN

Copyright © O.P. Kharbanda and E.A. Stallworthy 1988

British Library Cataloguing in Publication Data
Kharbanda, O.P.
   Takeovers, acquisitions and mergers :
   strategies for rescuing companies in
   distress.
   1. Consolidation and merger of corporations
   I. Title   II. Stallworthy, E.A.
   338.8'3   HD2746.5

ISBN 1-85091-459-1

Photoset in North Wales by
Derek Doyle & Associates, Mold, Clwyd.
Printed and bound in Great Britain by
Mackays Ltd, Chatham

All rights reserved. No part of this publication may be reproduced,
stored in a retrieval system or transmitted, in any form, or by any
means, electronic, mechanical, photocopying, recording or otherwise,
without the prior permission of the publishers.

Contents

Preface ix
Acknowledgements xi

PART ONE: IT'S A ROUGH ROAD

1 Going into Decline 3
  Why companies go into decline 3
  Managing success and failure 6
  How to avoid trouble 10

2 Meeting the Crisis 14
  The nature of the crisis 14
  Key questions 15
  The 'vulture' capitalists 17
  Annual reports and 'creative accounting' 19
  The crisis specialists 22

3 Strategies for Recovery 25
  A tailored strategy 25
  Is change of ownership the answer? 26
  Who applies the strategy? 27
  Takeovers 30
  Acquisitions 30
  The importance of communication 32

4 When Others Come to the Rescue 34
  The individual 34
  The company 36

PART TWO: ACQUISITIONS AND MERGERS

5 Motives and Methods 47
  Overview 470
  Policy considerations 48
  Signals for success 49

vi   **Contents**

    Acquisition: how to make it work   51
    UK government policy   52
    Acquisition and merger for the right reasons   54
    The shareholder's view   55

6 Merger Mania 57
    A frantic tempo   57
    Is it good business?   59
    Media mergers   60
    Food industry mergers   62
    Chemical industry mergers   64
    Synergy   65

7 The Megamergers 68
    What is a megamerger?   68
    The current trend   69
    Mergers past and present   71
    The year of the megabid   74
    The airline industry   75
    The Saatchi brothers   76

8 Success Amid Disaster 80
    How not to succeed   81
    'The decade's worst mergers'   82
    Successful mergers   84
    Cultural shock   85
    Successful mismatches   88
    Case studies   89
    The lessons   93

PART THREE: THE TAKEOVER SYNDROME

9 The Disease Spreads 97
    Takeovers as headline news   97
    Hostile takeovers   98
    A game without rules   99
    Raiders on the offensive   100

10 Who Takes Over Whom? 108
    The bankers always win   108
    A takeover triangle: Pennzoil, Getty Oil and Texaco   109

11 UK Takeover Battles 118
    The fight for Imperial   118
    Elders bids for Courage   121

    The Guinness saga   122
    The Westland victory   126

12 The Raiders   129
    Some definitions   129
    T Boone Pickens Jr   131
    Carl Icahn   133
    Irwin Jacobs   135
    Ivan Boesky   136
    The two 'Jims'   138

13 Takeovers Worldwide   140
    Japan   140
    Australia   147
    France   149
    The Commonwealth   151
    Takeovers elsewhere   152

PART FOUR: BUYOUTS: A STAKE IN SUCCESS

14 The Company Buyout   157
    A stake in the business   158
    Leadership and cooperation   159
    Involvement   162

15 Management Buyouts   167
    Background   167
    A new lease of life   170
    UK management buyouts   171

16 The Employee Buyout   176
    A real alternative?   176
    Ownership and control   180
    Problems and conflicts   181
    The impact of government intervention   183
    The John Lewis Partnership   184

PART FIVE: FINDING THE ANSWERS

17 Lessons from Case Analysis   189
    Acquisitions and mergers   189
    Merger and takeover fever   191
    A recipe for disaster   194

viii   **Contents**

18 Man Management   196
   The Japanese example   196
   'Corporate fat'   199
   Learning from the competition   200
   A profile for success   201
   Company culture   202
   Personnel selection   203

19 Is Change of Ownership the Answer?   205
   Restructuring   206
   Motivation   207
   Strategic fit   208
   Is Japan better?   209
   Conclusion   210

   Author Index   213
   Subject Index   215

Preface

The rescue and revival of companies in distress is an exciting subject. It is also a very challenging and vital job, not only for the companies concerned but also for the national economy. Decisive action is, unfortunately, rarely taken by the directors and managers of a company in distress; such action would be tantamount to an admission that their previous approach had been wrong. In this text we examine, by a study of a number of case histories worldwide, whether a change of ownership is the right or even a feasible answer to this problem.

The initial euphoria of a change of ownership soon comes to an end. In the excitement of acquisition or merger very real problems are swept out of sight, but once the partners settle down they become apparent. This is sometimes a nightmare, and can ultimately lead to divestment. In some cases success has been achieved, but more often the 'solution' only creates more problems. Why? Because the main motivation has been not the revitalisation of an ailing company, but the desire to build an 'empire' or to make a quick profit. It seems that human ego and greed are more often than not the driving force behind a change of ownership.

What, then, is the answer? Management is the key. Good management will ensure that a company is in good health, and will tackle and solve the problems that confront it, both within and without. We suggest that a change of ownership should always be accompanied by a change of management, although the degree of change will depend upon circumstances. Sometimes it is sufficient to change the chief executive. His replacement may well have to be tough, ruthless, take hard and even unpleasant decisions and ensure that they are implemented, but this is often the only way. There is, however, no single recipe or prescription for success. Every company is unique and a specific strategy has to be developed in each case. We highlight some of these strategies by taking specific examples and analysing their success or failure. Fortunately, many of these have been well documented in the economic, financial and management literature, bringing us a wide range of data and a valuable body of knowledge from which to learn.

One very positive contribution that the acquisition, merger and takeover mania of the past few years has made seems to have been largely overlooked. The very high failure rate of this route, involving change of ownership, has caused many companies to take a close look at themselves and set about their *own* restructuring to improve their efficiency and performance. Such restructuring may take many forms, such as downsizing, rationalising, or the streamlining of a bloated bureaucracy, but the end result should be a leaner but more efficient organisation. Unsuccessful takeover bids have not only driven threatened companies along this road, but also the 'acquiree', to use a word that seems to be coming into common usage in this context. Their own failure has caused them to look within to see what went wrong and why; they then apply the appropriate remedies and emerge fitter and stronger.

It is asserted throughout the book that management is primarily responsible for the health of its company. Good management should ensure that a company never goes into decline, but management is not an exact science and mistakes can be made. Others, particularly those on the outside looking in, can often see where things are going wrong long before those who are closely involved; but how much better it would be to recognise the necessary actions *before* others intervened. It is our sincere hope that the book will help our readers to learn from the experiences of others. To do this successfully we must first listen, then learn.

We hope that the references given at the end of each chapter will help those who are interested in a particular aspect of our subject to pursue further research.

O P Kharbanda, Bombay
E A Stallworthy, Coventry

Acknowledgements

While too numerous to mention individually, we hope that the references at the end of each chapter acknowledge our debt to the many who have written on the various subjects we touch upon in the course of our work.

Our grateful thanks go to librarians and their staff for their help in tracking down the material we were seeking. In particular, those looking after the libraries of the American Centre, the Bhabha Atomic Research Centre, the British Council, the Industrial Credit and Investment Corporation of India, the Indian Institute of Technology, the National Institute of Training in Industrial Engineering and the University of Bombay, all in Bombay, together with the librarians at the British Institute of Management, the Institute of Bankers, the London Business Library and the Science Reference Library all in London and last but not least, the New York Public Library, the Fairleigh Dickinson University Library at Rutherford, NJ and the Library of Congress at Washington, in the USA.

Lastly, and as always, our special thanks to our families and particularly to Sudershan and Dorothy, for their patience, understanding and loving support while this book was being written. Their contribution is far more than we can ever express in words.

OPK
EAS

Part One

It's a Rough Road

Chapter 1
Going into Decline

When we speak of companies in decline we have in mind, primarily, financial decline. However, financial decline is actually a symptom, not a cause. It results from one or more causes, either internal or external, and usually the former. The company in decline, however, tends to blame its troubles on external causes, factors such as a downslide in the economy or severe competition. These and other factors may well play a role, but a good management team should know how to anticipate and deal with them before the position becomes irretrievable.

Why companies go into decline

The corporate body has been likened by us to a human body; just as we sometimes becomes ill, so does a corporate body.[1] For both ourselves and a company, various symptoms appear as a recognisable prelude to sickness. Company decline is a symptom of an oncoming 'sickness', which if not identified and remedied, may well lead to failure.

Despite the accumulated body of knowledge on the management of corporate bodies and despite a large number of success stories in that context all over the world, some companies are always in danger. One estimate puts it at one in four. Initially, perhaps, this may be due to external factors but if the management is not alert to what is happening, the problems escalate and the company begins to have financial problems, such as cash flow and ultimately, of course, the balance sheet may be seriously affected. By then it may well be far too late; certainly the damage (disease) may have spread widely enough to make recovery much more difficult.

Managing resources

One of the basic problems is that in the highly competitive business environment that exists today, companies find it increasingly difficult to manage their human resources effectively, efficiently and innovatively. Man is by far the most important resource in any company; far more important than the other two key resources, money and machines. If the human resource is not managed properly and used to its full potential, trouble is at hand. Many large companies seem to be poorly equipped and ill adapted to motivate and manage their key managers and their competent and experienced professionals.

In a somewhat controversial but fully documented thesis, Ginzberg and Vojta demonstrate that large companies are increasingly vulnerable.[2] Using several case histories to make their point, they show that the growing scale and complexity of large companies leads to:

- Gross under-utilisation of human resources.
- Precious time and energy being spent on coordination and 'internal politics' rather than on the company's main mission – making better and more profitable products.

The case histories studied in connection with their thesis led the authors to discover the tensions between achieving corporate objectives and the performance of managers. In due course this tension leads to a non-fit between the company structure and the work of its managers.

The authors' consulting assignments at home and abroad brought such problems into sharp focus and led to the two major conclusions presented above. The principal source of their data was their combined total of nearly 75 years of experience in large companies (the senior author is one of America's leading human resources experts). This was supplemented by the body of literature already available on the subject and several hundred interviews specially conducted, mostly informal, for the purpose. So we can have some confidence in their conclusion that the proper use of the human resource is the key to success.

Means of escape

A company in decline is in financial distress. This leads to still further decline in the fortunes of the company and, if it continues for any length of time, to failure. What happens thereafter depends on the business climate, the regulations and laws of the country concerned. The company, in most countries in the free world, could go bankrupt and cease to exist, bringing with it a loss of jobs, and usually the near wiping out of the investment of a large number of shareholders.

In countries such as the USA the company may find a way of

escape by filing for bankruptcy under Chapter 11 of the US bankruptcy laws, which allows a company to continue operating, while agreeing to meet its liabilities in accordance with an agreed scheme. This has been done when a company has been threatened by a large number of lawsuits for liability in respect of the use of its product, or claims from an entire community that has been adversely affected by its operations. Finding its liability then to be far in excess of its assets it seeks protection under Chapter 11, since this allows it to continue to operate.

An example of this is the asbestos-product manufacturing company, Johns Manville, which was threatened with hundreds of thousands of claims by both its workers and the users of its products. All claimed to be suffering from adverse health effects due to their exposure to asbestos. The claims amounted to several billion dollars and Johns Manville had no choice but to seek protection under Chapter 11.

On the other hand, in countries such as India, due to a variety of social, economic and political factors, the government will go to almost any length to protect jobs. They therefore seek to avoid the closure of companies. This can go to such an extreme that sick units are 'nursed' along even when they appear to be no longer viable. This seems to us to be throwing good money after bad and we find the solution worse than the problem.[1] In the ultimate analysis the country's economy suffers. There is enormous overmanning, with a consequent disastrous effect on productivity. The economy then has to be 'protected' and 'sheltered' against the import of cheaper goods of equal quality and, by the same token, the country cannot compete in the fiercely competitive international market.

Predicting decline

In *Corporate Failure – Prediction, Panacea and Prevention*, we showed that company failure was *not* inevitable: it could be prevented if the appropriate steps were taken in good time.[1] That demanded prediction. In *Company Rescue – How to Manage a Business Turnaround* we showed a number of 'company doctors' at work, profiling the course of failure in a general way.[3] The profile, of course, varies from case to case. These two books are typical of the wealth of literature that has accumulated on this fascinating and important subject, and of the many books, we would like to mention just two.

In *Why Companies Fail*, based on several case studies, including Braniff Airways, International Harvester, Wicks and Dome Petroleum, the most significant causes of failure are outlined.[4]

Strategies are also suggested for detecting, avoiding and profiting from bankruptcy; that last interests those investors who see in bankrupt companies the chance of a lifetime for an attractive investment, an aspect which we develop at some length, particularly in Part 4. We ourselves have also dealt with some of these aspects (in *Corporate Failure*) including the prediction of failure, both by using quantitative techniques (numbers obtained from the annual accounts of a company) and qualitative techniques (involving the use of a discerning judgement and a 'feel' for what is happening).

Wilson's *The New Venturers* provides much revealing information in a chapter curiously titled 'Mr Fixit'[5] (the title refers to Frederick R Adler, a tough New York based lawyer who has earned fame and much money by rescuing companies in decline and has excelled in the role of 'turnaround artist'). This particular chapter carries a short conversation between a venture capitalist and presumably the author of the book – or it could well be with Mr Fixit himself:

'Do most startup companies encounter a crisis at some point?'
'All.'
'Is that a Murphy's Law of venture business?'
'Yes, it's not a question of if something will go wrong, it's just when.'

This means that the troubles encountered by any new business are part of the game. Anyone starting up a new business is taking a calculated risk, in anticipation of a breakthrough in performance and earnings once the management or entrepreneur can get over the initial teething problems.

Managing success and failure

Even though it seems to be the norm rather than the exception that companies will face trouble, much of the business literature is devoted to success stories and how to achieve success. Even the noted management 'guru' Peter Drucker has concentrated on success rather than failure in most of his writings. Why is there such a lack of literature on the subject of failure and disasters? It may be a result of our wishful thinking: we plan for and expect success in whatever we do. Planning is of course the proper thing to do, but we must also be realists, and accept that companies may go into decline and that inevitably there will be failures. It is due to the reluctance on the part of many to realise that disaster is a reality that we have written several books on the subject.[6,7] This resulted in our being labelled 'disaster' experts, an impression we sought to correct by writing *Successful Projects with a Moral for Management*,[8] yet once again we return to decline and disaster.

Of the books on the subject of success in the corporate world, we can perhaps just mention *The Winning Performance*.[9] This makes the valid point that the largest companies are not those with the fastest growth; that seems to be more predominant among the smaller companies. It maintains that one of the reasons for decline in new companies is that they grow far too rapidly for a steady and healthy balance sheet, since the management is unable to cope with and consolidate such growth.

It is also a common feature that as many as half of the companies which survive their first cash flow crisis get broken up in course of time, as the original founder of the company is unable to cope with its growth and continuing expansion.

The growing businesses are shown to be businesses which look after their workforce well and succeed in motivating them. The reverse also follows as a corollary: 'any manager ... who loses a key employee has failed the company.' It can be with such a simple and seemingly insignificant management failure that the decline of a company may well start.

A manager has to learn to manage both success and failure – both are part of the 'game' in the corporate world. Of the two it is the disasters that make media stories, especially in the popular and mass media. The coverage given is topical, somewhat superficial and even 'scary'. One has to look beyond such reports to find the key factors leading to such failures. It is only then that one can find where the management went wrong, which is a prerequisite to solving the problem and learning the appropriate lessons from past mistakes.

'When the mighty stumble'

A professor of commercial banking at the Harvard Business School sought to draw useful lessons from the decline of four major companies:[10] Massey-Ferguson Ltd, International Harvester Co, Dome Petroleum Ltd, and Grupo Industrial Alfa SA. In studying these four cases, he sought to identify the common characteristics of these companies in decline with a view to focusing attention on the key issues and the management decisions which led to their troubles. By deduction he then hoped to arrive at those decisions and actions that would lead to their recovery, revival and survival. These would then serve as lessons for managers and would become case studies for business schools throughout the world.

In the case of a company in trouble, such as the four mentioned

8   Takeovers, Acquisitions and Mergers

above, several groups – shareholders, employees, suppliers, customers and communities where the companies operate – have an interest in the destiny of the company concerned and they will all be keen to 'right the ship'.

The conclusions of the study can be briefly summarised as follows:

1. The decline can be arrested by following the advice of specialists who 'have been there before'.
2. Strategic and financial restructuring are essential.
3. If there is a great diversity of lenders and complicated financial arangements, dealing with the situation is much more difficult.
4. Restructuring outside the bankruptcy courts is to be preferred: both borrowers and lenders get a better deal.
5. Experience with companies such as MF, Alfa and other multinationals highlights the difficulty of restructuring within the diverse laws and procedures prevailing in different countries.
6. In agreeing to the concessions necessarily involved in restructuring, lenders often insist on having equity participation. Borrowers have to realise that they have no choice in the matter since they have nothing else to offer.
7. The decline of large and apparently invulnerable companies make the hazards of incurring excessive debt abundantly clear.

The last point, if nothing else, disproves the popular saying: 'Owe the bank a thousand dollars and the bank has you in its grip: owe the bank many millions and you are in control.'

This significant study of mighty companies in financial decline focused attention on the four major companies selected from a large number of companies which at that time were in financial trouble. It is instructive to review the group from which these four were selected for study in depth. They are set out in Table 1.1.

Table 1.1 *Companies in trouble*

Company	Debt	How handled
AEG-Telefunken (Germany)	A	Receivership and reorganisation
Allis-Chalmers Corporation (USA)	B	Restructuring of bank and insurance company debt
AM International Inc (USA)	B	Bankruptcy

Baldwin-United Corporation (USA)	A	Bankruptcy
Blocker Energy Corporation (USA)	B	Restructuring
Braniff International Corporation (USA)	B	Bankruptcy, then reorganisation
Burmah Oil Plc (UK)	A	Restructuring
Chicago, Rock Island & Pacific RR Co (and several other railroads) (USA)	B	Liquidisation or reorganisation in bankruptcy
Chrysler Corporation (USA)	A	Restructuring, with government loan
Commonwealth Oil Refining Co (USA)	B	Bankruptcy, and then operations reduced
Continental Airlines Corp (USA)	B	Bankruptcy
Dome Petroleum Limited (Canada)	A	Developing restructuring proposals at time of review
Eastern Air Lines Inc (and several other airlines, USA)	A	Deeply troubled
Goldblatt Bros Inc (USA)	B	Bankruptcy
Grupo Industrial Alfa SA (Mexico)	A	Hanging on (at time of review)
IBH Holding AG (Germany)	A	Bankruptcy
International Harvester Co (USA)	A	Three major restructurings before review
Itel Corporation (USA)	A	Bankruptcy filing, then reorganised
Lockheed Corporation (USA)	A	Restructuring with government assistance
Mamiya Camera Co Ltd (Japan)	B	Bankruptcy
Massey-Ferguson Ltd (Canada-based multinational)	A	Two major restructurings by time of review
Memorex Corporation (USA)	B	Restructured, but later taken over
North American Car Corporation (USA)	B	Restructured
Penn Central Corporation (USA)	A	Bankruptcy, reorganisation and partial liquidation
Sambo's Restaurants Inc (USA)	B	Bankruptcy
Security National Bank (USA)	A	Forced sale
Telecom Corporation (USA)	B	A major subsidiary filed for bankruptcy: debt issue in default
Tiger International Inc (USA)	B	Subsidiaries
Union Explosives Rio Tinto SA (Spain)	A	Efforts to restructure
White Motor Corporation (USA)	B	Bankruptcy
Wilson Foods Corporation (USA)	B	Bankruptcy, but continuing in operation
WT Grant Company (USA)	A	Bankruptcy and liquidation

Notes:
A Companies more than US$1 billion in total debt.
B Companies between US$100 and 999 million in total debt.
   In addition, 11 companies with less than US$100 million in total debt were reviewed.

How to avoid trouble

Having briefly catalogued the causes and reasons for companies going into decline we have also indicated broadly what can and should be done in such cases. The main reason for such a decline is a basic fault in the management.[1,3,6,7] To put it bluntly, it is mismanagement that brings the company into trouble. So one obvious solution is to change the existing management or at least the chairman or chief executive officer. This is one of the most significant routes to recovery for companies in decline; it is a most effective way of restoring sick companies to a state of health. Very appropriately the person who restores a sick company to health is called a company 'doctor' (see Chapter 3).

We find ourselves in somewhat strange company in laying the cause of company troubles at the feet of management. For instance, Carl Icahn is quite blunt when talking about the management of companies in decline. He says:[11] 'these managements need shaking up – they're horrendous.' His colleague, T Boone Pickens, doesn't mince his words either, saying: 'chief executives who themselves own few shares in their companies have no more feeling for the average stockholder than they do for baboons in Africa.'

Icahn, Boone Pickens, Ivan Boesky and their like exist not only in the USA, but almost everywhere in the world – the so-called free world at least. We consider them in detail in Chapter 12, but suffice it to say here that they are variously referred to in the press as 'financial wizards' and 'asset shufflers' while sometimes harsher terms are used, such as 'raiders' and 'respectable rogues'. The prime objective of such people is of course to make a quick profit, although they often describe themselves as social reformers. Unfortunately, since they as a group speak loudly enough to be heard in all quarters, they can gain respect even from the shareholders – at least from the laymen among them, since they do benefit, at least in the short term, from the activities of these 'asset shufflers'.

The trouble with the arguments offered by the raiders is that they presume that a company is merely the stock represented by the paper certificates. In actual fact:[11] 'The corporation is not a piece of paper and should not be bought and sold in that way.'

Having given you a little of the taste and flavour of this subject, we defer further discussion of it to Chapter 12.

Qualities for success

Each company and each case is specific and there can be no magic solution that will prevent companies going into decline and ultimately failing. We have indicated above that most of the failures occur during the initial years of a company's existence.[1] Most businesses start small, with an entrepreneur at the head. Some of the basic questions people should ask themselves before launching a new project are:[12]

- Do I have confidence in myself?
- Do I have confidence in my venture?
- Am I willing to make sacrifices?
- Am I a decision maker?
- Do I recognise an opportunity?
- Do I have a high level of energy and stamina?
- Am I willing to lead by example?

This is quite a catalogue, yet they are all basic qualities essential for success. If the answer to many of these questions is 'no', then perhaps the person concerned is not cut out to be an entrepreneur. Of course it is not as simple as that. An entrepreneur is in no position to judge him or herself realistically; more likely than not they will overrate themselves. Who then is to be the judge? Perhaps their colleagues? But they may well be biased, too, since at the start of any new venture everything appears so bright and exciting that any inherent weaknesses are likely to be overlooked.

For survival, let alone growth, the entrepreneur has to be a 'lion' in the corporate jungle, nothing less. The marketplace is a battlefield without any rules of battle except one, the survival of the fittest. Kiam, for example, told of a major sports event in the USA where it was impossible to find a parking space – except for chauffeur-driven cars. There was a parking lot without any charges adjacent to the stadium for such cars. This seemed patently unfair and Kiam felt cheated but at the same time saw it as an opportunity. He got himself a chauffeur's cap and the appropriate uniform. On his next trip to the stadium he insisted that his wife and their two friends sit in the back, dropped his passengers at the main entrance and was waved into the parking lot. After parking the car, he changed into his normal dress and rejoined his wife and friends.[12] The moral: in the corporate jungle you make your own rules and you have to *turn a difficult situation into an opportunity*.

Who is in charge?

It is very important to see who really runs and manages the affairs of a company. In theory, it is the company board, and this is the law, but what happens in practice? It has to be people – that is all there is. There *should* be one person, the chief executive or the chairman, who makes all the key decisions. In this way that person sets a course for the company to follow and is the only one with a complete overview of the company's operations, its resources of men, materials and machines. He is the one who can see the 'tree' in the midst of the 'wood' and he steers the company. He directs and controls the managers, who in their turn control the various operations of the company. He must, *inter alia*:[13]

- Evaluate and define the company's 'mission', its resources, the timing and rate of return on the investment.
- Select, monitor and give both responsibility and authority to the managers.
- Coordinate the efforts of his various managers.

Decline sets in when the board or the chief executive fails to discharge the above responsibilities. This is most likely to occur when:

- The chief executive is not a good leader or the board is not well constituted.
- They look within rather than critically outward and forward.
- Managers are not properly selected or are not removed when found to be inadequate or incompetent.

Then the chief executive and the board are performing poorly and this shows up in what is called the 'bottom line'. More specifically, there are declining real returns on the resources deployed, and declining contribution to the net creation of wealth.

It is said that 'the decline of the board is a universal phenomenon of this century' but we attribute far more importance to that person, the chief executive or chairman, who takes the lead. That one person is the *one*, above all, who can make or break the company.[3]

References

1. Kharbanda, O P and Stallworthy, E A *Corporate Failure – Prediction, Panacea and Prevention* McGraw-Hill, London, 1985.
2. Ginzberg, E and Vojta, G *Beyond Human Scale – The Large Corporation At Risk* Basic Books, 1985.
3. Kharbanda, O P and Stallworthy, E A *Company Rescue – How to Manage a Business Turnaround* Heinemann, 1987.
4. Platt, H D *Why Companies Fail* Lexington Books, 1985.
5. Wilson, J W *The New Venturers* Addison-Wesley, 1985.

6. Kharbanda, O P and Stallworthy, E A *How to Learn from Project Disasters* Gower, 1983.
7. Kharbanda, O P and Stallworthy, E A *Management Disasters and How to Prevent Them* Gower, 1986.
8. Kharbanda O P and Stallworthy, E A *Successful Projects with a Moral for Management* Gower, 1986.
9. Clifford, D K and Cavanagh, R E *The Winning Performance* Sidgwick & Jackson, 1986.
10. Williams, C M 'When the mighty stumble' *Harvard Business Review* **62**, July-August 1984, pp 126-39.
11. Law, W A 'A corporation is more than its stock' *Harvard Business Review* **64**, May-June 1986, pp 80-3.
12. Kiam, V *Going for it – How to Succeed as an Entrepreneur* Collins, 1986.
13. Mills, G *On the Board* 2nd ed, George Allen & Unwin, 1985.

Chapter 2
Meeting the Crisis

Having looked at why a company may go into decline, we now have to see how such a crisis can be met and overcome. Companies neither exist nor operate in isolation but within the business environment that surrounds them. There are matters such as government policy, the state of economy, the competition and a host of other factors external to the company over which it has no control whatever. The management has to adopt a pragmatic approach, accepting things as they are and then seeking to make the best of its resources.

The nature of the crisis

Before we can tackle and meet crisis, we must first know the nature of the crisis we have to meet. Crises in the case of new ventures are far too common; in fact, they are the rule rather than the exception. But even stable, reasonably successful corporations can easily get into a crisis situation when taking on a new venture. Starting in the 1960s, several otherwise successful American companies created new venture divisions which they thought might bring them a 'windfall' and put them in a commanding position in new and exciting technological areas. But within a decade their new ventures had failed miserably and there was nothing to show for their investments and all the managerial effort that went into them. Perhaps some specific illustrations may help us to understand what went wrong.[1]

In 1969, General Electric (GE) in the USA financed several small companies with great potential, with a view to acquiring them later, but lost some US$10 million in the process. What is more, one small company financed by them, having achieved success, turned down a GE bid to acquire it. Then in 1970 the company set up a technology ventures operation to translate potentially good technical ideas into practice, but were completely disillusioned after 10 such deals since none of the companies was successful. Ford followed a similar course, investing some US$14 million in start-up deals during 1968-71, but had to sell them off within two years at a loss, finding themselves unable to market the products effectively. Monsanto promoted an internal venture operation for three years and at the end all they had to show for it was: 'A warehouse full of plastic hobbyhorses we couldn't sell.' Yet Monsanto was a leader in the field of plastics and must have thought that they knew all the 'tricks of the trade'. But, being primarily a chemical manufacturer, they were not familiar with the requirements of the end user.

Receptive entrepreneurs learnt and profited from the lessons of these failures. A new generation of corporate venturers was born, who adopted a disciplined and pragmatic approach and were thus better equipped to meet the challenges of the marketplace.

It is estimated that between 1977 and 1983, the venture capital available to the new technocrat entrepreneurs shot up in the USA, from US$1 billion to US$2.5 billion. And it was no longer a fad, with entrepreneurs seeking to make a 'fast buck'. Not at all, according to writers in the financial press:

> It's different than it was the last time around, in that companies are thinking much more long-term about it. I just don't see them turning this off like they did before.

So, lessons are being learnt and applied and this should lead to a better success rate than before. But what are these lessons?

Key questions

What would the new project cost?

This is a crucial question, the final answer to which is seldom known when an existing or new company launches a project. With the scope of the project defined, estimates can be made of the capital cost. On the basis of such estimates the company proceeds to raise the necessary finance, sometimes from within but mostly from without. To the estimated project cost, of course, there must be added a provision for a number of other costs that will inevitably arise (such as start-up and precommissioning costs), but above all appropriate provision must be made for working capital. This latter is essential since a certain time will elapse before the project will start producing the desired product and thereafter more time will elapse before the product can be marketed and there is a positive cash flow. The working capital, therefore, has to cover all the expenses for this period, which can extend long after the project is ready for start-up.

A project may be delayed for one reason or another and this overrun in time will bring about a corresponding overrun in the project cost. In addition, the initial project cost may prove to be an underestimate for one or more reasons. Both these factors can lead to an overrun in project cost and its extent may affect the viability of the project and even result in its being no longer viable.

It is virtually impossible to know exactly how much money a new business will need to complete its project, together with the cash requirements during the first few years of operation. But it is possible to arrive at certain realistic estimates and every effort must be made to make such estimates. For this it is necessary to prepare realistic financial forecasts, including: the expected sales and the consequent income; the prospective balance sheet; the cash flow statement.

The cash flow statement is the most crucial of all. Numerous books and articles have been written to guide the entrepreneur in such an exercise. Typical of these is the article 'Growing Concerns – How Much Money Does Your New Venture Need?'[2] The author shows in a step-by-step fashion how an entrepreneur may, perhaps with the help of an accountant, prepare a financial forecast for, say, the first five years of operations. This forecast is also used as the basis for determining the necessary equity investment and the amount of financing required to complete the project and run it for five years. It is an extremely useful guide which purports to chart the direction of the new venture from year to year. Use of computer spreadsheet programs can help to simplify the calculations, especially with a detailed and complex forecasting exercise.

The steps involved in the exercise can be summarised thus:

- Beginning the process
- Getting to the cost of goods sold
- Establishing key expenses
- Completing the balance sheet

and finally, the all-important

- Cash flow statement

How much cash is needed?

An entrepreneur, who usually does not have much financial background or experience, even after having made a forecast as outlined above may well agree with the venture capitalist if, studying the forecast, he says:[2] 'Fine, but you don't need all this money now, at the start. Let's put up some of the required capital, and when you need the rest, ask for it.'

But he should not agree. Such a policy is sure to lead to a crisis situation, for when the additional capital is requested from the financial bodies involved, including the venture capitalist, they may well retort: 'Sorry, but my funds are tied up right now. You'll have to wait a while.'

In effect, the entrepreneur is being given the message that the financiers want to see some return on the investment before risking any more of their venture capital. Nor can they be blamed for such conservatism. Who knows but that they have already 'burnt their fingers' on some of their recent ventures and don't wish to add to their sleepless nights. The author of the article referred to above had exactly this experience with his very first venture and this experience led to the enunciation of his first law of entrepreneurship:

> If you want to fly to financial paradise, have enough gas to make the trip, as there are no service stations along the way!

This is sound advice, based on first-hand experience, but the author doesn't tell us what to do if the entire gas tank capacity is not sufficient. Further, there can be hills, traffic snarl-ups and traffic lights on the way, so that the mileage obtained may be far less than was first anticipated. Then what? Perhaps a second supplementary gas tank is necessary? If the additional gas (and of course 'gas' equals capital in this analogy) is not available when needed, all that the new venture can show is a 'trail of red ink' on the financial statements, indicative of impending decline and disaster.

The 'vulture' capitalists

The nature of the crisis facing many new entrepreneurs was brought into sharp focus in early 1980s with a spate of investment activity arising from a peak in new company formations. Encouraged by the success of many new ventures, especially ventures in the high-tech area, like those prevailing in the now famous Silicon Valley in California, there was venture capital available aplenty – an endless supply, it seemed. However, Gordon Moore, chairman of Intel, one of the more successful high-tech ventures, observed:[2]

> There is some optimum amount of venture capital. It's clearly not zero, because at zero a lot of things die without seeing the light of the day. But the possibility exists of there being too much venture capital, in which case everything gets fragmented and all the continuity in things that established companies can do gets lost. From the mid-1970s to now, we've gone from one extreme to the other.

William J Perry, a very successful entrepreneur, expressed a similar concern in early 1984:

> I believe firmly that venture activity has been a tremendous catalyst in innovation. But I'm also willing to believe there's some level at which it could become problematic, given the exponential increase since 1978.

That too much may be as dangerous as too little is confirmed by one of the most respected entrepreneurs in the Silicon Valley, in the course of a BBC interview in March 1984:

> I think there's a little too much venture capital available today, which makes it possible for some people to get into things when they're really not quite prepared for it.

Why have we dwelt with the issue of oversupply of funds and quoted several experts to that effect, especially when in the previous section we have pointed out that shortage of funds before a project starts to bear fruition can create a crisis situation? Well, an oversupply of funds is not desirable either, for it too leads to a crisis situation, but of a different kind. What happens is that projects which may not otherwise be viable can readily be funded by a venture capitalist rising on the crest of success with some of his recent investments. This can bring its own havoc: not only are the venture funds at great risk, but even a few failures amid several success stories can bring about a crisis of confidence in the marketplace. When someone then comes along with an attractive, viable project, it may not attract sufficient funds. The crisis is further accentuated by the following factors:

- The funding of an excessively large number of similar ventures, some without proper leadership, results in both money and talent being wasted without adding much to the furtherance of technology and even creating an artificially overcompetitive situation.
- Venture capital may, unknowingly, encourage some of the best technocrats to leave their 'safe and secure' positions in successful companies and venture forth on their own, using perhaps pirated technology. The already established success may simply be replaced by another one under a different name and at a different place: once again without adding much to the national economy.

Even a highly successful company such as Intel – built up by technocrats practically from scratch on the basis of sound technology and the unique but simple slogan 'Intel delivers' into a billion-dollar business by 1983 – has suffered in this way. When the recession set in some of its key people started leaving – perhaps 100 or so out of a total of over 20,000. But that was enough to hurt Intel, from whose success they had benefited.

Intel was by no means alone in this respect. The ex-employees of Hewlett-Packard went on to form at least 10 new ventures between 1980 and 1982, all of them competing with Hewlett-Packard. The same thing happened with a number of other companies, such as Advanced Micro Devices, National Semiconductor, Tektronix and Texas Instruments. They all suffered serious defections which left them weaker and at the same time exposed them to fierce competition from the new ventures formed by their ex-employees, who were operating with much lower overheads.

There are plenty of instances available where the helpful venture capitalist has been instrumental in encouraging 'vultures' to build upon the strength of their previous company and emerge as one of its fiercest competitors. We are not concerned here with the question of ethics, but are merely stating a fact which causes a crisis situation where there was none before. The ex-employees, together with the 'vulture capitalist' backing them, may well profit in the short term, but there is, of course, the chance that they may fail, especially if the parent company is able to meet the new venture head on, by cutting costs savagely. The new venture will not be able to cope with such a strategy and the venture capitalist may well abandon it in midstream, since all that matters to him is the prospective profit.

Crises such as these, arising from an over-abundance of capital, have a way of solving themselves. The laws of classic economics can help to correct the capital oversupply situation. According to another venture capitalist, Paul Wythes:[2]

> We'll all have some problems in our portfolios in the next few years that we created in this euphoric cycle. Some of the money that's come into our business is going to wish it hadn't come in. We'll see the spigot turn off rather dramatically. And those of us who are in it for the long haul will work with the money we've got until we can prove again that we are ready for that next uptick in the cycle.

(For those of our readers not familiar with American English, a spigot is a tap.)

Annual reports and 'creative accounting'

We usually place great confidence in numbers. After all they are precise – or are they? Well, that depends on what sort of numbers we are talking about. In the present context, we are referring to the host of numbers which appear in any annual report of a company. These reports have been prepared by the company's accountants, who are required by law to be chartered, certified or the equivalent, depending on the country. It is their duty to make sure that the accounts are correct. They then have to be audited, by law, by an outside firm of independent auditors. With the checking in-house and cross-checking by an outside independent auditor, one should have a great deal of confidence in such numbers – but they can be very deceptive indeed. Judging from the many reports we read in the financial columns of the dailies and the business journals, deception seems to be a common feature in a great many annual reports.

Why is this? Every company wants to present a good public image. A company's annual report and accounts has been likened to a 'studio portrait', taken on a specific day. When sitting for a portrait we dress well, are well groomed, and take every care to present the best possible appearance. It is just the same for the annual accounts of a company.

The auditor is required by law to qualify a company's published accounts with footnotes that highlight any discrepancy or unusual accounting practice, even though what is being done is perfectly legal. The objective is to make sure that unpleasant facts are not being hidden by 'cosmetics'. Further, in most countries, of which the UK is typical, the auditor is required to assess the status of a company by means of a 'going concern qualification'.[3] However, between 1977 and 1983, only some 25 per cent of quoted companies in the UK were qualified on a going concern basis. Of those 70 per cent had obvious problems, so that was no surprise. What is significant is that most of the companies so qualified *did not fail*. The failures occurred with companies where the accounts presented a good picture and there was no qualification. In other words, despite the fact that the accounts had been audited there were no footnotes and they failed to convey a true picture of the financial situation of the company. This comes about through what has been called 'creative accounting', a term designed to give respectability to a very misleading procedure. But of course the auditor has failed to carry out his duties as required by law.

In the USA so many companies on the point of collapse have presented accounts that display a very satisfactory position that it has become a public scandal, prompting congressional probes. One sub-committee, for instance, focused its attention on Ernst & Whinney, one of the 'big eight' US accounting firms, for giving an 'unqualified' opinion (that is the best rating) in January 1983 with respect to the United American Bank of Knoxville. Within three

Meeting the Crisis   21

weeks the bank had been declared insolvent, setting off a chain of bank failures that became perhaps the largest commercial banking collapse in American history.

Figure 2.1 shows that the Securities and Exchange Commission (SEC), the US government regulatory body, has not been very active in monitoring the activities of accountants and that the number of actions pursued by the SEC over the years shows a marked falling off since 1977. But that is part of their job and it is very apparent from the many incidents reported in the press that

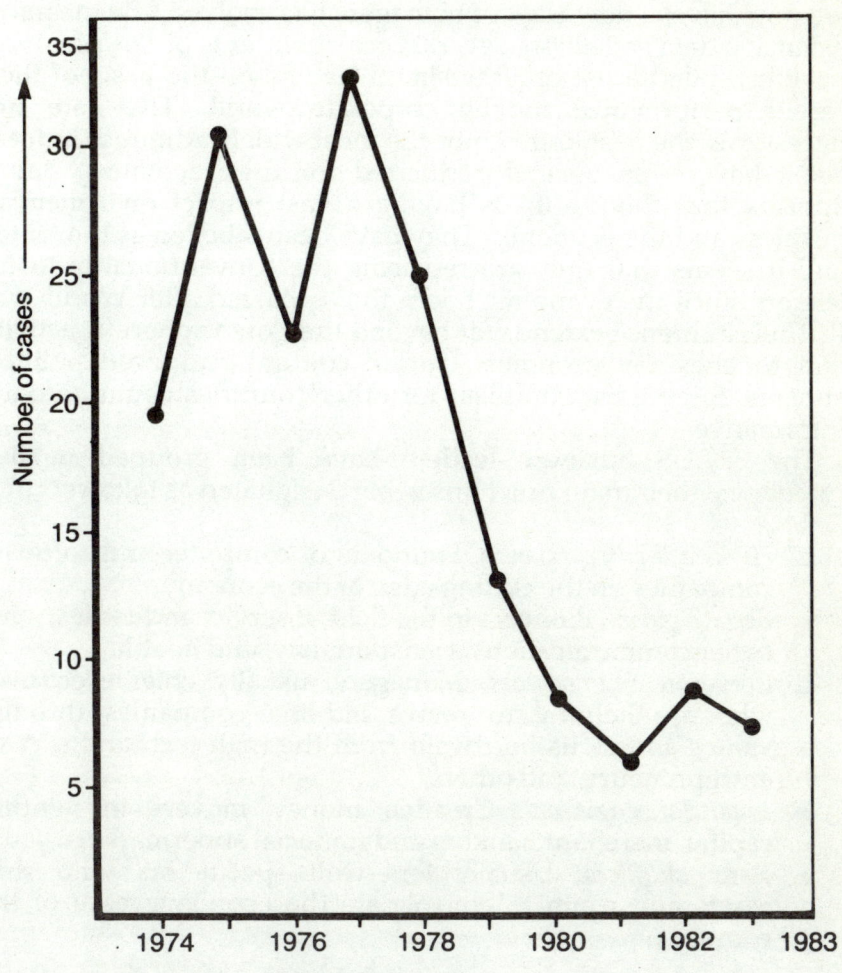

Source: Securities and Exchange Commission,
American Institute of Certified Public Accountants

Figure 2.1 *Policing by the SEC*

we do indeed need to call upon auditors to 'audit' their own activities. There is little the onlooker can do about it, although a change of auditor can be significant: perhaps the auditor who is being displaced is insisting on the company keeping to the rules.

The crisis specialists

Times changes and so do people. The corporate world is much the same. To meet the changing needs of the times and to cope with the highly complex and dynamic business environment that we now have, a new class of managers has evolved.[4] By means of extensive data collection, several correspondents of *Business Week* have compiled a list of 50 business leaders on the basis of their recent performance in the corporate world. They are not necessarily the best known nor the most widely admired. Indeed, some have been severely criticised for their activities. But it appears that this group is having a vast impact on American business and the economy. They have been labelled as the 'élite', and it seems that they are replacing the conventional industry leaders since the economic boom that occurred after World War II. Their influence extends far beyond their own sphere of activity and touches the economic, social, cultural and even political spheres. Such a list compiled for other countries could be quite informative.

The 50 US business leaders have been grouped in five categories, their main functions being designated as follows:

- 17 *High-tech entrepreneurs*. Founders of computer and software companies on the cutting edge of the economy.
- 9 *Service gurus*. Pioneers in the field of service industries, such as telecommunications, transport, law, and health.
- 15 *Corporate rejuvenators*. Managers, usually chief executives who are helping to revive old-line companies through values and skills borrowed from the high-tech and service entrepreneurs, and others.
- 6 *Financial engineers*. Creative money movers in venture capital, merchant banking and financial supermarkets.
- 3 *Asset shufflers*. Usually lone-wolf speculators who shift assets and claim to consolidate the economic base of the country.

As far as our present subject is concerned, we are chiefly interested in the last two categories. The financial engineers are, no doubt, rendering a much needed service but their activities in conjunction with the last category, asset shufflers, lead, we think, to very undesirable results. One cannot help but get suspicious about their motives. Is the national economy, that they claim to strengthen through their activities, really benefiting, or are they pursuing their personal gains at any cost? The results, so far, appear to confirm the latter. In their relentless drive towards enriching themselves, they may well be seriously undermining the larger interest of the economy.

A quotation about the credentials of T Boone Pickens Jr (mentioned in Chapter 1) may be in order:[4]

> Chairman and president of Mesa Petroleum. Oil patch raider extraordinaire; one of the great asset shufflers of all time; catalyst for the reorganization and consolidation of the American oil industry; self-styled corporate populist who speaks of shareholders' rights while making sure partners make millions of dollars in profits; big political player in Republican Party; fund raiser for Reagan's Presidential campaign in Texas.

This, we feel, says it all. Such asset shufflers seem to be on the increase all over the world. They create crisis situations in the business marketplace in the process of securing their personal gains. Of course, they see themselves as serving the shareholders' best interests and justify their activities by asserting that they are correcting or displacing an erring management. T Boone Pickens Jr, for example, is quite blunt:[5]

> It is questionable how much more long-term planning shareholders can stand. What many managements seem to be demanding is more time to keep making the same mistakes.

The activities of these 'short-termers', as they are called, are known to have caused widespread upset in the free market conditions. There is really no proof that the target companies, whose management the short-termers seek to remove for their acts of omission and commission, are mismanaged. On the contrary they have often performed better than the companies of the short-termers themselves.[6] Also, while the stockholders of the target companies may seem to have gained from the activities of the short-termers, this may well have been at the cost of a multitude of other shareholders. In any case the gains made are known to be of a temporary nature.

Nevertheless, despite the criticism that is levelled at them, the short-termers will continue their efforts. They are very determined. In a candid dialogue between another short-termer, Carl C Icahn, and CE Meyer, president of TWA, a company where Icahn sought to gain control, tells it all:[7]

M: 'All you want is the fast buck.'
I: 'If we are psycho-analysing each other, why don't you admit what you really care about is your job, and you're afraid I'm going to take it away from you?'

Candid enough? This and many similar dialogues will go on while the crisis in corporations and the marketplace continues and even intensifies. We will be talking more about this later, but suffice it to say here that in our view – and we are by no means alone in this – the situation is serious enough to justify bringing in legislation which will stop the activities of short-termers such as Boone Pickens, Icahn and their like.

References

1. Wilson, J W *The New Venturers* Addison-Wesley, 1985.
2. Stancill, J M 'Growing Concerns – How Much Money Does Your New Venture Need?' *Harvard Business Review* **64**, May-June 1986, pp. 122ff (9pp).
3. Taffler, R J and Tseung, M 'The audit going concern qualification in practice – exploding some myths' *Accountant's Magazine* July 1984, pp 263-9.
4. Cover story: 'The new corporate élite – they're changing the face of US business, and gaining political power' *Business Week* 21 January 1985, pp 62ff.
5. Pickens, T B Jr 'Professions of a short-termer' *Harvard Business Review* **64**, May-June 1986, pp 75-9.
6. Law, W A 'A corporation is more than its stock' *Harvard Business Review* **64**, May-June 1986, pp 80-3.
7. Johnston, M *Takeovers – The New Wall Street Warriors* Arbor House, 1986. Reviewed by Jerome Zukosky in *Business Week* 3 November 1986, pp 10-11 under the heading 'A you-are-there glimpse of the takeover wars'.

Chapter 3
Strategies for Recovery

Having discussed both the causes and reasons for the decline and consequent financial distress of companies, and the indicators that show us the situation, we now look at possible strategies that can be adopted by the company management to stop further decline. The strategy should, of course, do more than that: it should also get the company on the road to recovery.

A tailored strategy

There is no single strategy that will fit all situations. It has to be specific to each case, designed to tackle and solve the problems confronting that particular company. There are several books that deal with such strategies and typical of these are *Corporate Turnaround*,[1] *Corporate Recovery*,[2] and *How to Turn Around a Financially Troubled Company*.[3]

We too have dealt with the subject of turnaround and recovery of companies.[4,5] Our own approach to this subject is very like that of Sloma.[6] We assert that a sick company, like a sick person, needs to have a 'doctor' to diagnose the problem and prescribe and administer the treatment. The parallel between the human body and the corporate body is very close indeed, as illustrated in Table 3.1 on page 26.

As with the person, so with the company: the doctor can play a vital role in restoring the patient to health. In both cases, depending on the complaint, a specialist may be needed, although a general practitioner may make the initial diagnosis. Like the human patient, the corporate body can only describe the symptoms; it needs a doctor to identify the basic cause. In both cases the patient's condition and history have to be documented, certain tests have to be carried out and an analysis of these will lead to the final diagnosis. Thereafter, of course, the prescription is written out and the treatment starts.

In both cases, one person can make all the difference and if he is experienced and competent enough, a cure follows. The new breed of managers which we among others have chosen to call

Table 3.1 *The parallel between the human and corporate body*

The person	The company
Conception	Concept
Pre-natal care	Feasibility report
Birth	Company start-up
Healthy person	Profitable company
Patient	Company with a problem
Sickness	A problem, usually financial
Doctor	Management consultant
Specialist	Technical and financial consultants
Hospital	Bank or other financial institution
Intensive care	Turnaround techniques
Cured	Turnaround accomplished
Death	Financial collapse
Undertaker	Receiver

'company doctors' were rare just five years ago, but their numbers have been increasing fast to meet the demands of the marketplace. To be effective, such doctors have to be firm to the point of being ruthless. They have to be decisive, make quick decisions and be strict disciplinarians. The company may be in serious trouble and unless something is done fast, it is as good as dead. The options at this point are very limited: there is the possibility of survival and revival but the action taken has to be immediate and drastic if it is to succeed.

Is change of ownership the answer?

In this book we deal, however, with a different type of turnaround strategy from that described above. We consider the strategy that involves a change of ownership, represented by terms such as: 'acquisition', 'merger' and 'takeover'.

These terms are by no means mutually exclusive. For example, company A may acquire company B and then let the latter operate under its original name but with a change of top management. Alternatively, company B may be merged into company A, in which case B will lose its identity. Such acquisitions are usually negotiated deals between the two companies, but if company B is in trouble, it may have rather limited options.

Why would company A wish to acquire company B, especially if it is in financial trouble? There could be a variety of reasons. For instance, the acquisition might strengthen its own position where it has an established product line; alternatively it might wish to diversify into another related or even unrelated area. The main attraction, of course, is that because company B is in trouble, it can be acquired at a 'bargain price' which company A can largely dictate. Further, the losses of B can be offset against the profits of A, this bringing substantial tax savings.

Some countries actually go so far as to offer fiscal incentives to a healthy company for rescuing an ailing company. Then there is the further benefit that the additional facilities are available for immediate use – there is no waiting period required to formulate the project, execute it and run all the the risks of time and cost overruns – and the merits of such a takeover or acquisition become very clear. The new assets acquired may prove to be most valuable to company A and in the process company B may well have a better chance of recovery and revival. It should therefore be supported by the workforce and management of company B, although they will have to sacrifice part of their management function to their new 'master', company A.

Acquisitions and mergers are usually brought about through a process of negotiation, often friendly, since the process is expected to benefit both companies. Takeovers are in a rather different category, since more often than not they are not so friendly. These are the so-called 'hostile takeovers'. They can be initiated by a 'raider' (see Chapter 12), whose main interest is personal gain, although he presents himself in the guise of one who can bring benefits to the existing shareholders. Takeover battles have been most common and most fierce in the USA, but the phenomenon has become quite common in Europe as well, and other countries such as Australia and India are by no means immune. Even Japan has caught this 'infection', despite the conservatism that prevails there and the fact that Japan has a business style entirely its own.

The three financial strategies, acquisition, merger and takeover, were designed for the recovery of companies in distress, but the results have not been in accordance with the expectations, as we illustrate in Parts 2 to 4 of this book. There have been some success stories but these have been eclipsed by a much larger number of failures and even disasters.

Who applies the strategy?

After company A has acquired or taken over company B, the former has to formulate a strategy for the recovery of company B. Who does that? This question, of course, can also be posed if company A is itself in decline and wants to plan recovery from within. As part of the overall strategy, it may seek to be acquired or merged by or with another company, preferably in its own field of activity, but which is quite healthy and doing well. But in either of these cases, who within a company is responsible for planning and executing the strategy for the recovery of the company?

The practice varies from company to company but, in general, management is presented with a series of questions such as:

- How do we manage the beast we have become?
- How do we add value to the separate entities under our control?
- What are we really here for?

The last question is basic for any management and beyond our present terms of reference. The first two questions are, however, relevant to our subject. Has the company become too large to manage successfully and to anticipate and arrest its decline? Is the time ripe to break it up into small entrepreneurial sections? Perhaps it might even be appropriate to divest (this is the opposite of acquisition) sections of the company, selling them to others? These are all possibilities that can be considered.

There is also the anomaly that while many managers believe that small is beautiful, the capital markets think otherwise and continually seek to encourage growth by acquisition, seeking to make the most of the economy of scale, and hoping that they are thereby averting decline at some future date. In a comprehensive three-volume study, the Centre for Business Strategy reviewed the management styles of 16 large British multinationals in formulating strategy. The analysis that the study offers is strong and its prescription subtle. The conclusion: there is no magic formula for ensuring success and thereby preventing the decline of a business. A strategy has to be selected and implemented to suit each particular firm.

The 16 companies selected for study were grouped under three broad headings depending on their type of management style with respect to who planned their strategy for survival. There are:[7]

1. *Strategic planners*. This group included BOC, BP, Cadbury Schweppes, Lex, STC and United Biscuits.
2. *Strategic controllers*. This group included Courtaulds, ICI, the Imperial Group, Plessey and Vickers.
3. *Financial controllers*. This group included BTR, Ferranti, GEC, Hanson Trust and Tarmac.

Although somewhat oversimplified, the above classification does help to put the issue before us in perspective. It is also true that in some companies the division of function may not be as clear-cut as would appear from the above classification and grouping. (Note that the Imperial Group, said to be run by strategic controllers, has since been taken over by financial controllers, namely Hanson Trust.) Some of the significant conclusions may be briefly summarised thus:

- Financial control and central planning are indicated when there is a large number of separate businesses within the group.
- The larger the investment, the greater should be the involvement of the centre in the planning decisions.
- When cash is tight, strategy has to be sacrificed to cash flow.
- Accountants should not be put in charge of strategically controlled companies. In general, the personality of the chief executive should fit in with the style of the company.
- The chief executive should be aware of the drawbacks of his own personal style.

In general, companies run by strategic planners usually have a small number of core businesses and their subsidiaries help to implement global plans to their mutual competitive advantage. As companies become more diverse, the strategic controllers at the headquarters concentrate on helping their subsidiaries formulate their own detailed plans for review at the centre. Lastly, in the case of financially controlled companies, the managers at the centre judge their subsidiaries by numbers representing the financial targets they have been prescribed. So there is a tight control by the centre on finances, the headquarters staff is small but consists predominantly of accountants and the divisional managers enjoy a great deal of autonomy in their day-to-day business.

Which of these various management styles is best in ensuring success and thereby preventing company decline and the consequent financial distress? There can be no single answer. The management style with respect to company strategy has to be fitted to the specific requirements of each business and each style has its own set of pros and cons. The two must be balanced in each specific case before a final strategic system emerges. Also it is really a process of evolution and not a matter of imposing a particular style from the centre.

Takeovers

Takeovers have been seen as an answer to the problem of decline of companies. But a takeover, especially a hostile one, has proved to be no answer to the problem (as demonstrated in Part 3 by means of several case studies). Of the several books written on the subject of takeovers, one of the most interesting, which brings the battles that have been fought in this context very much alive for the reader, is *Takeover: The New Wall Street Warriors*.[8] The drama and trauma of takeovers are vividly described by focusing attention on three of the major takeover battles that took place in 1985. There was Icahn's three-month fight to win control of TWA, Pickens' failed quest for Unocal and Sir James Goldsmith's triumph over Crown Zellerbach.

The reader is taken inside the hotel rooms, boardrooms and even court rooms where takeover battles were plotted and fought, often reading the words of the participants themselves. Squadrons of lawyers, investment brokers and bankers spent hundreds of manhours, for which they were paid something of the order of US$500 per hour. An equal number of fruitless hours were spent by managements trying by every means possible to fight off the threat of the raiders.

If the raider is successful, he gains handsomely and all his time and effort pay rich dividends, but almost everyone else in the game loses. Where the raider fails, he learns a lesson which he can use in connection with his next raid.

We see that no publicly owned company is safe from the raiders, thanks to the rich availability of 'predatory capital' there for the asking. The bulk of the capital is in the form of what are popularly called 'junk bonds', but are really high-yielding bonds that are just pieces of paper (in the form of IOUs, which someone has to guarantee) until they are converted into cash. Companies whose stock is undervalued on the stock market are particularly vulnerable to raids. One of the foremost among raiders, Icahn, is quoted as saying: 'The only real defense is to have your stock price up.' He also candidly observes: 'In takeovers, the metaphor is war.'

Acquisitions

A detailed examination of mergers and acquisitions shows that many of them fail because of their flimsy rationale and poor and inadequate execution.[9] Indeed, in many cases they later have to be divested, usually at a loss. The only parties to profit are the lawyers, the merchant brokers and the go-betweens, who get

Strategies for Recovery 31

paid by the hour, or, in the case of a 'win', reap a commission which is a percentage of the value of the deal. When billions of dollars are involved, even a fraction of 1 per cent is a handsome sum for effort spread over a few weeks or months, and far more than is paid in annual salary to the highest paid business executive. No wonder it is an attractive business and that some of the best brains get involved in such deals.

This is the finding of a critical study and analysis of the subject by a highly respected and admired Harvard Business School professor, Michael Porter, who has been a pioneer in the field of competitive strategy.[9] The study is largely based on an analysis of friendly takeovers using synergy or portfolio management rather than on the raiders' activities, which are seen as an aberration of the takeover phenomenon. The basis of the study was some 4,000 cases of takeovers, joint ventures and start-ups by 33 prestigious US companies that took place between 1950 and 1986. Nearly half of these were in the form of acquisitions, made to enable the company to enter a new product area or alternatively a new market. Half of these acquisitions had later to be divested. The conclusion, very briefly: 'The corporate strategy of many diversified companies has failed – much diversification just doesn't work.'

The reason for the many failures lies in the fact that the three key tests, which must be applied *before* any acquisition is seriously considered, were not in fact applied. These are:

1. *The attractiveness test.* A 'fit' is a must and the temptation to amass portfolios just for the sake of it must be resisted.
2. *The cost of entry test.* The cost must not offset future profits to an uneconomic extent.
3. *The 'better off' test.* The new business must gain competitive advantage from the existing company, or vice versa.

Porter's study has also led to appropriate and effective guidance on portfolio management, restructuring, transfer of skill, and shared activities.

What does all this mean? Acquisitions are made in an effort to diversify or strengthen the acquirer's position in relation to its normal business and with the intent that the acquired company, usually in decline, would be lifted up and put on the road to success for the benefit of both parties. But that rarely happens. On the contrary, the successful diversifiers have relied unusually heavily on internal start-ups rather than on takeovers and acquisitions. This is particularly true where they have been entering fields unrelated to their ongoing business. So acquisitions are *not* always the right course for the company seeking success.

The importance of communication

The processes of acquisition, merger and takeover are designed to help to put a company on the path of recovery, but as we have seen, more often than not the exercise actually proves to be counterproductive. While the drama is being played in the back rooms, the workers, together with the middle and senior management of the companies concerned (and especially those in the company that is being targeted) keep wondering or trying to guess what is happening. Their fate is being decided without their having any say whatever and, what is worse, they are seldom informed of what is in store for them if the deal goes through. This failure in communication demoralises everyone concerned and the grapevine takes over. For success, frank and open communication is essential. We have dealt with this subject at length elsewhere,[10] but the essentials are simple and straightforward.

There is no doubt that the importance of effective communication throughout the corporate structure is well recognised but, unfortunately, largely absent. Peter Drucker asserts in the foreword to a book on the subject of management communication that the great majority of us do not know what to say, when to say it, how to say it, nor to whom to say it.[11] A devastating assessment, but we believe it to be true. We would go a step further, and point out that the weakest link in the communications process is listening. If no-one listens, any attempt at communication collapses.

Since listening is an integral part of the communication process those who manage must realise its importance. There is no doubt that successful companies have learnt – or rather, their chief executives have learnt – the art of getting people to listen. One company, Sperry, once built an advertising campaign around the theme, saying: 'We understand how important it is to listen. When you know how to listen, opportunity only has to knock once.'

Listening is a skill we learn at our mother's knee. While it is the most used skill, it is never taught: merely 'acquired'. We are taught how to speak, read, write, but not how to listen. So when it comes to one company dealing with another, whether for acquisition, merger or takeover, it is of first importance not merely to publicise what is going on, but to ensure that the message is being heeded. Then there is a much greater chance of success.

References

1. Bibeault, D *Corporate Turnaround* McGraw-Hill, 1981.
2. Slatter, S *Corporate Recovery* Penguin Books, 1984.
3. Kibel, H R *How to Turn Around a Financially Troubled Company* McGraw-Hill, 1982.
4. Kharbanda, O P and Stallworthy, E A *Company Rescue – How to Manage a Business Turnaround* Heinemann, 1987.
5. Kharbanda, O P and Stallworthy, E A *Corporate Failure – Prediction, Panacea and Prevention* McGraw-Hill, 1985.
6. Sloma, R S *Turnaround Managers' Handbook* Macmillan, 1985.
7. Gould, M and Campbell, A *Strategic Decision Making* London Business School, 1986, reviewed in 'British company, know thyself' *The Economist* **299**, 28 June 1986, p 69.
8. Johnston, M *Takeover: The New Wall Street Warriors* Arbor House, 1986.
9. Reviewed by Lorenz, C in 'Diversification – the trouble with takeovers' *Financial Times* 8 December 1986.
10. Stallworthy, E A and Kharbanda, O P *Total Project Management* Gower, 1983.
11. Parkinson, C N and Rowe, N *Communication: Parkinson's Formula for Business Survival* Prentice-Hall, 1977.

Chapter 4
When Others Come to the Rescue

There is no doubt that companies and those who run them have to walk a rough road, full of ups and downs. Chapter 1 dealt with the how and why of decline, the second chapter considered how such a crisis could be met and Chapter 3 dealt with some of the recovery strategies that could be adopted. Now we review what happens when those strategies are put into practice. There are a number of pitfalls and traps and we deal with some of them in the hope that forewarned is forearmed.

The individual

The rescue or recovery of a company in decline is typically provided by either an individual or another company. In the former case, if the individual has the right qualities and experience, he can work wonders.

One such individual is Victor Kiam who has shared his experiences in a fascinating book.[1] He spent four years with Lever Brothers, then 13 years with Playtex, moving fast up the corporate ladder and becoming president of one of their divisions in his late thirties. However, he became disenchanted with the direction Playtex had taken following a takeover and left for greener pastures. A firm of headhunters saw in him the makings of a successful entrepreneur and his attendance at a conference of the Young Presidents' Organisation sealed the issue. He bought into the Benrus Corporation and helped to turn it around.

Encouraged by this initial success, he acquired the Remington company, being spurred on to do this by a casual remark he saw in an article by J P Lyet, chairman of Sperry Corporation, who owned Remington at that time: 'We'd rather sell one computer installation than 100,000 Remington shavers.' This gave Kiam an indication that Remington could be up for sale, which proved to be correct. After prolonged negotiations, a financial package acceptable to Sperry was formulated and Kiam did indeed put Remington back on its feet.

This story shows clearly that a company in decline can be

turned around by one person. He doesn't need to be a genius; a point that Kiam in all modesty has made. To him turning around companies in distress is like playing entrepreneurial tennis. Armed with the seven entrepreneurial principles enunciated in Chapter 1, he succeeded.

The product, a shaver, was good to start with, and the company's main problem was diagnosed by Kiam as cash flow, so that became his top priority. A ruthless cost-cutting exercise was put into practice and both distribution and marketing were improved and streamlined. Turnaround followed quickly, but Kiam acknowledged that it was all the result of teamwork – thus giving credit where it was due; a sure sign of a good leader. As a result a company with one of the smallest market shares was transformed into the second largest. The net income of Remington is said to have been some US$10–15 million over 1984 to 1986, this to be compared with a loss of US$5 million five years earlier when Kiam acquired the company. He himself has been featured in a TV advertising campaign built around the claim that Remington shavers, 'shave as close as a blade or your money back'.[2]

Kiam has proved that, as Al Burak, president of Helena Rubinstein, once said: 'You can make big money buying trouble.'

The rewards

If we look at the UK, not noted for high salaries when compared with the USA, Sir Ralph Halpern, chief executive of the Burton group, is said to earn more than £1 million a year.[3] Now 49 (1987), he worked his way up from a £5 a week job selling net curtains for Selfridges to become head of a retailing giant. His remuneration is linked to the profits of the group, as are the salaries of some 75 per cent of the group's employees. To quote Sir Ralph:[3]

> Most companies are prepared to pass power and responsibility down the line, but then the people who are asked to exercise that power get no reward for their performance ... I'm aiming to encourage a system which is meritocratic – where people are encouraged to do well and are allowed to share in the success they generate.

The present Conservative government has been criticised for the patronage it extends to the sort of business leaders who are dubbed 'fat cats' in the USA. Patronage is extended by the granting of 'honours', and while money cannot precisely buy this ultimate perk, it does seem that business profits help. There is no doubt that inclusion in the honours list is an incentive and a plum for executives. Harold Brooks-Baker, publishing director of Burke's Peerage, a publishing and research business that maintains the social register of Britain, says:

> No matter what you may hear, the honours are considered incredibly important for their prestige among business leaders. They provide that extra bit of entrée to certain board directorships, and a social entrée too.

In the UK perhaps one-third of the 1,200 or so names on the honours list each year come from the business world and the list of Britain's 100 highest-paid executives currently includes 28 lords or knights, plus a comparable number of empire honours.

This point is driven home convincingly by the fact that of the 10 top chief executives interviewed by the authors of the book *The New Elite*, eight of the nine Britons (the tenth was an American) had been knighted.[4] Sir John Egan of Jaguar, numbered among this 'new élite', favours high salaries for chief executives if only to attract the best talent into the wealth creating industrial domain.

Returning to Sir Ralph, he not only rescued Burton from oblivion, but has raced along the takeover trail. His latest acquisition is Debenhams, the departmental stores group, secured for some £570 million after an acrimonious struggle, but which has boosted Burton's 1986 pre-tax profits from £80 million to £147.8 million. It is said that his knighthood came not only as a result of his efforts in the high street but also as a reward for his efforts on behalf of the unemployed in setting up a new job creation scheme.

The company

Acquisition

We shall consider acquisition in more detail in Part 2, with the help of several case studies, but let us now look briefly at two success stories and at a case where change of ownership did not help.

The successes
Metropolitan Telecommunications, headed by Russell Banks, made their final acquisition in 1961, buying Grow Solvents, a company four times bigger than themselves. It took a lot of doing, with complex dealings with the underwriters and in the new-issue market, but the effort was well worth it. Metro, as a result, changed its name to Grow Corporation and two years later, as the process of acquisition continued, to Grow Chemical,

When Others Come to the Rescue 37

since some companies in the paint and coating field were acquired. Banks spent the next 20 years acquiring one company after another. So the Grow group grew. Thirty acquisitions later, the end still seems nowhere in sight. Market analysts see the company in a positive light, thanks to its flexibility and its mix. According to Ray Yavneh, president of Forbes Investors' Advisory Institute:[5]

> One of Grow's strengths is its ability to move with the times. They have changed greatly over the past few years. When the auto industry shifted from volatile solvents to powdered pigments and water-based coatings, Grow was able to supply those products.

Banks' ambition now is to become a billion-dollar company. That goal would have seemed distant and perhaps impossible in 1961 when the company made its first acquisition, but he has already taken the company nearly halfway towards his target. Although this series of successful acquisitions have been on a company-to-company basis, there is no doubt that the real driving force has been an individual, as was the case with Remington.

To take another example, a British group, Cookson, with a turnover of US$1.3 billion per year, a diversified chemical company, wanted to get into the US market with a flame retardant for use in plastics, antimony oxide. Although a leading supplier in the UK and Europe, it found entry into the US market difficult since that was controlled by a few well-established American firms. However, a chance came its way at the end of 1978 when NL Industries (formerly National Lead) decided to divest some of its traditional business, including antimony oxide. Starting with this Cookson have made further acquisitions in the USA; their North American Division sales are expected to be nearly US£1 billion by early 1988.[6]

One acquisition included A J Oster, a brass distributor, and this provided Cookson with its North American management team, led by Richard Oster, who now heads Cookson America. Oster, earlier his own boss, fitted into the larger organisation like a 'hand into a glove'. It seems that Oster was looking for something 'bigger' and Cookson found in him what they were looking for in the USA. A spate of acquisitions followed. According to Oster, Cookson's acquisition strategy can be summed up as follows: 'Look for good late-maturing markets where we can find niches in embryonic stages.'

The secret of their success? Once the acquisition is completed it is left alone, apart from assistance at the top management level. Such independence and non-interference helps to keep and even boost the morale of the workforce, thereby increasing motivation.

The failure

Joseph Cavedon Sr formed the Cavedon Chemical Company in 1958 to manufacture lubricants, detergents, cleaners and defoamers. Later, bactericides and fungicides were added to the list. But Cavedon had difficulties and thought the way out would be to be 'acquired' by one of the companies with whom he did business, such as Great Lakes Chemical who supplied ethyl bromide for the manufacture of bactericides, which were used for bleaching newsprint. Meanwhile a British firm, Lunevale Products, obtained a licence to manufacture Cavedon products in Europe.

A chance meeting with a vice president of Great Lakes during a transatlantic flight led to its acquisition of the Cavedon Chemical Company. Joseph Cavedon, at the request of the Great Lakes board, then helped it to acquire Lunevale. The objective was to get a foothold in manufacturing and marketing overseas. As a result, Joseph Cavedon became a director of Lunevale.[7] Meanwhile, the only company, it seems, in the Great Lakes group that was not prospering was the Cavedon Chemical Company: it was suffering by neglect while the rest of the group prospered.

There was fierce competition in Cavedon's line of flame retardants, margins were squeezed and profitability declined to such an extent that Great Lakes decided to divest it in 1976, some seven years after having acquired it. The Cavedon Chemical Company was bought back by its founder, who weeded out the 'me-too' products and concentrated efforts on the 'niche' products. During his years with Great Lakes and Lunevale, Joseph Cavedon had gained valuable experience in locating and selecting the right type of people for key positions and 10 years after its new beginning the Cavedon Chemical Company is thriving – thanks to the experience its founder had gained at someone else's expense. It is clear that Cavedon Chemical Company was neglected while part of the Great Lakes group; no doubt they were concentrating their attention on their newer and perhaps more profitable acquisitions.

Mergers

Merging a company in distress with another healthier company is supposed to rescue the former; in practice it doesn't always work out, as we shall demonstrate in Part 2, using a host of examples worldwide.

The motivation for buying and selling companies varies considerably, but it is important that both parties understand what they want from one another. First, what is the buyer looking for?[8] It could be:

When Others Come to the Rescue 39

- An opportunity to grow faster, with a ready-made market share.
- To eliminate a competitor by buying it out.
- Better integration – horizontal or vertical.
- Diversification with minimum cost and immediate profit.
- To improve dividend yield, earnings or book value.
- To forestall the company's own takeover by a third party.
- To enjoy the prospect of turning around a sick company.

On the other hand, why are companies available for sale? Some of the reasons are:

- Declining sales or earnings.
- An uncertain future.
- Owner wants to slow down or retire with no successor in sight.
- Desire to maximise growth under the umbrella of a larger company.
- To raise cash for a more promising line of business.
- A lack of adequate financial and management skills.
- To concentrate time and effort on what it can do best.

The stages that have to be gone through in order to conclude a deal, either directly or through an intermediary, include:

- Search and exchange of information about each other.
- Preliminary investigation followed by serious negotiation.
- Contract development and closing the deal.

Mergers and acquisitions have been widespread in the chemical industry. In the four years 1981 to 1984, a total of 251 transactions with a total value of US$4 billion took place worldwide. The pace has since not only continued but even accelerated because of the felt need for the restructuring of chemical companies to meet a fast-changing and difficult market-place.

Despite all the care and attention that is paid to the proper completion of a merger, one hears of more and more mergers that have not worked out.[9] Perhaps this is partly because the 'homework' before the deal is not thorough enough: the negotiators are excited and wish to conclude the deal in a hurry. A more important reason, however, seems to be that there is not sufficient follow-through after the deal to ensure that the companies are properly integrated. The post-merger integration requires far more attention and planning than that required to set up the merger. The two parties are so relieved to have concluded the deal that they fail to realise that the real problems come when dealing with the 'nuts and bolts' of the merger. This applies particularly to areas such as accounting and finance, operations, personnel and the organisation of sales and marketing.

In retrospect it has been found that the problems of post-merger integration need to be addressed by the buyer and seller *before* the deal has been closed and not after, as is usually the case. By tackling the problems beforehand, it is possible that the problems encountered will result in the merger not succeeding, and this is far better for both the parties than for the deal to go 'sour' after it has been struck.

Takeovers

We devote Part 3 of this book entirely to the subject of takeovers, documenting several recent case histories around the world. The motivation for a takeover, especially a hostile one, is such that it creates more problems than it solves. It could not be otherwise, for the raider, while professing to safeguard the shareholders' interests, has his own personal interest very much at heart.

However, one learned professor rather surprisingly supports the activities of the raiders, arguing that hostile takeovers[10] are good for the shareholders; serve a unique economic function; and that criticism is largely unfounded and unproductive.

His treatment is extensive, since he deals not only with hostile takeovers but also with mergers, tender offers, leveraged buyouts and proxy offerings. All of these are sometimes associated with the activities of the raiders, such as Carl Icahn, whom the author describes very respectably as a 'takeover artist'! To be fair, the professor does not ignore the other side, quoting Lee Iacocca's view of the Bendix-Martin Marietta takeover:

> It's not a merger, it's a three-ring circus. If they're really concerned about America, they'd stop it right now. It's no good for the economy. It wrecks it. If I were in the banking system I'd say no more [money] for conglomerates for one year.

He also supports the contrary argument by quoting what a former director of Bendix had to say about that same takeover:

> I think ... it's the kind of thing corporate America ought not to do, because the poor stockholder is the one whose interest is being ignored in favour of the egos of directors and ex-executives. And who the hell is running the show – the business of making brakes and aerospace equipment – while all of this is going on?

When Others Come to the Rescue

But having quoted such knowledgeable persons, the professor then defends takeovers by refuting what he calls the 'myths', and summarises what he describes as the 'most important scientific evidence' in that context:

- Takeovers by outsiders benefit the shareholders, they do not harm them.
- Takeovers use assets productively and do not waste resources.
- Takeovers do not siphon commercial credit.
- Takeovers do not create monopoly power.
- Plant closures, layoffs and dismissals help to increase efficiency.
- Anti-takeover action harms shareholders and managers.

It is very clear where the author's sympathies lie. In general, he asserts, the activities of the 'takeover specialists' benefit the shareholders. Why attempt the takeover at all? Again the author's bias is quite clear:

> Takeover specialists like Icahn risk their own fortunes to dislodge current managers and reap part of the value increases available from redeploying the assets or improving the management.

In order to be seen as fair and balanced in his assessments, the author should have added that Icahn and those like him take a calculated risk with a view to making a fortune.

It appears that while the editors of the *Harvard Business Review* published the article, even though it was one-sided, they were uneasy and hoped that there would be a rebuttal. One such was published a year later.[11] The author, chairman of a merchant bank, traces the reasons for the increased activity in the takeover field and points out the fallacy in the belief that takeovers enhance the shareholders' wealth. This is largely illusory and it is at the cost of jeopardising the long-term interests of the company. The huge debt required to service the takeover activity makes sense in the short term for the raider when the cost of the debt is below that of the equity. But to fend off the raider, the target company must substitute debt for equity and thus resort to unhealthy leverage. Takeover attempts can thus leave an otherwise healthy company that had a strong balance sheet with a heavy debt which then limits future expansion, increases the risk for the creditors and the shareholders and puts the company in jeopardy if the cash flow falls short of expectation.

It is also demonstrated that the widespread takeover activity creates a feverish atmosphere under which a prudent board and shareholders are unable to act in the best interests of the company. The author strongly recommends restraint, either voluntarily or by law. The management guru Peter Drucker is quoted in this context as follows:

> Business had better think through what the policies [on takeovers] should be instead of waiting for the 'scandal' that pushes the politicians into demagoguery.

A prominent corporate lawyer, Martin Lipton, recommending strong legislation in this regard, is quite outspoken, asserting that at present there is no defence against a 'two-tier, front-end loaded, bust-up, junk bond takeover'.

The need for self-restraint
The situation may indeed have reached an alarming stage, since the above article in the *Harvard Business Review* was followed by yet another in the next issue, with the title 'Takeovers: the last chance for self-restraint'.[12] The author, the managing director of a broker company, who usually benefit greatly from hostile takeovers, feels that the raid battle is heating up to the point of being destructive. He feels that it may soon undermine the fundamental aspects of corporate management, so that unless the corporate world reforms itself through self-policing, government intervention by way of legislation is a must.

The implications of hostile takeovers go far beyond the fact that the raiders line their pockets while the managements of otherwise healthy companies are driven to the wall. To quote Peter Drucker once again:

> A good many business leaders now hold takeover fear to be a main cause of the decline in America's competitive strength in the world economy.

The raiders are using the corporate world and the capital markets as their playground. Felix Rohatyn, senior partner of Lazard Freres, and a veteran merger adviser, puts it thus:

> [there is a] growing feeling today that the capital markets have become the property of insiders and speculators, of raiders and other professionals to the detriment of the general public.

The author also provides an agenda for reform, designed to safeguard the interests of the various parties involved and to restore confidence in the marketplace. This could include:

- Paying directors in stock.
- More and better information available to shareholders.
- Creation of a new class of stock that would put value on continued ownership.

It would also be of vital importance to provide a voting concentration charter to make any potential change in control a rational, informed decision-making process which would be fair to all the parties involved.

Thus, far from solving the problem of getting companies in decline back on the road to recovery, the takeover, especially the hostile takeover, is seen to create rather than solve such problems. The success rate is very low, as we shall see in Part 3.

References

1. Kiam, V *Going for it – How to Succeed as an Entrepreneur* Collins, 1986.
2. Lueck, T J 'Remington boss out there pitching' *International Herald Tribune* 27-28 December 1986.
3. Laurance, B 'The boss who is worth £1m a year' *Daily Express* 11 November 1986, p 8.
4. Ritchie, B and Goldsmith, W *The New Elite* Weidenfeld & Nicholson, 1986, reviewed by Riley, B 'Why they're in the top ten' *Financial Times* 7 March 1987.
5. Preminger, H 'Grow's 30th acquisition is its biggest' *Chemical Week* 2 April 1986, pp 30-2.
6. Katzenberg, D and Cooke, S 'Cookson shops for more acquisitions in the US' *Chemical Week* 18 December 1985, pp 23-4.
7. Cavedon, J Sr 'How I got my company back' *Chemtech* **16**, April 1986, pp 201-3.
8. Rosenbloom, A H 'Mergers: some work, some don't' Part 1, *Chemtech* **15**, December 1985, pp 724-7.
9. Rosenbloom, A H 'Mergers: some work, some don't' Part 2, *Chemtech* **16**. January 1986, pp 28-9.
10. Jensen, M C 'Takeovers: folklore and science' *Harvard Business Review* **62**, November-December 1984, pp 109-21.
11. Saul, R S 'Hostile takeovers: what should be done? *Harvard Business Review* **63**, September-October 1985, pp 18ff (5 pp).
12. Fogg, J G III 'Takeovers: the last chance for self-restraint' *Harvard Business Review* **63**, November-December 1985, pp 30ff (7 pp).

Part Two

Acquisitions and Mergers

Chapter 5
Motives and Methods

Part 1 set the scene for the rescue of companies in decline. Part 2 takes up one of the possible strategies for their rescue: acquisition and merger, now very much in vogue and part of the 'way of life' in the business world. Of course, companies in good health are also the subject of acquisition and merger for a variety of motives.

Overview

A comprehensive list of motives for mergers contains as many as 13 items, the more important among them being:[1]

- Larger scale for better economies and profitability.
- Expand market share and eliminate a competitor.
- Diversify and thereby restructure to weather the 'storms'.
- Better and fuller utilisation of managerial and financial resources.

Other motives could include these points:[2]

> Acquisition is a cheaper and faster method of entering a new market or a new country. It's easier too, since entrepreneurial skills, which are required when you start from scratch, are rarer.

There are indeed a multitude of motives, although one or two may predominate in a specific situation. The decisions taken are often based on inconsistent and even incomplete information. With a particular acquisition or merger, some of the motives may even be conflicting and incompatible. What is worse, they may be deliberately suppressed during the negotiation stage, their later revelation leading to serious conflict once the deal has been consummated. This can pose problems which would have been much easier to solve had they been aired during the negotiations, well before signing and sealing the deal.

Acquisition and merger can help a company to attain better integration – vertically or horizontally – and they are also a way of ensuring that you do not have all your 'eggs in one basket'. But one surprising feature of the acquisition and merger phenomenon is that even competing companies can find it rewarding to cooperate and merge, provided the law of the land (on monopolies, for example) permits it. In the 1960s, there were serious personnel and industrial relations problems as a result of acquisitions and mergers, but these seem to be fewer now that management is more alert to them.

There is a lack of detailed information on this aspect, however; perhaps the problems are swept under the carpet in order to present a brighter picture. More work and research is required in this area so that the pitfalls are highlighted and can serve as lessons for companies considering acquisitions and mergers. The research should include the long-term results of acquisitions and mergers on management and other personnel, the degree of centralisation, wage differentials, the impact on pensions, fringe benefits and working conditions. The time period on which such a study is based should ideally include a complete business cycle, with its highs and lows.

Policy considerations

Having established that the motives for acquisition and merger are complex, diverse and change over time, it is difficult to form a clear-cut picture of the policy that relates to them. Each country's policy is unique, being based on multiple techno-economic and socio-political criteria. Over a period of time the national merger policies seem to have become less liberal in Europe.

There are also somewhat contrary trends in that mergers involving large companies are subject to close scrutiny in some countries, because of the need to conform to the laws relating to monopoly and the like, whereas in some other countries, such as Italy, small and medium size companies are shielded and protected against bids for merger made by large companies in order to gain control of the market.

More and more countries are regulating and controlling, either explicitly or implicitly, the acquisition and merger business. This has been a growing feature of the attitude taken by governments since the mid-1970s. While initially merger control was merely an instrument for the control of competition, the matter has now become much more complex. Merger control is now often used as an instrument for policies relating to the labour market – by safeguarding employment; and the industrial structure – control of capacity and competition.

Most countries now have a Monopoly Commission or a Cartel Control Board. To take one example, steel manufacture was a growth industry during the 1940s and 50s. Britain was one of the largest steel producers during the nineteenth century, and around the turn of the century US and European firms expanded considerably. This development continued, with new entrants, notably Japan and the developing countries, becoming major manufacturers of steel. As late as 1973 this dramatic growth was expected to continue, with the total world demand in 1985 being estimated at some 1,100 million tonnes. The oil crisis, however, brought about a drastic change, and all of a sudden there was overcapacity everywhere. This led to considerable restructuring of the steel industry in many countries.

For example, Sweden, with a capacity of 5 million tonnes in the mid-1970s and plans for a 40 per cent increase, had to shelve them all. A national Commission appointed in 1976 estimated that for healthy survival the Swedish steel mill capacity would need to be cut by approximately one-half by 1980 and by two-thirds by 1985. A committee was set up to implement this policy decision, the members of the committee being drawn from government, industry and the unions. Its recommendations included merger, with the accompanying loss of some 4,000 jobs, lower steel production and the closing of some mines. All aspects including personnel, forecasting and organisation were considered and decisions arrived at by consensus. Some of the conflict between the diverse groups had to be resolved at higher national levels in order to save the country's steel industry from further distress. This required sacrifices from all the parties concerned, but it ensured that the steel industry was brought down to a slimmer but healthier state.

Without action of this sort at national level, there would have been chaos and the decline and distress of individual steel producers would have continued unabated for a long period. So merger was successfully used as an instrument of policy. This phenomenon occurred elsewhere too, for example in the British steel industry.

Signals for success

The merger of two companies involves the 'marriage' of two corporate cultures, often quite different. Merger failure is usually ascribed to a clash between the cultures of the two parties, but this need not be so. Problems supposedly arising from clash of two dissimilar cultures can and have been surmounted by the acquiring company sending the right signals.[3] The word 'merger' is usually dreaded, because there have been so many failures in the past – all the more reason that care should be taken by the acquiree (the current in-word for the company making the acquisition) to send the right types of signal. These are that there will be:

- A foundation for a new employment relationship.
- A spirit of mutual adjustment.
- Integration by cooperation.

The last item means that a firm *merges*, it is *not* merged: a subtle but most important difference.

Two examples will help to illustrate the point. During 1983 the Mellon National Corporation acquired two Pennsylvania banks, Central Counties Bank (CCB) and the Girard Bank (GB). The first merger went off smoothly, whereas with the second just about everything that could go wrong did. What was the difference? The right signals were sent in the first case, with a clear programme for the employees and the management of CCB, involving them, guaranteeing them employment and security and even letting their loan officers 'hold the line' on charging off loans – thus showing fairness and indicating respect for their opinion. Such signals created a spirit of mutual respect. The CCB president was allowed to exercise his normal powers and the CCB employees were deliberately involved in the merging process. The process seemed logical and natural.

The wrong signals

The GB, however, with a well-known name and a respected clientele, viewed Mellon as a rival with a reputation for arrogance. They had business relationships with each other, both professional and cordial, but somewhat at 'arm's length'. Once the merger was signed and sealed, there were swift and devastating changes at GB and according to a GB employee: 'Mellon marched in with all the finesse of the Russian army insisting that everything be done its way.'

Thanks to GB's severe loan loss problems, Mellon moved in with a vengeance, seemingly to 'clean up', and some of the senior lending officers were either forced out or reassigned. New and more restrictive loan policies were imposed and Mellon also proceeded to reform the retail banking and trust operations of GB to bring them in line with their own practice. Several GB managers were eased out or they defected leaving the bank understaffed.

The signals sent by Mellon were all of the wrong type. There was no foundation for the new employment relationship, integration by force (that is the acquired firm was merged) and, not surprisingly, active and passive resistance to change. Mellon's signals to GB demonstrated a lack of understanding and this set up a destructive cycle.

An essential ingredient was missing: 'A big helping of conversation and more than a grain of humour.' That was the prescription for a successful marriage according to Jane Austen, and a merger is no different. Wrong signals are sent or the right signals are not sent, because the acquiring firm uses formal channels of communications instead of the much more effective informal channels, such as the telephone, face-to-face informal meetings and 'huddling'.[4] Other examples of wrong signals are:

- No 'pep talks' to encourage unity and common purpose.
- No talks to share company philosophy and morals.
- No integration ceremonies or rituals, such as a party.
- No joint task forces.
- No two-way movement of employees.

The reverse of the foregoing, of course, constitutes the right signals. Since so many mergers fail, it must be because more and more firms are being merged rather than merging, as a result of the wrong signals being given.

Acquisition: how to make it work

Although acquisitions and mergers are on the increase, they do not necessarily live up to the expectations of those who initiate them, even when the recipe for success is closely followed. We have outlined above the types of signal which, if sent to the acquired company, can ensure success. Another recipe for success is stated to be a strategic and organisational fit between the two companies. Of course, a perfect fit is neither possible nor should it be sought. Failure in this context can occur because:[5]

- The agreement, instead of being a cohesive whole, is fragmented due to the involvement of outside specialists and experts, each with their different opinions and independent goals.
- The hurry to close the deal leaves some integration issues unresolved.
- Both parties leave certain aspects unsaid, sometimes deliberately.

These factors cause conflicts as the two companies get on with the detail of integration. During the negotiations there is hectic activity among so many different people, some from within the organisations but many from without, that it is hard to tell who is doing what. These people have never worked together as a group before, nor do they share a common expertise or even language (jargon), so that proper communication is extremely difficult. Line managers who have to implement the deal are seldom associated with the negotiations and they may not be aware of the real 'spirit' behind the 'letter' of the agreement.

Some words of wisdom from Bernard Schwarz, who purchased a highly profitable leader in the defence electronics industry, Loral Corporation, in 1971:

> I like to spend a lot of time before the acquisition – even before you get to money terms – to talk about attitudes, to talk about what drives people. I've done a lot of acquisitions ... but the real test ... is what happens after the lawyers and bankers are not there anymore and you have to run the business. Then it comes down to people. So I think the investment you make before you make your deal – in terms of people's relationships – is very significant.

The article by Jamison[5] also includes diagnostic questions as a guide for managers when approaching an acquisition. The important point is that these questions must be asked and answered *before* concluding the deal. The questions are under three broad headings: integrating perspectives; managing the rush to close; agreeing on the essentials.

UK government policy

We noted earlier that each country has its own laws to control and regulate the process of acquisition and merger. The details are too technical for our present purpose, nor do we have space to enter into a comparative study of laws in different countries. To illustrate the type of process and the thinking going on in this field, we shall discuss the policy in Britain, with specific reference to two merger deals which occupied the media headlines for several weeks.

When GEC proposed a merger with Plessey, the Monopolies and Mergers Commission ruled that GEC's bid should not be allowed to proceed. This ruling was based solely on the issue of competition in relation to the proposed merger. The 'public interest' criteria were ignored, it being said that they did not arise in this particular case. The Commission, which according to the government reached the right conclusions for the right reasons, took notice of the widespread opposition – particularly from the two companies' suppliers and competitors. Their customers, unions, local authorities and even MPs raised their voice against the merger. The Ministry of Defence, one of GEC's most important customers, was the strongest and perhaps the decisive critic of the proposed merger. The main arguments *for* the merger can be briefly stated thus:[6]

- There was an urgent need for rationalisation in the field of digital telephone exchanges in relation to domestic manufacture.
- It was uneconomic for both Plessey and GEC to cater to the domestic market and at the same time try to break into the export market.

But Plessey pointed out that a merger is not necessary for rationalisation, which can be achieved simply by either company selling its digital telephone exchange interests to the other or alternatively by creating a jointly owned enterprise. Further Plessey was big enough to enter the international market on its own. For instance, L M Ericsson, the Swedish group, was only half the size of GEC and yet could hold its own in the international markets.

The following argument against the merger was found to be convincing enough for the Commission to opt against it taking place:

> Reduced competition in defence electronics and equipment. Also the potential for competition would be reduced if, for example, Plessey was to enter new lines or re-enter those which it had discontinued, such as the manufacture of torpedos.

The Commission's report raises the wider issue of economy of scale, which industry could well take note of when contemplating acquisitions. Much duplication of effort is thereby eliminated, but this aspect must be considered *before* a merger proposal is drawn up and it should be duly quantified. The failure of several mergers in the past has been put down to vague assumptions being made about the assumed synergy which later proved untrue.

Now for our second illustration, BTR's bid for Pilkington. In contrast to the proposed GEC/Plessey merger, the government decided not to refer the BTR/Pilkington case to the Monopolies and Mergers Commission. This evoked a storm of protest in the light of Pilkington's good image. The company had a reputation for community care and a commitment to long-term research. On the other hand, BTR had a poor image: the company was seen as an asset stripper, the emphasis being on short-term profits. But this seems misleading.[7] The government decision, although completely the opposite to that taken on the GEC/Plessey merger, nevertheless seems to be right. BTR is a well-run company and is known to have improved whatever business it has acquired in the past. Also it is a much more diversified company than Pilkington, which is almost exclusively involved in glass manufacture.

The record of conglomerates is patchy, not only in the UK but also in the USA, but BTR appears to be an exception to the rule. In 1982, BTR's bid for the engineering company Serck was referred to the Commission who found the merger proposal not to be against public interest. There was a shift in policy in 1984 when it was decided that large conglomerate merger proposals would not normally be referred to the Commission unless it was seen to reduce competition, which was of course the case with the GEC proposal discussed above. Otherwise the marketplace is not interfered with.

If company A thinks that it can better manage company B, possibly in trouble, and help to improve its operations or arrest its downslide and put it on the road to recovery, it is perfectly free to persuade the shareholders of company B with facts and figures. This can be overdone, however, as occurred with the Guinness/Distillers' affair in 1986, when the public was bombarded with full-page advertisements from the parties concerned. The management of company B can of course counter company A's claim and put forward its own case. Then market forces will decide the final outcome.

There is a lot to be said for minimum government intervention, but existing merger legislation in the UK and many other countries provides wide enough powers for the government to intervene. Unfortunately it sometimes intervenes in cases where it serves no useful purpose.

An editorial in the *Financial Times*[7] brought an interesting observation from a reader.[8] This was to the effect that the 'public interest' criterion for referring proposals to the Commission should include the windfall profits that predators (such as raiders) make as a result of their financial 'conjuring tricks'. Such profits should be detailed in the published annual accounts. Acceptance of such a proposal could, we feel, help to reduce a lot of the 'tricks' and the wheeling and dealing that takes place, resulting in a much healthier marketplace.

Acquisition and merger for the right reasons

Acquisitions and mergers are seen as an instrument for preventing the decline of companies and restoring them to a condition of health.[9] To use a simple but effective analogy, industry is likened to a coal stove: fresh coal is fed in at the top, and ash withdrawn from the bottom. This keeps the fire going and the stove is not 'choked'. Likewise companies can stay viable and healthy by acquiring an attractive business. Such a business may well be in decline but still offers great potential to an alert management, while at the same time the seller may be relieved to be rid of it. Remember that someone's trash can be someone else's gold mine: this is a basic principle in the recycling of waste and when this happens everyone gains.

Not all such transactions are made on a rational basis, nor do they all succeed. Some are made merely to grow big and create an 'empire' without regard to true value. There was a 'merger fever' in the chemical industry in the 1960s. The fever abated somewhat in the early 70s, but picked up again in the mid-70s and still continues. Acquisitions and mergers in the chemical field have been dictated by a desire to move from commodity chemicals, which were in oversupply, to the high value-added speciality chemicals. They also enabled entry into newer and seemingly more attractive markets; some of the European and Japanese companies entered the US market in this way. However, many of the acquisitions and mergers of the 1960s turned sour and were ultimately divested, although there was always someone else ready to acquire them.

The failure of many acquisitions and mergers was one reason for the decline of many chemical companies in the early 1970s. However, the conglomerates have quite often been able to improve the performance of the companies they acquired and they have certainly prevented their decline, putting them back on the road to recovery. As each case is unique, it is difficult to make any broad generalisations.

The shareholder's view

Shareholders are usually the 'pawns' in the battle between the acquiring and the acquired companies – unless the shareholder is someone like Boone Pickens Jr. According to him[10] – or should we say *because* of him and those like him – the 42 million American stockholders are beginning to assert their rights, but their activity is being curbed by the imposition of a moratorium on mergers in the oil industry, through legislation introduced in 1983.

This seems to have been done at the instance of *Business Roundtable*, representing the 200 largest US corporations, and this despite the fact that both the *Securities & Exchange Commission* and the *Council of Economic Advisors* have shown that takeovers benefit the stockholders. A study by Michael Jensen has shown that shareholders gain as much as 30 per cent on average from such transactions.[11]

Boone Pickens Jr asserts that the moratorium legislation has been prompted by managements in order to safeguard their own interests. According to a Lou Harris poll: 'What executives really want is for the acquirer to be hemmed in, but not themselves ... [further] their hearts don't bleed for shareholders.'

Managements see acquisitions, mergers and takeovers, particularly hostile takeovers, as a threat to themselves. Usually they own very little of their company stock and are therefore not concerned about any gain or loss that the shareholders may make as a result of acquisition, merger and takeover activity. Boone Pickens Jr, as one would expect, blames managements for not being alert to the business environment and he even suggests that they adopt very questionable practices in order to keep their jobs and salaries, their bonuses and 'perks' intact – even at the cost of company performance and the shareholders' interests.

This is, of course, a very one-sided verdict designed to suit his activities in this field, but there may still be some truth in it. Raiders such as Boone Pickens Jr, naturally enough, have their *own* interest rather than that of the shareholders uppermost in their minds, but in the process shareholders cannot but benefit (see Chapter 12).

References

1. Ansoff, I et al, *Acquisitions Behaviour of US Manufacturing Firms* Vanderbilt University Press, 1971.
2. Goldberg, W H *Mergers, Modes, Methods* Gower, 1983.
3. Perry, L T 'Merging successfully: sending the "right signals" ' *Sloan Management Review* Spring 1986, pp 47-56.
4. Merrell, V D *Huddling – the Informal Way to Management Success* American Management Association, 1979.
5. Jamison, D B and Sitkin, S B 'Acquisitions: the process can be a problem' *Harvard Business Review* **64**, March-April 1986, pp 107-16.
6. 'Mergers and competitiveness' *Financial Times* 7 August 1986.
7. Editorial: 'Hot air about mergers' *Financial Times* 20 January 1987.
8. Lucking, A J Reply to 'Hot air about mergers' *Financial Times* 24 January 1987.
9. Copulsky, W 'Buying and selling businesses' *Chemtech* **15**, October 1985, pp 591-3.
10. Boone Pickens, T B Jr 'A stockholder's view of mergers and acquisitions' *Chemtech* **15**, November 1985, pp 648-9.
11. Jensen, M 'Takeovers – Folklore and science' *Harvard Business Review* **62**, November-December 1984, pp 109-21.

Chapter 6
Merger Mania

In the previous two chapters we dealt with motives and methods; now we take a look at the worldwide craze for mergers. The apparent purpose is to put companies in decline on the road to recovery, but this is not always done successfully. This is because the main motive is the desire to grow bigger, but unfortunately this does not necessarily mean better.

A frantic tempo

There is no doubt that acquisitions and mergers in industry worldwide have become quite common. The list of such deals in any one year in the USA alone would fill several pages of this book and the subject is exciting and important enough for continuing media attention. In addition books are constantly being issued on this and related subjects. Typical of these is 'Deal Mania',[1] a summary report in *Business Week* dealing with what the writer considers to be at stake in the merger game and its impact on the vitality of the American economy. Subsequent articles in this particular issue of *Business Week* take up various aspects of the same subject, such as:

- Who calls the shots? Apparently the opportunistic middlemen of Wall Street, who have much to gain from such deals.
- Whose interests do investment bankers really represent? This is illustrated with 'shady' deals.
- Impact of foreign investors. With the weak dollar, billions are being poured into the USA for acquisitions in various industries. What is the long-term effect?
- Is it good news or bad? There's a hot debate on about how the mania for acquisitions and mergers is eroding the economy.
- Management anxiety. Chief executive officers are using anything and everything within their armoury to fend off raiders and other unwanted suitors, and thus stay independent and in charge.

- The market's new rules, if any! It seems that the market forgets about the profit-earnings ratio and Wall Street is agog with dealing and wheeling. Where will it all end?

In 1986 there were 38 billion-dollar deals on the US stock market, ranging in size from US$1 billion to US$6.3 billion. They can be classified thus:

23 Acquisitions or mergers
8 Leverage buyouts
5 Recapitalisation schemes
1 Initial public offering
1 Joint venture

No wonder there is talk of merger mania in the USA – and not only in the USA, although data for other countries is not so readily available nor so well documented. The subject is serious enough to call for an in-depth study of its influence on the overall economy, both national and international, since many of the deals are across national boundaries.

Such frantic activity on the stock market has never been seen since the pioneering days in the USA. Then, in 1901, J P Morgan merged three industrial empires into US Steel to form the first billion-dollar corporation. Now, in 1986, some 4,000 of America's largest companies, including US Steel (now the USX Corporation) have conducted transactions involving some US$200 billion in activities such as those listed above. This should be compared with a mere US$50 billion in 1983 and one US$125 billion deal in 1984.

All this is being done ostensibly for the purposes of restructuring, for the good of the companies involved. With the enormous sums of money that have to be found, the executive power seems to have shifted to Wall Street. All this financial activity is taking up a lot of precious management time and company resources and one cannot but wonder whether the main mission of the corporations – the manufacture of products and the provision of services, the looking after of suppliers, customers and employees – is taking second place. A lot of management time is being wasted in shrinking and streamlining the bloated bureaucracy of business – termed 'corporacy' by a government bureaucrat!

With much overcapacity and a sluggish market, together with intense foreign competition, companies are having to restructure themselves for mere survival. But this seems to be proceeding in an unplanned and rather painful way. The objective is economic regeneration, but we rather doubt whether this objective is in fact being achieved. Unfortunately, in the absence of any coordination or direction from the government, all the action is left to the free market: a market not so free from manipulators, deal makers and raiders, concerned only with their financial enrichment.

Is it good business?

It is certainly good business for all the middlemen: the investment brokers, lawyers and other experts in the field. In Chapter 3 we made mention of the mind boggling fees that such people receive, of the order of US$500 per hour. We have assembled some published data on major US deals over the three years 1983 to 1985 in Table 6.1 and have indicated the fees paid to the middlemen. The deals involved both domestic and foreign markets, were either mergers or acquisitions, and included companies buying their own shares.

Table 6.1 *US deals of the year*

	No of deals above US$1 billion	Total value of the 50 biggest deals US$ billion	Single biggest deal US$ billion	Fee as % of value of deal Buyer	Seller
1983	29	48.2	2.3	0.06	0.29
1984	12	38.4	13.2	0.13	0.37
1985	37	94.6	5.6	0.18	0.26

Source: Various issues of *Fortune* 1984-1986

But is such activity good for the economy as a whole and even for the companies concerned? We have mentioned the enormous drain on management resources and the valuable time spent on such activities. Quite often the action taken is completely unproductive, in that it is taken to protect the company against a bid from an unwanted raider. Part of the problem is that no-one is safe from such raiders, since they do not require large sums of money but a certain manipulative power. Nominal financial resources can easily be supplemented by market finance, most of it in the form of junk bonds (see p 30).

A survey of 600 acquisitions in the USA led to four significant findings:[2]

1. The higher the premium above the market price, the less is the likelihood of success.

2. The more the acquiring company knows about the acquired company, the greater the chances of success.
3. If the management of the acquired company is left to itself, the success ratio is higher.
4. The bigger the buy, the greater the chances of success.

These findings proved to be correct when applied to 10 major acquisitions in Britain and seem to be generally valid. They make sense too – common sense! But there can be exceptions.

Things have changed drstically in recent years, however. The restructuring is now entirely finance-driven and the so-called 'nuclear finance', or high-powered debt with junk bonds allows raiders to threaten and even capture the largest of companies. In order to protect themselves, these companies have to take steps which in the long run may harm their fortunes and growth. But restructuring with a sharp focus on corporate goals can be rewarding provided it makes the company competitive in a business it knows best, even though it may become leaner in the process. The important point is that it should be able to provide the products and services of the best quality at the lowest cost. Lawrence G Franko, international business relations professor at Tufts University puts it thus:

> In the 70s and 80s companies that diversified out of their core areas did worse internationally in terms of market share and profitability than those that did not. The message is clear: focused firms do better.

A very negative point in the current wave of restructuring is that companies are not giving much attention to the financial aspects of acquisitions and mergers. Junk bonds and bank credits have ensured ample and even unlimited finance, but the cost is high. Interest can be as much as 13 to 16 per cent, apart from the risk inherent in such high leverage. Just one serious recession or any other factor which might adversely affect the cash flow required to service the huge debt that has been created could bring the company into serious trouble.

Media mergers

It seems that acquisitions have suddenly become the rage in the entertainment and information industries, to the extent that some TV stations are paying such ridiculously high prices that profits may be unlikely for several years.[3] It seems that the financial markets have fallen in love with these particular industries. As a result, this once insular and highly lucrative business is beginning to suffer. To illustrate this, let us mention some recent developments:

- Prices of television stocks have been zooming, practically doubling in just six months.
- The best TV deal: Capital City bought ABC for US$3.5 billion and thereby formed the largest group so far, capturing one-fifth of the total US market.
- The worst TV deal: Rupert Murdoch acquired six TV stations from Metromedia for US$1.55 billion, roughly twice as much per dollar of cash flow as the Capital City-ABC deal mentioned above.
- A good deal: Tribune Co, a newspaper publisher owning TV stations in five markets, including New York and Chicago, bought Los Angeles independent KTLA for US$510 million.

TV companies are beginning to be compared with valuable and irreplaceable assets such as real estate and oil reserves. But the comparison is already proving fallacious: it is easy to go wrong and pay far too much, without the genius to devise a TV programme which catches the public imagination – and this event is rarer than one might think or hope.

Rupert Murdoch aims to become one of the major players in this TV game, not just in the US but worldwide.[4] With his vast experience in the newspaper field, Murdoch is clear that the two media are quite different: 'I think a newspaper should be provocative, stir 'em up. You can't do that on TV. It's just not on.'

We have yet to see how Murdoch will live with the rules, which do not permit ownership of newspapers and radio or TV stations all in the same market. But he is quite clear on one aspect: if he wants an adequate return on the money invested in buying the TV stations, he will have to offer very different fare from that available on the other networks, which are far too alike.

Starting with a small family newspaper, the Murdoch empire has now grown into an international media conglomerate valued at some US$3 billion. An Australian turned American, he has built the first formidable global media conglomerate incorporating newspapers, magazines, TV stations, book publishing and movie studios. He seems to run it all solo, rolling up his sleeves and periodically taking charge of any new acquisition or project.[5] His decisions have usually proved right, but in time he may well need a bit of good luck as well.

Food industry mergers

There has been a wave of mergers in the food industry in recent years.[6] But for non-food companies who have entered the food business through acquisition, the message is simple and clear: 'Shoemaker, stick to your last.' People – and especially companies – seem to have to learn such basic principles the hard way. Food companies, normally quite conservative and even debt-shy, seem all of a sudden to have developed an appetite for taking risks and have been making many jumbo size deals, some in the billion dollar range. Examples include Beatrice acquiring Esmark and Nestlé acquiring Carnation. At the same time, the smaller companies have been active. There is a clear trend towards consolidation according to James L Ferguson, chairman of the General Foods Corporation:

> ... it is impossible not to take note of the trend toward consolidation ... From our standpoint, consolidation is a means of improving growth, and I think others probably see that too.

But the successful merging of two companies, especially when they are large, can be a herculean task. Integration is difficult, as Ferguson observes: 'Any time you get two big companies and put them together, there are going to be some gears that don't mesh.'

Beatrice, when acquiring Esmark, were attracted not only by the product portfolio but also by the company's management talent. Yet after the deal they lost the marketing miracle in that company, Frederick B Rentschler. Perhaps Beatrice interfered unnecessarily in Esmark's management; a common mistake. If they were happy with things as they were – and that seems to be why they bought the company – then they should have left the management alone.

Another factor is the debt load, which can easily prove to be too heavy to bear. In the Beatrice-Esmark deal, the debt to total capitalisation ratio doubled to 67 per cent and in addition Beatrice had to asborb Esmark's debt load of US$900 million, which in turn had arisen from Esmark's own acquisition of Norton Simon. So we see a chain reaction, a 'snowballing' effect. Fortunately food companies usually have a strong enough balance sheet to absorb such shocks. For the large companies, the debt ratio is less than 25 per cent, which is well below the industrial average of 33 per cent. Since many of the diversification attempts made during the 1960s failed, the food companies have now learnt to expand in their own field, which of course they know best.

The food business, although noted for low growth rates, has something new going for it. Very few (some 7 per cent) of households today are traditional in form, with the husband working while the wife looks after the home. The dual career approach, where both husband and wife go out to work, now predominates, and such families are willing to pay more for pre-prepared meals. In addition, the higher consciousness that has now developed in relation to health and fitness has given further impetus to specialised high-cost 'natural' products. This new emerging market is highly sophisticated and can bring high profit margins.

Where will the food companies go now, in their endeavours to cater for this profitable emerging market? Companies such as Beatrice have opted for acquisitions and mergers. On the other hand, companies such as Campbell Soup, Consolidated Foods and Quaker Oats have opted for internal product development, supplementing this with small but selective acquisitions. The former route can be quite expensive, as indeed it has proved for Beatrice. The price paid was some 16 times Esmark's earnings and some 40 per cent more than Beatrice's own equity. This must have been an all time high. The leveraged buyout which resulted shocked an otherwise conservative food industry. But chairman James L Dutt was quite clear about his objectives: 'If we want higher returns and higher growth, we're going to have to take more risks.'

There is no doubt that with the Esmark acquisition Beatrice has emerged as the industry's leading marketing powerhouse, with well-known national brands, such as Hunts tomato sauce and Wesons oil, part of Esmark's portfolio. These can help Beatrice's own brand names tremendously. Dutt sees a great deal of synergy between the two companies and according to him this deal comes close to the perfect merger. Of course, he has to justify his action in paying an exhorbitant price and time alone will show whether the merger was indeed perfect.

One reason why the food industry caught the acquisition fever was the comparatively low stock prices throughout the industry. The price/earnings ratio was between 6 and 10 in 1983, while margins were rising: from 3.5 per cent in 1980 to 4.0 per cent in 1983. This was the period when the food industry became conscious of the advantages of acquisition. It takes US$10 to 15 million in consumer marketing costs to launch a new brand and the chances of its success are placed as low as 12.5 per cent. Hence the acquisition of companies with a well established portfolio of brands is to be preferred. This fact provided Beatrice with yet another motive for acquiring Esmark.

Chemical industry mergers

There has been a tremendous increase in acquisitions and mergers in the chemical industry, the number having doubled in the last six years. but in terms of value they have practically quadrupled. In 1980 there were some 1,900 acquisitions and mergers, worth some US$47 billion. By 1986 there were some 3,000, worth some US$173 billion. Of these, the chemical deals show an even greater growth rate, and that too over a shorter period. The acquisitions and mergers in the chemical industry doubled from 308 in 1982 to 729 in 1986. Further, of the world total of 1,200 acquisitions and mergers, 60 per cent took place in the USA, 28 per cent in Europe, with the rest (12 per cent) being scattered across a number of other countries. The average value of an acquisition in the chemical industry is about twice that of the average for all industries: US$88 million against US$44 million in 1985.[7]

It seems that more and more non-US companies, such as BASF, ICI, Beecham and Hanson Trust are acquiring US chemical companies. Most in demand has been the electronic and diagnostic chemicals area of the industry. This trend seems likely to continue. The increased activity in this field is an indicator of the dynamic nature of the chemical industry, but the success ratio is rather low, particularly in case of hostile takeovers. A cultural mismatch, with the acquiring company going about the merger in a heavy-handed way is a sure recipe for failure (see examples in Parts 2 to 4).

The acquisition of Conoco by DuPont in 1981, hailed as the largest ever at the time, is now seen as unwise. This has been partly corrected by disposing of a host of assets that do not fit in with the main business stream. Monsanto Chemical is another chemical company that is following the same route, divesting itself of many commodity operations in favour of higher value added speciality products. Union Carbide, spurred to action by the takeover attempt made by GAF is having to take the opposite course. It is having to dispose of some of its 'crown jewels' in order to lighten the debt burden imposed while fending off GAF and other possible unwanted suitors.

In all these cases the companies have emerged healthier and stronger. Union Carbide's stock has risen and is now rated as an attractive investment and the shareholders have been suitably rewarded. Monsanto, however, is using the cash from divestures in order to acquire suitable companies rather than using it to reward the shareholders.

In an effort to have adequate representation in the USA, the world's largest chemical market, the German chemical giant BASF went on a shopping spree, acquiring companies right, left and centre. As a result its 1984 sales of US$2.5 billion jumped by some 40 per cent in the following year.

Since there is worldwide overcapacity in petrochemicals, many of the major chemical companies, like DuPont, ICI, and PPG have sold off such of their operations in the petrochemical field that they considered to be liabilities. Surprisingly enough there have been ready buyers for these cast-offs. The attraction for the acquirer is to get hold of valuable assets at some 20 to 30 per cent of their replacement cost. As is normal in this field, these acquisitions are financed through the use of high debt or leverage. The buyer then needs to provide a mere 10 per cent of the purchase price, the rest being provided by lenders who see in the transaction a once-in-a-lifetime investment opportunity. But both the buyer and the lender must know the type of business concerned and be confident that their gamble will pay off.

Gordon Cain, a 75-year-old industry veteran, a former vice president of Conoco and president of Alaska Petrochemical and PetroTex Chemical, has excelled in acquiring and buying chemical companies. He heads the Sterling Group, which acquired some of the assets of Conoco which DuPont desired to dispose of. Cain has already logged some 15 buyouts, his latest and his fourth in the chemical industry being by far the biggest. Cain raised some US$1.1 billion recently in order to acquire seven recently built plants in Texas including ethylene and high density polythylene (from DuPont and Corpus Christi), together with the ethylene oxide and glycol plants of ICI and PPG. These have been profitable acquisitions and the plants are surviving despite a downturn in the market; they are likely to thrive once an upturn appears in the petrochemicals' cycle, as it must.

Thus companies and plant units in decline in the chemical industry have been put on the road to recovery through a change of ownership.

Synergy

Is synergy, where the new acquisition fits in neatly with the acquiring company, the answer that will ensure success? It could be. United Technologies' chief executive, Harry Gray, is quite clear about his company's acquisition policy. His four criteria in selecting the target firm are:[8]

1. A technology match.
2. A market leader, profitable in its own field.

3. Competent management.
4. In-house development and marketing capability.

Further, having made an acquisition, United Technologies does its best not to change the successful formula on which the acquired company was built. In addition, United Technologies does not go for companies requiring a turnaround. Some companies are good at turnarounds, but not United Technologies. It doesn't have a 'stable' of management experts who can go in and do everything better than the people who have built up the business. This is of course its individual company policy and United Technologies is therefore willing to pay the right price for a going profitable concern.

Companies which are good at turning around a company will look for those in decline which can be picked up at a bargain price and after the turnaround can perhaps be sold off at a profit. They then keep repeating that particular formula: they are specialising in turnaround management and look specifically for companies in distress that have real potential.

Let us sound a note of caution. The apparent bargain in acquiring companies in decline with a view to turning them around, may not prove so in the long run. The turning around of ailing companies through acquisition is reported to be notoriously risky, especially when the acquirer is a large company with its hands already full with its normal day-to-day operations. Its management resource is fully utilised in achieving its main mission, as we noted in case of United Technologies.

Some of the more notable failures in turnaround situations have been:[8]

- Philip Morris, who acquired Miller Beer and turned it around, but could not repeat this in case of the soft drinks company 7UP, which was acquired at a considerable premium (four times the book value) and ultimately had to be divested.[9] (We have already made the point: the higher the premium, the less the chance of success.)
- Colgate Palmolive acquired Helena Rubinstein in 1973 for US$142 million, but having failed to turn it around had to sell it off for a mere US$20 million in 1980.
- Exxon acquired Reliance Electric on the basis of synergy: the former's technological strength in electric motors and the latter's strength in manufacture, distribution and sales. But Exxon failed to achieve a turnaround, as we demonstrate later.

There is no magic formula; what works in one case may not work

30in another very similar case. Each situation is different and no generalisations are possible. Synergy can help, but it is the bottom line which finally matters. There are certain economies to be had when two large firms agree to merge: a lot of duplication in departments such as law, accounts, personnel and sales can be eliminated and the staffing reduced. Such scale economies are more likely to be achieved through mergers with firms that are not direct competitors of the acquiring firm. Acquisition is always cheaper than building anew, but acquisition just for the sake of growth may prove to be very costly. Some companies are 'worth more dead than alive', but it is not easy to identify such companies. Some solid but seemingly dull companies can be very good bargains, but again this is not easy to predict.

It seems that it has become the fashion for large companies to acquire smaller companies simply in order to grow. Growth is a very desirable public image. If a company is not seen to grow, then the question will be asked in the marketplace: 'What's wrong with them? Aren't they in business any longer?'

Growth is, most unfortunately, identified with sales growth rather than the far more important profits growth. Before going on an acquisition binge it is advisable to take note of the warning by an American university president, Richard Berenzden: 'Growth for its own sake is the ideology of the cancer cell.'

References

1. Nussbaum, B 'Deal mania: the tempo is frantic and the future prosperity of the US is at stake' *Business Week* 24 November 1986, pp 74-6.
2. Van de Vliet, A and Isaac 'Mergers' *Management Today* February 1986, pp 38-9.
3. Sherman, S P 'Are media mergers smart business?' *Fortune* **111**, 24 June 1985, pp 98-103.
4. Vamos, M N 'Rupert Murdoch's big move – his goal: a new network from Metromedia's TV stations and Fox's Films' *Business Week* 20 May 1985, pp 70-4.
5. Moore, T 'Citizen Murdoch presses for more' *Fortune* **116**, 6 July 1987, pp 67-72.
6. 'The new food giants – merger mania is shaking the once-cautious industry'. Cover story *Business Week* 24 September 1984, pp 132ff (6 pp).
7. Nordhoy, F 'Acquisitions: a profit-oriented strategy in the chemical industry' *Chem Eng Prog* **83**, February 1987, pp 9-13.
8. Daily, J E 'Do mergers really work? Not very often – which raises questions about merger mania' *Business Week* 3 June 1985, pp 64-70.
9. Porter, M G 'From competitive advantage to corporate strategy' *Harvard Business Review* **65**, May-June 1987, pp 43-59.

Chapter 7
The Megamergers

In the previous two chapters we have seen that acquisition and merger activity is on the increase and is a worldwide phenomenon. Not only are there more and more deals, but the value of individual deals has been going up constantly. The big companies want to grow ever bigger, but in the process do they become better? This is a difficult question, but in an attempt to find the answer let us look at some of the big deals of recent years and see how they have fared.

What is a megamerger?

Megamergers are in fashion, such is the urge for large companies to grow ever larger. For our present purpose a megamerger indicates mergers where the value involved is of the order of one billion US dollars, in line with a recent book on the subject, *Megamergers – America's Billion Dollar Takeovers*.[1] It seems that here as elsewhere in the literature, not only mergers and takeovers, but also acquisitions, are all embraced under the term 'merger'. Sometimes the words are used interchangeably. So a megamerger may denote an acquisition, a merger, a consolidation or even a combination of these when very large firms are involved.

Let's be quite clear: a megamerger is not something new. The first megamerger occurred as early as 1901, when US Steel was formed by combining Carnegie Steel with its leading competitors. The motivation at the time was not spelt out and was probably a mixture of a number of factors: the desire to create a monopoly, increase profits and improve production efficiency. The present chairman, David Roderick, who took charge in 1979, has transformed the company to such an extent that its main interest has shifted from steel (once bringing 80 per cent of its total revenue) to oil and gas.[2] The company's name has as a consequence since been changed to USX. Some US$10 billion in oil assets has now been acquired and over half of the total steel-making capacity has been shut down. This drastic restructuring had become essential in order, once again, to fend off the raiders.[3]

The current trend

The current wave of megamergers is completely unprecedented. Davidson's book on the subject is exhaustive and he paints a picture of what is happening in the field of megamergers without arguing for any particular viewpoint.[1] A lively debate on the pros and cons of mergers and takeovers is vividly portrayed in five parts:

1. Acquisition process, takeover battles, merger mercenaries and shareholders' rights.
2. Mergers past and mergers present.
3. Decisions to acquire, bright ideas, bargains and blunders.
4. The megamerger wave.
5. The consequences of mergers.

In reviewing the current wave of megamergers we have to accept that many such transactions have no valid explanation. They are certainly not all in pursuit of a common or coherent economic objective, and in any case far too many of the large mergers combine entirely unrelated companies. But why this wave at the present time? Megamergers represent a mixed bag for companies, shareholders and society. The present wave has perhaps been triggered by factors such as: tax laws giving incentives to retain earnings; lack of spending opportunities, other than acquisitions; and the desire to build an 'empire'.

It seems that there are somewhere between 50 and a 100 takeover battles in the USA every year and of these only about 5 per cent are said to be hostile, although it is the latter that attract much more media attention. Some of these megamergers have involved fierce takeover contests, at times with two, three or even more firms bidding for the same target firm.

Who really wins?

One instance of this type of contest is the Conoco takeover. Conoco had three suitors: Mobil, Seagram and DuPont. It was DuPont who finally succeeded. But did anybody really win?

Let us look first of all at the winner, Dupont. Its size doubled, but its long-term debt was increased some five times, the stock fell in value and its bond rating was lowered for the first time in the history of the company. Seagram now owns 20 per cent of

DuPont and has three directors on its board. Now Conoco: it has become a wholly owned subsidiary of a smaller company. Will Conoco now be better run by DuPont? That is obviously a very open question. What about Seagram? Seagram had to sell the Texas Pacific Oil Co for US$2.3 billion to buy 20 per cent of DuPont stock for US$2.6 billion and in the process earned US$100 million as income. That same US$2.3 billion put on deposit in a bank would have earned Seagram twice as much. Seagram paid US$92 million for Conoco stock and then exchanged it for DuPont stock. Then, in just three months after the Conoco takeover, Seagram's investment in DuPont, originally US$2.6 billion, fell in value to US$1.8 billion.

Well, who won? No-one really. It was an expensive exercise for everyone, it seems. In retrospect, DuPont's acquisition of Conoco has been termed one of the greatest follies in the corporate world.

Nevertheless, there were some who did win, although they were none of the above three parties. The chief winner was the investment banker who handled the deal. The investment banker and their financial and legal experts earned fees of the order of US$400-US$600 per hour. In 1982, for transactions worth some US$20 billion the fees were said to be US$100 million or more. The merger units at the three leading dealmakers, Golden Sachs, First Boston and Morgan Stanley, each earned some US$200 million in fees during 1985, and this does not include their commissions for helping to raise the necessary finance for the deals.[4]

Does the time and the work these companies put in justify such fees? It appears that those using them cannot even count on their loyalty. Once all the information is in their hands, they may well end up in the enemy's camp, if the fees are more attractive.

Like a patient with a rare and perhaps incurable disease, the doctor's fee is never taken into consideration while there is hope for the patient. The chairman of a company making a large acquisition in 1984 was said to be willing to pay almost any amount. Why? To quote him:

> I can screw up badly. So I get the best people and pay what I have to pay. You pay investment bankers for knowledge of the game. They're good at it; they created it.

No wonder then that they can and do get a 'blank' cheque. Another young dealmaker at a major firm says:

> We always deal with the same players – the same lawyers and bankers – and there are accepted protocols that guys from the sidelines just don't know.

There is yet another factor that comes into play, which can be summarised as 'once hooked, always hooked'. The company concerned has to tell its investment bankers everything about itself – the good, the bad and the indifferent – and will not want such information to be floating around the market. This is what would happen by going to different bankers every time, changing banker in pursuit of a lower fee.

A few corporate chiefs have successfully done the deals themselves, but they need to have extraordinary financial talent. The fees may be high, but a good dealmaker is worth any fee that he may charge. A dealmaker whose fee was the equivalent of 40 US cents a share, takes pride in what he has been able to achieve for his client: 'We got one bid raised from $75 a share to $83. Ask yourself whether we provided the equivalent of 40 cents a share in value.'

Mergers past and present

How is it that the number of mergers is increasing despite many countries having antitrust laws which forbid the merger of rival firms in order to retain competition in the marketplace? American laws are the most strict in this respect and the EEC, West Germany and other countries are lately falling in line with American practice. The antitrust laws are designed to prevent monopoly power and not growth *per se*. This has at times led to the merger of totally unrelated businesses. For example, Greyhound, although primarily a bus company, now earns most of its income from non-bus operations and its name may soon disappear from the US bus scene. Competitors such as People Express are now undercutting bus fares by as much as 20 per cent.[5] Penn Central, once a famous railway company, has long been out of that industry. But in both cases, their name has been retained, presumably for the sake of the goodwill it carries.

It seems that the antitrust laws have been successful in preventing the formation of cartels and monopolies in the USA. This happened in Germany in industries such as steel, rubber, and coal around the turn of the last century. But the same laws have pushed companies into mergers with unrelated businesses and there seems to be no limit to this. In this century there have been broadly four merger waves:

   1898-1902 Creation of monopolies as in Germany, mentioned above.
   1925-1929 Acquisition of related firms, such as customers.
   1966-1968 Large conglomerates built up of unrelated businesses.

1974   Dramatic increase in megamergers, driven on to
onwards   some extent by the activities of raiders.

Megamergers help in that they allow the reinvestment of windfall profits into the existing enterprise. It seems to be one of the best alternatives for this purpose: certainly better than, for example, paying increased dividends, starting a new business or putting the money on deposit in a bank. A merger is much less risky than starting up a new business, and in addition it offers substantial tax benefits. It is an attractive solution for a successful company with plenty of cash, and if the acquisition is of a company in decline or distress, then all the better, since with the injection of the surplus cash and the provision of better management, the company that has been acquired can be put on the road to recovery. Since the company was in decline, it can be picked up at a bargain price: certainly at a much lower price than would be required to start a similar venture from scratch. What is more the complete facility with all the necessary backup is immediately available. There is no time lag waiting for engineering and construction and no risk of time and cost overruns.

'The merger tango'

Acquisitions and mergers have indeed become a game and can even be seen as a dance on the corporate dancefloor. No wonder, then, that we see a *Time* feature on the subject of mergers with the cover heading: 'The merger tango'.[6] The opening sentence is most arresting:

> I suppose you read in the paper today that General Electric just bought RCA. But it's OK, nothing's going to change, because I just bought General Electric.
>
> (Johnny Carson)

Johnny Carson is a well-known TV personality in the USA and it is all supposed to be a joke, but it is a dramatic indicator as to how fast deals are being made these days. The numbers of acquisitions and mergers has grown rapidly since 1980 in the USA. In 1980 it was 1,600, the following year it shot up to 2,300 and by 1984 it had risen to a peak of 2,900.

The average citizen must wonder what is going on as he watches not only the smaller companies but the giants seeking out and acquiring or merging with other giants. There nearly always seems to be a battle, since for every target company there are usually several suitors. The target company is attractive because it is somewhat underpriced on the market. The necessary background data is available to everyone and many may well reach the same conclusion at the same time. But some basic questions are raised: is the current rash of mergers good for the country? For business? For the shareholders? For the employees?

Above all we must ask whether the merger game has not already gone too far. The cover feature noted above followed General Electric (GE) buying RCA for over US$6 billion. This was the biggest acquisition ever of a non-oil firm. It came in the wake of Texaco fighting for its life, faced with a liability of over US$11 billion in damages for 'derailing' the Pennzoil and Getty merger of 1984. A US$4 billion takeover bid for Union Carbide had also been made by the rather smaller firm, GAF. This is another common feature: small companies make a bid and at times buy up far larger ones.

These megamergers, once confined mainly to oil and gas giants now know no boundaries having extended to film makers and even missile manufacturers. The principal architect of the GE/RCA merger, Felix Rohatyn, a senior partner in the investment banking house Lazard Freres notes:

> In my 35 years of business, I have never seen anything remotely approaching this year's [1985] wave of takeovers, mergers and buyouts of every size and shape, including both very good and sound ones and extremely ill-conceived ones.

The really troubling feature of these deals is the enormous amount of debt that is being created. During 1984 and 1985 alone, some US$200 billion worth of stock has vanished from corporate treasuries and has been replaced by IOUs (junk bonds). Even the biggest of firms in every industry are players in this 'game' and the rules are so threatening that otherwise healthy companies are having to resort to this unhealthy means to protect themselves against an unwanted suitor. Precious resources and management time are being frittered away in these completely unproductive activities instead of being deployed for the growth and health of the company. Where will all this lead to? Isn't the so-called solution to the turning around of declining companies posing more problems than were originally there?

These deals may be good business for the investment brokers, but are they doing the economy any good? Serious debate on this and related issues is under way and there is even legislation being enacted in some states in the USA and in some other countries in an attempt to curb the activities of the wheeler-dealers. Similar legislation in many other countries is inevitable in the process of time, as the damage to the commercial and business climate becomes ever more apparent.

The year of the megabid

Megamergers are by no means confined to the USA: the UK has also had its share. So much so that 1986 was described by one commentator as 'the year of the megabid'.[7] By way of example, it was back in 1984 that Blue Arrow joined the Unlisted Securities Market. Since then its chief executive, Mr Berry, has built up a following among the financial press that is the envy of many of the bigger blue-chip companies. In 1984 Blue Arrow was capitalised at a mere £3.1 million, but in only two years its stock market value had grown to £90 million and it had graduated to a full listing. This was after the acquisition of Brooke Street Bureau, Hoggett Bowers (The US market-quoted head hunter), and a string of smaller, privately owned companies. Then, in that same year, Berry turned his attention to the lucrative US temporary employment agency sector and, armed with an extra £30 million following a very successful rights issue, paid US$8 million for Positions, a Boston company, and secured Temporaries of Washington for a down-payment of US$10.7 million. He began 1987 by turning his attention back to the UK market and completed a hat trick by the purchase of Career Employment Services for $10.3 million. Notice how strictly Berry confines himself to the business with which he is familiar.

By way of contrast, Geoffrey Mulcahy, chief executive of Woolworth Holdings, earned a lot of praise for his successful defence of the £1.9 billion unwanted bid from Dixons in the summer of 1986, although the company is still very vulnerable to takeover. Under the Takeover Panel rules in the UK, Dixons must now wait a year before trying again, but that does not prevent other predators from trying. But Mulcahy could avert this by pursuing a restructuring programme of his own, which could well include acquisitions and mergers that would increase the value of the company for his shareholders.

Still further contrast in the 'year of the megabid' was provided by John Gunn. He resigned as chairman of Exco International, the money broker and financial services group in September 1985, following differences between himself and the rest of the Exco board. He joined the board of British & Commonwealth Shipping almost immediately and was appointed chief executive in October 1986. His first task as chief executive was to launch a £672 million bid for his erstwhile company Exco and within three days he had received acceptances from the two biggest shareholders. The newly merged company is worth £1.2 billion, but Gunn is unlikely to stop there.

The airline industry

The airline industry seems to have taken acquisition and merger to heart to such an extent that with several deals now finalised, there are only nine major carriers in the USA controlling some 90 per cent of the market.[8] During 1985-86 there have been as many as 25 mergers, all involving just these nine major carriers, and although more acquisitions and mergers are in the pipeline, the activity is unlikely to be as dramatic as in 1986. Finally, perhaps the number may be reduced to six to eight, but competition will be retained and although fares are expected to rise, they should not rise as fast as the rate of inflation. Rising fuel costs will put a squeeze on profits, but this may be offset by better economy of scale resulting from the major consolidation effort of 1985-86. Texas Air, as a result of five acquisitions (including Eastern, Continental and People Express) is stated to have emerged as the largest company with 20 per cent of the market share, followed by United (15.7 per cent), American (13.5 per cent) and Delta (11.9 per cent) after acquiring Western.[9]

It is still to be seen how this large-scale consolidation in the industry will affect the cheap fares originated by People Express, with its 'no frills' flights in the early 1980s. Consolidation may well retain the benefits of deregulation and although the low fares may not end, the ridiculous US$99 transcontinental fare will have to go. People Express introduced this 'magic figure' fare not only from West coast to the East, but also from the West Coast across the Atlantic to Europe. How could they have survived? Cheap fares, yes, but not so cheap as to involve inevitable loss. For mere survival, the fares will have to be reasonable but with the competition prevailing even after the consolidation, the traveller can still be assured of a good deal.

We now see the same movement developing on the other side of the Atlantic. Most of the Western European countries have one state-owned airline, but of course these companies are in competition worldwide. In Britain the state-owned airline British Airways was privatised in 1986 and now, only a year later, a merger with British Caledonian, its major competitor in the UK, has been agreed, with British Airways buying up British Caledonian for £237 million.[10] The reason is the same: consolidation is required to effect economies and to enable worldwide competition to be met. British Caledonian was in some financial difficulty, having made a loss during its last financial year. The relative size of the two companies can by gauged by the number of aircraft they have: BA has a fleet of 164, while B-Cal has 27. The tie-up is regarded by City analysts as a neat and logical fit, while the two chairmen involved declare that they are creating a 'mega' airline to compete with the American giants. The chairman of BA, Lord King, says that the deal is in the best interests of the shareholders, adding: 'It makes a lot of sense. BA needs to expand and be strong enough to stand up against the mega carriers.'

The proposal is that sales and marketing operations be combined, and with the merging of other parallel operations BA is looking for annual savings of around £50 million (US£75 million). The B-Cal board is recommending the offer to its shareholders and the biggest, Investors in Industry, with 40.1 per cent of the company, has already accepted this offer. However, the merger has now been referred by the government to the Monopolies Commission, and this text has had to leave our hands before the outcome of that referral can be known.

The Saatchi brothers

From practically nowhere to the top spot in the world in a mere 16 years – that is the meteoric rise of the Saatchi brothers in this fast changing field with a single motto: the survival of the fittest.[11] As if that is not enough, their next target is the consulting business, where they want to repeat their earlier performance. Their top position in advertising was assured in mid-1986 when they concluded the purchase of the third-ranked Ted Bates agency.

The Saatchi brothers teamed up in 1970 to start their advertising agency, when still in their mid-20s. The elder brother, Charles, got an early start when, at the age of 18, he joined an advertising agency as an office boy and rose quickly to be a star copywriter. At 25 he formed his own creative consulting firm. His younger brother Maurice, now 40, graduated with distinction from the London School of Economics and started work with a trade journal publisher developing new magazines until 1970, when the brothers took the plunge, starting up on their own. From then on there was no looking back. In less than 10 years their advertising agency became the biggest in Britain. This was in 1979. Two years later they were number one in Europe and five years later number one in the world.

Much of this growth occurred as a result of acquisitions and they learned to grow 'wholesale', rather than company by company, as is normal. This lesson came to them in 1976 when Compton Partners, a long-established London advertising agency that had gone stale handed over control to Saatchi & Saatchi in exchange for fresh blood and talent, which that company had in abundance. This deal brought them a prestigious client, Procter &

Gamble, and what is more, Compton Partners had a listing on the London Stock Exchange. This provided Saatchi & Saatchi with a 'dynamo' for growth. Thereafter furious acquisition activity started across the Atlantic with the purchase in 1982 of New York based Compton Communications, a minority shareholder in Compton partners. Subsequent acquisitions included McCaffrey & McCall, Dancer Fitzgerald Sample, and Becker & Spielvogel.

With its fast-expanding assets and its name, Saatchi & Saatchi floated a £400 million (US$590 million) stock rights offer in London. This in itself was almost the largest such offer ever to come on to the London stock market. With this money they bought the highly profitable company, Ted Bates, and thereby achieved the number one position in the world. All this from the smallest of beginnings and very little capital only 16 years earlier. Hard work and their intimate knowledge of the industry went a long way in helping them to achieve this top position.

It now seems that the best and the largest of the Madison Avenue advertising agencies are being acquired by their smaller British counterparts. In less than two years (since 1986) more than a dozen American agencies have fallen prey to the British invasion, as set out in Table 7.1. The aggressive UK expansion on Madison Avenue has been encouraged by the weak dollar and different accounting rules in certain areas, such as the treatment of goodwill. We have described the way in which Saatchi & Saatchi attained the top slot in some 16 years, but their ex-finance director, Martin Turrell, has done even better. Branching out on his own, under the WPP Group, he acquired four American agencies within the six months up to March 1987 and then bought J Walter Thompson for US$566 million. This company was some 20 times bigger than the WPP Group, and the growth of Saatchi & Saatchi now pales into insignificance when compared with the growth of WPP.[12]

An advertising agency is a service business and its main asset, of course, is its employees. Saatchi & Saatchi employed some 500 people in London in 1976, but that number grew by 1985 to 7,000 in 150 offices in 28 countries, and soared to 12,000 in mid-1986 when the Bates deal was signed and sealed. Their billings in 1985-86 reached US$2.2 billion, 83 per cent up from the previous year and their net profit was US$43 million, over 100 per cent up on the previous year. The profits in 1986-87 are expected to touch US$100 million. The pre-tax profits of Saatchi & Saatchi over the last decade have increased at a compound average annual rate of 53 per cent, a remarkable growth rate. Here is a model case of a company acquiring companies in decline – such as Compton Partners, whose margins were doubled within three years – and

Table 7.1 *The British invasion*

UK group	Company bought	Category	Date
Boase Massimi Pollitt	Ammirati & Pris New York	Advertising	May 1987
WRCS Group	Delta Femina Travisano & Partners	Advertising	Aug 1986
	HBM Creamer	Advertising	Jun 1986
	Masiov Gold & Rothschild	Design and marketing	Dec 1986
	Robert A Becker Inc	Medical ad agency	May 1987
WPP Group	Pace Communications	Real estate communications	Oct 1986
	Harvard Capital Group	Financial communications	Dec 1986
	Sidjakov, Berman, Gomez & Partners San Francisco	Packaging and design	Mar 1987
	Walker Group ICNT New York and Los Angeles	Retail design	Mar 1987
Saatchi & Saatchi	Dancer Fitzgerald Sample	Advertising	Feb 1986
	Becker & Spielvogel	Advertising	Apr 1986
	Ted Bates Worldwide	Advertising	May 1986
Lowe Howard Spink & Bell	30% of Lowe Marshalk	Advertising	Nov 1985
Shandwick	Henry J Kaufman & Associates	Public relations	Dec 1986
	Rand Public Relations Inc	Public relations	Dec 1986
	Rogers & Cowan Inc	Public relations	Apr 1987

Source: Advertising Age

putting them well on the road to recovery through proper management. Evidence indeed that a change in ownership can help a company to realise its full potential.

References

1. Davidson, K M *Megamergers – America's Billion Dollar Takeovers* Ballinger Publishing, 1985.
2. Kharbanda, O P and Stallworthy, E A 'Steel and the Americans' in *Company Rescue – How to Manage a Business Turnaround* Heinemann, 1987, ch 5.

3. Merwin, J 'Not in the next thirty days' *Forbes* 17 July 1987, pp 72ff (7 pp).
4. Petre, P 'Fees that bend the mind' *Fortune* **113**, 20 January 1986, pp 18ff (6 pp).
5. Cameron-Jones, C 'Greyhound Bus may face final run' *Financial Times* 1 July 1986.
6. Greenwald, J 'Let's make a deal – A wave of raids and acquisitions is changing the face of the US industry' *Time* 23 December 1985, pp 30-4.
7. Clark, M 'Men who hold the aces' *The Times* 1 January 1987, p 20.
8. 'After mergers, 9 airlines control 94% of US market' *International Herald Tribune* 27 January 1987.
9. Russell, G 'Flying among the merger clouds – Consolidation is the game in the buffeted airline industry' *Time* 29 September 1986, pp 42-3.
10. Gribben, R '£237m B-Cal deal heads off foreign bid' *Daily Telegraph* 17 July 1987, p 1.
11. 'Saatchi & Saatchi will keep gobbling' *Fortune* **113**, June 23 1986, pp 36-40.
12. Hall, W 'British bulldogs on Madison Avenue' *Financial Times* 29 June 1987, p 23.

Chapter 8
Success Amid Disaster

Despite all the care time and attention that is paid to the preliminaries preceding an acquisition or a merger, it still seems more likely than not that the 'marriage' will run into trouble. This becomes evident when we examine the statistics. Despite the merger mania described in Chapter 6, and the increasing number of megamergers discussed in Chapter 7, the record indicates that some half to two-thirds of them do not work. What is more, this dismal record does not seem to deter the market. The craze for acquisitions and mergers still flourishes.

It is evident that no industry is immune from acquisition and merger.[1] The overall record of recent years shows that one out of three acquisitions or mergers is later undone and the number of divestitures has therefore grown rapidly. Successful mergers seem to have some common factors:

- The companies concerned are in closely related fields.
- The deal is financed by stock swap or cash rather than by borrowing.
- There is no undue premium in the purchase price.
- Management of the acquired company usually stays on.

Some of the success stories include international known companies, such as Nabisco-Standard Brands, Allied-Bendix and Heinz-Weight Watchers.

Some very well known companies, such as Johnson & Johnson, Proctor & Gamble, Raytheon and United Technologies seem to have done well with acquisitions, judging by the fact that only somewhere between 10 and 20 per cent of these have been divested. Other majors, such as General Electric, Xerox, RCA and CBS have had to divest themselves of most of their acquisitions. RCA was itself taken over during the course of an exhaustive study involving 33 large and prestigious American companies who made in all nearly 4,000 acquisitions over the years from 1950 to 1986.[2]

How not to succeed

To take a few typical examples, Philip Morris sought to apply its cigarette success skills, following its acquisition of 7UP, and so turn that company into another Coca-Cola. It has been unsuccessful, despite having spent millions of dollars on this elusive mission. Philip Morris has also been unwilling to accept the fact that lemon-flavoured soft drinks have a limited appeal. Likewise, Coca-Cola's skills in the marketing of soft drinks did not seem to help it in its foray into the wine field.

The oil majors' argument for acquiring mining companies was that it was an allied field: both oil and mining are part of the natural resource business, and can also be considered as part of the energy field, but the argument does not hold water. None of their ventures into mining has been marked with much success, apart from Shell's acquisition of Billiton; but Billiton remains a completely separate organisation.

Yet again, much of the talk about synergy seems to have been mere lip service. In practice it has not happened. Westinghouse Electric sought to become a profitable player in cable TV with its in-house management expertise and financial resources, which it injected into the Teleprompter Corporation's strong market position in that field. But it has been an expensive and disastrous experience; after four years and an expenditure of some US$1.5 billion it seems no further forward.

Conflicting corporate cultures have been another source of trouble, breaking up or putting off many a 'marriage'. In this field we have the Exxon Corporation's attempted acquisition of the tiny Vydec Corp in order to break into the field of office automation.

Earlier we indicated some of the 'dos' for success in acquisitions or mergers. We believe that the 'don'ts' are equally, if not more important:

- Don't leap before looking.
- Don't pay too much cash.
- Don't assume a boom market will always remain so.
- Don't stray too far behind or afield.
- Don't swallow something that is too big.
- Don't marry different or contrary corporate cultures.
- Don't count on the key managers of the acquired company staying on.

Disregard of these basic aspects and insufficient time and attention paid to assessing both the risks involved and the management skills required to ensure success have brought disaster to many companies. As one consultant put it: 'If you don't understand what you've got your arms around, it's damn hard to manage it.'

'The decade's worst mergers'

Failures and disasters have great value, in that they are a powerful means for driving home lessons to management. Fortunately, when we look at acquisitions or mergers we have a compilation of such major failures. For this we have to thank the Wall Street analysts, the acquisition and merger specialists and investigative reporters. Typical of these is Anne B Fisher.[3]

Some 23,000 deals valued at about US$400 billion were surveyed and analysed by several acquisition specialists and security analysts. In the initial list about 40 of the worst mergers were listed and the list was then further shortened to seven. What can we learn? It seems that of all the mergers in the past decade: one-third enriched the acquirer's shareholders; one-third have been a total failure; one-third have cost the investors heavily.

What then are the lessons from this analysis? They can be summed up as follows:

- Think twice before acquiring an unfamiliar business for cash.
- Beware of overborrowing.
- Thorough analysis is a must.
- Beware of the synergy argument.

It is the first rule in our 'don'ts', and the first of the four set out above, that has been broken the most. Investors would have done far better if they had put the cash in their own stock or in the bank. Let us look at three of the seven worst mergers to see what happened.

Exxon acquired Reliance Electric in 1979 for US$1.24 billion. The main business of Exxon was oil and gas, which was now to be combined with electrical equipment. All the signs of synergy were there, since they were two energy-related companies. During the negotiations, Reliance Electric acquired the Federal Pacific Electric Corporation who, it turned out, had been cheating for years on the underwriters' laboratory tests of its circuit breakers. Reliance had what was called a synthesiser (a magic motor controller) and this had been one of the main attractions for Exxon. However, it was found to be too costly to produce and was therefore scrapped in 1981. Then the acquisition of Federal Pacific brought a tangle of lawsuits and product recalls, which proved quite expensive. Altogether a sad story.

Pan Am acquired National in 1980 for US$400 million. Here we have two airlines, so synergy would seem to be assured. Pan Am had international routes, while National ran domestic routes. But flying from Houston to Paris via New York meant a change of terminals at Kennedy Airport. With the advent of deregulation it seems that Pan Am would have been permitted domestic routes anyway, without the upheaval in its organisation that came with the acquisition of National.

Atlantic Richfield acquired Anaconda in 1977 for US$700 million; an oil company branching out into copper mining. Synergy was assumed on the basis that both oil and copper are natural resources with common features, such as exploration and working underground. But the similarity ends there. Winning oil and mining copper ore are two entirely different types of operation. The 1982 recession brought a dramatic fall in the demand for copper and, in retrospect, the merger qualified as one of the seven worst.

The main features of those seven worst mergers are indicated in Table 8.1. Five of the seven acquisitions listed were certainly

Table 8.1 *Mergers that failed*

A: Acquiring company T: Acquired company	Year	Price (US$ billion)	1983 profit (US$ billion) A	T	A's earning (1983) per share with T (US$)	without T (US$)
A: Mobil T: Marcar	1974	1.86	1.5	0.041	3.70	6.12
A: Sohio T: Kennecott	1981	1.77	1.51	0.136	6.14	8.01
A: Exxon T: Reliance Electric	1979	1.24	4.98	0.058	5.78	6.17
A: Baldwin-United T: MGIC	1982	1.16	0.67	0.148	32.68	[*]
A: Atlantic Richfield T: Anaconda	1977	0.70	1.55	0.155	6.03	7.51
A: Pan Am T: National	1980	0.40	0.05	[*]	0.58	[*]
A: Wilkes/Gamble T: Skegma Retailing	1980	0.20	0.025	0.005	1.72	10.86

[*] Not calculable

money losers and failures on that score alone. The other two were probably the same, although the calculation cannot be made with any certainty. The profit/loss figures for 1983 for both the acquiring and the acquired companies is indicated, together with the assessed earnings per share of the company making the acquisition. The companies listed are four oil companies and three service companies, all of them listed in the journal *Fortune* as among the top 500. Two of those listed in Table 8.1, Baldwin-United and Wickes, have filed for bankruptcy since their mergers and another, Pan Am, only just managed to escaped that fate.

Successful mergers

To balance the above stories of mergers that failed, let us consider some mergers during the past 10 years that have worked, in the sense that the benefits from the merger would not otherwise have occurred. The steel industry provides our first example: the merger of LTV and Lykes. When the merger was announced in 1977, the steel industry analysts were aghast. Lykes seemed to be heading for bankruptcy, while LTV was only making a small profit on its steelmaking. Over the past years LTV had lost some US$50 million, yet the company paid US$188 million for Lykes.

In the words of one Wall Street analyst: 'This isn't a merger, it's a suicide pact.' What observers failed to see was that by combining some of the facilities and closing down the less efficient ones, costs could be reduced very considerably. Also one of the Lykes units, Continental Emsco, who made oil drilling equipment, made enough profit in the three years following the acquisition to pay for the entire purchase price.

To take another example, United Technologies (UT) paid US$398 million in 1976 for the lift manufacturing company, Otis. Their chief executive, Gray, followed this up by purchasing Carrier for US$1 billion some three years later. What did he have in mind? His strategy only became apparent when in the following year he added Mostek to his collection. UT formed a separate division, the Building Systems Corporation, that linked together the three companies that had now been acquired. Using microprocessor technology developed by Mostek, Building Systems designs 'intelligent' buildings. Computers control the air conditioning, heating, lifts, communications, security and the like in high-rise blocks. Set up in 1982, Building Systems had sales of US$147 million within a year and goes from strength to strength.

One final example concerns American Express, which of course is known worldwide. The company decided to buy Shearson

Loeb Rhoades (SLR) for US$902 million in 1981, a price judged by analysts at the time to be far too high. But by 1983 SLR profits had jumped 41 per cent to US$175 million, a very adequate return on the original investment. The merger made sense for other reasons as well. It gave SLR's 4,000 brokers access to the 17 million cardholders of American Express. It also seems that the management of SLR was of high quality: their Sanford Waill is now president of American Express. A securities analyst at Paine Webber, Rodney Schwartz, now says:

> American Express bought a different corporate culture. Shearson people are hungry, driven and strong on the nuts and bolts of making systems work. American Express needed that.

Cultural shock

We have just cited a case where companies with two very different cultures nevertheless merged very successfully. In that case it was the acquirer who not only took the company on board, but also its culture, with great benefit to both. But it can happen the other way round, in which event a different and perhaps very alien culture will be imposed on the acquired company, who may well not like it, but may eventually take to it when convinced that it may do them good.

For a convincing example of this we turn to the UK and the acquisition of Dunlop Holdings by BTR in March 1985 for £101 million. The plot of the PAS-score for Dunlop, set against the industry trends, shows that the company, despite its international reputation, had been very much at risk since 1980, as is illustrated by Figure 8.1.[4] The PAS system used in this figure allows companies to be picked out as potentially at risk on the basis of a downward trajectory, well in advance of their moving into the so-called 'at risk' area.[5]

BTR Plc is one of Britain's largest, fastest-growing and broadest-based conglomerates. Suddenly it offered to take over poor, weak, limping Dunlop. This caused apprehension in the market and management circles because of BTR's past record in this respect. It had a name for being an aggressive acquirer, seeking short-term profits.[6] Everyone was asking: Would there be a drastic change in the management? Would parts of the group be sold, like the European tyre-making operations that had been sold by Dunlop to Sumitomo only months before? Would Dunlop degenerate?

Two years later, Dunlop is thriving, undoubtedly because it has a new owner. Both profits and its level of investment have risen sharply, presumably because of the imposition by BTR of rigorous

86 Takeovers, Acquisitions and Mergers

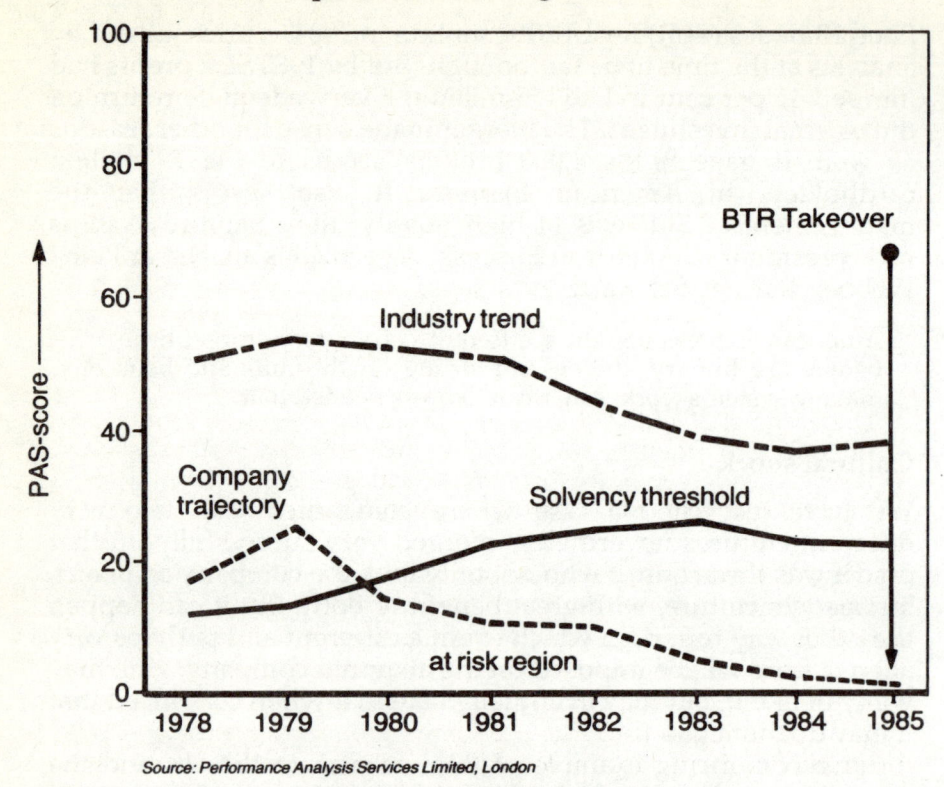

Figure 8.1 *Dunlop in context*

Source: Performance Analysis Services Limited, London

financial controls. John Roberts, who had more than 30 years with Dunlop and is now head of BTR's aerospace group, declared: 'It produced real culture shock, but it has proved a vigorous and disciplined way of controlling operations.' This is a reference to the financial and other control methods which have helped to transform BTR from its small beginnings in the rubber sector to one of Britain's largest companies under the stewardship of Sir Owen Green.

When considering the transformation at Dunlop, credit is also due to Dunlop's own managers for the fine groundwork they had already done when Sir Michael Edwardes was brought in at the end of 1984 to rescue the debt-laden company. A £142 million capital reconstruction plan was devised and BTR's first task was to convince Dunlop's managers that despite what had appeared in the press: 'BTR takes a strategic view of its businesses ... We've proved that we've each got only one head and a couple of eyes.'

The task of integrating the various Dunlop companies into the BTR structure was completed in just four weeks. The existing

Dunlop management and talent was retained virtually intact and this helped to restore the confidence of the Dunlop managers. BTR's financial reporting system with the relevant forms was introduced and the Dunlop managers were quick to adopt it:

> At first I thought this odd ... BTR was on my territory. But then I warmed to it. If my people aren't delivering, then it helps the business to have others come in. People said it would lose us customers but it hasn't.

Another Dunlop manager concurred with his colleague, saying:

> Under the old Dunlop, there were financial corners you could hide in. In BTR, if the strategy is going off the defined track for the year it is very evident and you have to take action ... It is surprising how much else appears to fall into place when return on sales is right.

In fact, the new system has not only given Dunlop managers better control over their operations but even freedom of action. There is much less interference from the head office; BTR have a small, unprepossessing headquarters in London. Taking a long-term view of the business, BTR has helped to rationalise and update Dunlop's factories. Technology has been upgraded, productivity is up and some of the production operations have been brought back from the Far East.

The fear was that BTR would 'milk' the new acquisition and harvest short-term gains but this has not happened. An ambitious capital spending programme, together with the development of computer-aided design is going forward and research and development expenditure, 10 per cent of the sales, is being kept up. Profit and sales for 1987 are targeted to give an 18 per cent growth and long-term development plans are being implemented.

The labour unions, like the management, were not so happy initially. The labour force was cut by 10 per cent, a reduction which was long overdue, but the old Dunlop management did not have the cash to effect this change. It is clear, in retrospect, that this particular acquisition has benefited both companies: BTR has profited by having a new market niche while Dunlop has not only been allowed largely to manage its own affairs but has also been provided with the necessary financial support and management help that it so badly needed. Dunlop knew what had to be done – even before the acquisition a turnaround had been planned and put in place – but BTR helped to accelerate its implementation.

Successful mismatches

In 1978 the marine oil construction giant McDermott acquired the electric-utility boiler manufacturer Babcock & Wilcox (B & W). The price paid was US$750million. The two companies were thought to be an odd couple, but they have forged what must be the model for a perfect 'marriage'.[7] Why were they an odd couple? One was noted for construction work carried out under difficult conditions, often offshore, while the other was noted for shop fabrication. Also, whereas McDermott's growth had been uneven, as is mostly the case with construction companies, B & W had been growing smoothly. McDermott's managers were known to be tough, a cigar-smoking, duck-hunting crew, whereas B & W were seen as 'gentlemen', taking their cues from a top management made up of 'organisation' men.

Others mergers, some discussed in this chapter, have been between seemingly much more compatible partners and yet have ended in disaster. So the McDermott/B & W merger was confidently expected to go badly and the initial signs confirmed this expectation. Many of the B & W managers and four of the top five senior executives left, instead of shifting from New York to McDermott's headquarters in New Orleans. At the same time, McDermott hit a low point in marine construction and as a consequence of the Three Mile Island nuclear power plant disaster B & W, who had built the nuclear reactor, was facing disaster.

Three years later, however, things were much brighter. B & W had helped to smooth out the highly cyclical nature of McDermott's business and has provided the bulk of the combined US$1.1 billion cash flow in the four years since acquisition. For 1981-82, the profits doubled to US$200 million on total sales of US$4.8 billion. Half of the total cash flow went on acquiring the new plant and equipment required to meet an upsurge in marine construction work.

Looking back at how it all started, McDermott began as a one-man show in 1923, the founder R Thomas McDermott making wooden drilling rigs, and the company being called J Ray McDermott, after his father. The 'J Ray' was dropped in 1980. A pioneer in its field, McDermott was organisationally primitive, each division having its own accounting system. Million-dollar deals were made with a handshake and inventories were kept in a notebook by each manager concerned. In the 1960s the company was charged for illegal campaign contributions and also for price fixing. Nevertheless, business flourished and the company landed major contracts for North Sea platforms, which each cost somewhere between US$75 and US$100 million. The company grew tremendously because of the rapid development of the resources in the North Sea and profits in 1977 peaked at about US$200 million. As a result McDermott was flush with some US$500 million in cash and so was able to outbid United Technologies for B & W.

But fiasco followed in both companies. In McDermott's eagerness to get a prestigious offshore project at the Bombay High field (India), the local managers quoted too low a price and the project ended with a US$50 million loss. At the same time a number of other projects also brought losses totalling another US$50 million. Meanwhile, B & W had its own problems at TMI. The chief operating officer, James Cunningham, took charge and with the right blend of know-how and feel for financial matters was able to steer the group out of stormy waters.

A certain amount of discipline has been introduced. Instead of division managers having the authority to purchase a US$1 million barge following just telephone approval from headquarters, they now have to send in a formal request for any item exceeding US$100,000. McDermott has contributed to a massive reduction in office paperwork at B & W, including memos, reports and manuals of operating rules. B & W divisions used to pay no interest on the funds that they were using and the managers could boost operating income just by selling more. McDermott has now introduced an equitable cash-management system whereby the divisions are charged market rate for funds used, thus introducing a significant degree of financial discipline.

Case studies

Avis

Acquisition can prove traumatic for the company that is acquired, yet some companies have not only survived but even thrived despite being acquired time and again. Avis, the car hire firm with a reputation worldwide, is one such, since it still survives despite having changed hands eight times since it was founded. One thing it shows is that it must be an extremely high-potential company to have so many suitors. Here's the record:[8]

 1946 Avis founded by Warren E Avis.
 1954 A Hertz licensee, Richard S Robie, acquires Avis.
 1956 Avis acquired by a group of Boston investors.
 1962 Avis bought by Lazard Freres, an investment bank.
 1965 ITT purchases Avis.

1973 Avis floated as a public company.
1977 Avis acquired by Norton Simon.
1983 Norton Simon, in turn, bought by Esmark.
1984 Esmark, in turn, bought by Beatrice.
1985 Beatrice acquired by Kohlberg Kravis Roberts & Co.

As a result, Avis has had to adjust its accounting year three times to suit that of its changing owners. Such changes bring with them a number of practical problems. Senior managers may well have to change their homes, headquarters and bosses every time their company changes hands. When one considers that each change may well lead to a mismatch, one shudders to think of the enormous risks involved, not only for individuals but also for the company.

The magazine *Fortune* surveyed half a dozen companies that have had two or more changes of ownership in the previous 20 years. All six have survived but there were differences: two went through genuine travail, and overall there was no improvement; one endured pain but survived; one had first an interfering owner and then one who kept his hands off; two remained profitable, as if ownership was irrelevant.

Returning to Avis, one chairman, Patrick Barrett, has survived under three owners. He has probably provided a consistency of purpose within the company by persuading the new owners to leave him and his team alone. Barrett, chief financial officer of Norton Simon, was asked to head Avis when it slid into the red in 1982, going from an operating profit of US$38 million in the previous year to a loss of US$35 million. It seems that Barrett is a good persuader: he persuaded 13 of the 14 senior managers in Avis to leave. Norton's chief of planning Juergen Ladendorf, a former Harvard professor, records Avis' reaction to the then new owners:

> The Avis people hated us from the first day. They thought that Norton Simon could do nothing to enhance their business. Mahoney [Norton's chairman] ruled by dictat and fear, and couldn't extend loving care to his children.

The Avis executives were pestered with all sorts of irrelevant questions and Norton Simon were said to have grown at the cost of Avis. When Esmark acquired Norton Simon, Avis managers were once again apprehensive, but Esmark's chairman, Donald P Kelly, while dining with Avis executives – in itself a very unusual but wise move – put them at ease and said that he would let Avis mind its own business so long as they produced the right numbers. But things moved far too fast for Avis, since Esmark was bought by Beatrice, who in turn were acquired by Kohlberg Kravis Roberts & Co, a leveraged buyout specialist company which had planned to dispose of Avis. So now there will be yet another owner.

Pullman

Successive acquisition seems to have revitalised Pullman, which was otherwise heading for extinction. The name Pullman is known worldwide in connection with the railways. Pullman Incorporated, the dying vestige of Pullman Palace Car Co, founded in 1867, was acquired by Wheelabrator-Frye in 1980. Despite a sudden boom in demand for railway freight cars, Pullman was near bankruptcy and Wheelabrator-Frye had no alternative but to intervene. With a bloated headquarters staff, Pullman was on the verge of closing down its passenger car business.

Some quick surgery was required since the Wheelabrator-Frye chairman, Michael D Dingman, believed in a lean headquarters. With just one public relations person at his headquarters in Hampton, New Hampshire, Dingman could not tolerate a seven-person public relations staff at the Pullman headquarters in Chicago. Thomas M Begel was deputed to Pullman (he later became its chief executive) and within six months the entire headquarters staff of 400 at Pullman was almost totally eliminated and a cut of similar proportions was effected at its subsidiary, Pullman Standard. This was a hard and unpleasant job, but it had to be done for survival. In 1982 Signal bought Wheelabrator-Frye and in 1985, the Allied Corporation merged with Signal.

Between these deals Pullman was spun off and it is now a slim but profitable and independent company with Begel still at its head. The headquarters moved to Princeton, New Jersey, and the revitalised Pullman now makes aircraft seats and galleys, storage tanks and truck trailers. This is of course a far cry from its original business of railcars, but there is still a remote connection.

Pullman has now merged with the Peabody International Corporation and while at one time a target Pullman is now looking for companies to acquire. Naturally enough it is looking for companies such as it once was: fat, troubled and requiring a turnaround. Its chairman has the necessary experience! Having achieved a major transformation at Pullman, Begel lets us in on the secret of his success: 'It creates a lot of stress, but some people thrive. The whole point is to create value for the shareholders.' And Begel ought to know: he himself has thrived on a job well done.

Takeovers, Acquisitions and Mergers

Successful mergers

Some of the corporate marriages that appear to be working include:[1]

Allied and Bendix. The Bendix company seems poised for growth and many Bendix executives and managers have been kept in place for integration and growth.

Conagra and Banquet. This was a good acquisition at a comparatively low price. A new top management has been put in place.

Dayton-Hudson and Mervyn. This merger seems to be a good fit. Both companies are in the same business (retailing) and are doing well. A proven management team has been retained.

Nabisco and Standard Brands. A book-value marriage of near equals with a similar business and complementary products, technology and marketing. The management was integrated in an orderly fashion.

Sara Lee and Hanes. This merger was thoroughly studied before it was consummated. It was a good bargain, since the two companies have compatible marketing and distribution facilities.

Unsuccessful mergers

Of course, many other 'marriages' have gone sour. Typical of these are:

Mobil and Marcor. Mobil took on an unfamiliar business, retailing and containers. It also paid too high a price for a business that was in much worse shape than was first realised.

Schlumberger and Fairchild. Schlumberger paid too high a price. Then key personnel left due to a corporate culture clash and as a result the product development programme suffered severely.

Wickes/Gamble and Skogmo. Wickes took on an unfamiliar business: there was no strategic fit. They took on too heavy a debt burden in order to acquire a diversified retailer that had very serious problems.

This brief review of a series of case histories will, we hope, provide useful lessons for our readers. They certainly have for us! Companies, however, seem to refuse to learn. Wickes, which was protected under Chapter 11 from 1982 to 1984, started looking for a large acquisition in January 1985 when it emerged from bankruptcy proceedings. A building products and retail group, it bid unsuccessfully (US$1.23 billion) for National Gypsum in mid-1986 and was set to take over a leading producer of textile products (Collins & Alkman) for US$1.2 billion.[9]

Various studies and analysis of mergers have led to very disappointing conclusions:[10] most diversification plans fail; most mergers turn out to be rotten; and 90 per cent of mergers never live up to expectations.

The lessons

It is estimated that about one-third of all acquisitions are sold off within five years. According to another study, for every seven acquisitions, there are on average three divestitures, although these were once potentially good acquisitions. The most common cause of failure is a clash of corporate cultures, or 'the way things are done round here'. Changing this is not easy. One well-proven way to bring about cultural change in a company is to start by asking questions, instead of providing a series of ready-made answers.

It seems that most of those who have succeeded in the acquisitions and mergers game have learnt the hard way, by direct practical experience. This may well be the best way, but it is certainly not the easiest. The easiest way, at least to begin with, is to attend a school designed specifically to teach the necessary skills.[10] Alfred Rappaport, a merger specialist at Northwestern University's J L Kellogg Graduate School of Management, runs a week-long programme, called the 'merger week', during which some 80 executives learn how to:

- Search for the right acquisitions.
- Value them, using known indicators.
- Negotiate the deal to their best advantage.
- Make the 'marriage' work.

After an initial introduction to the subject by some of the guest faculty, Rappaport moves on to the hard parts: discounted cash flow analysis, value analysis of acquisitions and the synergies they may create, illustrated by case studies. The participants discuss the strategies and so get a 'feel' for what they are all about. Participants pay US$2,400 for one week of classwork. Of course, it may turn out to be one of the best investments they or their companies have ever made, if only they can take some lessons home and apply them to the next merger they get involved in.

References

1. Daily, J E 'Do mergers really work? Not very often – which raises questions about merger mania' *Business Week* 3 June 1985, pp 64-70.
2. Porter, M G 'From competitive advantage to corporate strategy' *Harvard Business Review* **65**, May-June 1987, pp 43-59.
3. Fisher, A B 'The decade's worst mergers' *Fortune* **111**, 30 April 1985, pp 262ff (4 pp).
4. Kharbanda, O P and Stallworthy, E A 'Dunlop's Dilemma' In *Company Rescue – How to Manage a Business Turnaround* Heinemann, 1987, ch 13.
5. Taffler, R J 'The assessment of company solvency and performance using a statistical model' *Accounting and Business Research* **13**, Autumn 1983, pp 295-307.
6. Dickson, M 'A culture shock that won ardent converts' *Financial Times* (London) 13 January 1987.
7. Tully, S 'The mismatched merger that worked' *Fortune* **105**, 19 April 1982, pp 166ff (7 pp).
8. Main, J 'Companies that float from owner to owner' *Fortune* **113**, 28 April 1986, pp 34ff (6 pp).
9. Hodgson, C 'Wickes buys big textile producer for $1.16b deal' *Financial Times* 10 November 1986.
10. Dobrzynski, J H 'Inside a school for dealmakers' *Business Week* 7 July 1986, pp 82ff (3 pp).

Part Three

The Takeover Syndrome

Chapter 9
The Disease Spreads

In Part 1 we dealt with the issue of companies in decline, the causes and the possible remedies. In Part 2 we looked at acquisitions and mergers. In Part 3 we look at takeovers worldwide. Takeovers also involve a change of ownership, as do acquisitions and mergers, so let us now see whether this particular remedy is any better at putting companies in decline on the road to recovery.

Takeovers as headline news

The literature on the subject of takeovers is growing rapidly, both in the form of articles in the economic, financial and business media, and a host of books. To give a 'flavour' of what is being written and said about the subject, we give you a selection of headlines that have appeared in the recent past:

- Takeover madness – corporate America fights back
- Takeovers – folklore and science
- Takeovers – last chance for self-restraint
- Takeover ethics, anyone?
- Takeover frenzy
- Have takeovers gone too far?
- It's time for a takeover moratorium
- How to ward off takeover sharks
- Is any company safe from takeovers?
- Companies will do anything to thwart takeover artists
- The takeover game
- You never know when a takeover attempt will strike your company
- Is any company safe from takeover?
- US takeovers – the storm's last gust for now
- First Chicago: arming itself for the coming takeover battles

To be fair to the takeover artists, who if hostile are called raiders, there is at least one article in their favour.[1] In its subtitle,

'Takeovers, and the bonds that finance them, are helping make American business less flabby', lies the argument that the raiders offer in defence of their activities. We would normally have ignored it, except that it appears in *The Economist*, a highly respectable economic weekly, the best in its field and unique in the world. The article is based upon what Richard Darman of the US Treasury is quoted as saying about big business in America. Apparently he described it as 'bloated, risk averse, inefficient and unimaginative'. There is no mincing of words here. As one would expect, the statement is supported by the raiders themselves, such as Icahn, but it seems that it is also supported by learned academics such as Professor John Galbraith, although perhaps for a different reason.

Hostile takeovers

Acquisitions and mergers are supposedly friendly, carried out with the consent of the company concerned. A hostile takeover or raid is different. It is not wanted by the company that is being taken over. The raider usually buys a certain percentage of the shares of the company he is after and once his share is large enough, he may offer to buy some of the rest of the stock at a price much higher than that prevailing in the market in order to gain control. Such an offer is attractive to the shareholders, for they benefit by selling their stock, but the management of the company concerned is afraid of losing control of the company or, in an extreme case, even their jobs. The management therefore resists the takeover by all possible means. The survival of the fittest is the name of the game, and some companies will go to any lengths to repel and get rid of the raider.[2]

The target companies have several options to resist a raid. They can restructure the company so as to cut costs and improve efficiency. Another course is to buy their own stock, thereby helping to boost their share price to a level too high to attract a raider. If the target company does nothing, which of course is exactly what the raider is hoping for, it risks being taken over.

The raider's main interest is to make a windfall profit, and he therefore focuses his attention on those companies which seem to be undervalued in the market in relation to their assets. This undervaluing is, according to him, due to mismanagement, leading to a failure to achieve the full potential of the company. A takeover deal is usually financed by the issue of high-yield bonds (popularly but wrongly called junk bonds in the USA, although this term is now spreading to other countries as well).

But is the raider really interested in the long-term well-being of

The Disease Spreads 99

the company? Judging by their activities so far – and raiders are now quite widely spread all over the world – it does not appear to be so. Of course, the threat of takeover by a raider may well alert the management, bringing them to a realisation that something has to be done, and quickly. But by then it is often too late.

A game without rules

Not only for the raiders, but also for the investment bankers, the consultants and the lawyers taking part in takeover battles, it is all a game of chess, where companies are the pawns and the raider is out to checkmate the company by threatening the king or queen. At times, in desperation, a company may seek protection by turning to a 'white knight', a desirable and acceptable owner when compared with the raider.

Chess has accepted rules, but the game of takeovers seems to have none. In some countries laws have been passed, supposedly as a safeguard against hostile takeovers, but the raider and his accomplices are clever enough to find a way around such laws.

Taking the fictitious case of *Sleepy Giant International* in Britain, a typical takeover has been depicted as a game in the *Financial Times*.[3] Notice that the fictitious name chosen is apt: the management is assumed to be 'asleep' and hence ripe for a takeover. The moves depicted are even reminiscent of some of the takeover battles that have taken place in the UK recently, such as the Argyll-Distillers-Guinness and Imperial-Hanson Trust-United Biscuits battles (see Chapter 11). Interestingly enough, Lord Hanson, one of the players, is depicted as a raider. Substitute the real names and the entire game comes to life.

We have noted that no company is immune from raids and a bank offering advice and a service against such activities advertises thus:[4]

> An unfriendly takeover can come out of the blue ... the most effective defenses are built upon a thorough understanding of your true assets ... An acquisition may be a good defensive or a divestiture ... And there are elements of your business [that] have the potential to thwart a takeover ... the best defense is a plan that's well grounded.

To fend off the raiders, Atlantic Richfield restructured itself so as to be slimmer and more efficient. Union Carbide had to make major divestitures in order to pay off the heavy debt the group incurred by buying its own stock when faced with a takeover threat from GAF, although in the process Union Carbide may have gone too far for its health.

A Louis Harris poll of executives in the USA has clearly established that hostile takeovers do more harm (66 per cent) than good (19 per cent) and further that in a hostile takeover situation, the raider has the advantage (70 per cent) over the target company (19 per cent). The percentages expressing the opinions shown were of those executives that responded to the poll.[5]

Raiders on the offensive

It does seem that the raiders have everything going for them. Earlier, size was a deterrent, but no longer. With banks and other institutions willing to lend vast sums, perhaps no company is safe. There have been some very large company takeovers, and each was a record in its turn when it happened. In 10 years the size of takeovers has gone up more than 30 times, as can be seen from Table 9.1, which indicates the value of the largest takeover during any year.[6] We are quite sure that the record will be broken before this book is released. In some cases the unfriendly and the unwanted bidder won. But in some cases the 'white knight' won, as when DuPont snatched Conoco from Seagram, although on analysis, as we saw in Chapter 7, nobody really won.

Table 9.1 *The growth in size of takeovers*

		Cost (US$ billion)
1975	United Technologies buys Otis Elevator	0.398
1977	McDermott Intl buys Babcock & Wilcox (Chapter 8)	0.748
1980	United Technologies buys Carrier	1.000
1981	Elf Aquitaine buys Texas Gulf	2.300
1982	DuPont buys Conoco (Chapter 7)	7.800
1984	Texaco buys Getty (Chapter 10)	10.100
1984	Socal buys Gulf	13.400

Raids, unfortunately, will continue until the banks lose their appetite for such deals. This could happen if interest rates rise or enough of the takeovers turn sour. Alternatively, legislation of the type currently being enacted in some of the states in the USA and elsewhere in the world could put a stop to such deals, or at the least restrict them very considerably.

Meanwhile, the initiative has shifted from offence to defence.[7] Rising stock prices have made takeover deals more expensive and therefore less likely. With uncertain economic conditions, financing is becoming more difficult and the legislation that is in prospect could also curb the activities of the hostile raider, although these ambitious gentlemen will not give up their trade as easily as all that. Guided by the action of Union Carbide who fended off its raider successfully, many companies are taking certain preemptive restructuring steps. Unfortunately, the threat remains, with some of the more recent court decisions favouring the target company management and the raider almost equally.

The raiders are constantly changing their techniques and using new tools from the armoury of weapons available to achieve a successful takeover. One recent technique is the proxy fight. The pressure this brings to the management puts it in an unfavourable position – psychologically, if nothing else – and in the process it may well do precisely what the raider is hoping for.

Four of the prominent raiders, Icahn, Pickens, Goldsmith and Jacobs, having had good 'appetisers', seem to be hungrier than ever. No hurdle, not even the legal hurdle, seems to be high enough to deter them and those who follow in their footsteps. Money is the least of their worries, since each big takeover brings in hordes of financiers seeking to cash in on the situation.

Even the 'poison pill' doesn't deter the raiders – but what on earth is that? Let us give a typical example. If a raider acquires a company against its wishes, the shareholders are permitted to buy stock in the surviving company at half the price. This could be fatal to a raider. However, the grand master of the takeover chess game, Sir James Goldsmith, has found a way around it.[8] Thus, when the San Francisco forest products company, Crown Zellerbach, rebuffed Sir James' partial tender offer, he simply went on buying their stock on the open market until he owned over 50 per cent and then installed himself in the chair. The residual shareholders could not exercise their rights, because Sir James was now a major shareholder, with rights of his own. He had managed to turn the poison pill into a placebo.

The raiders always seem to find a new strategy for an offensive and they clearly have the initiative. Even the bold restructuring moves taken by Atlantic Richfield (Arco), such as divesting itself of a string of petrol stations and a large refinery may only give it a little more time. It seems that Pickens is hard on its trail and is honest enough to declare: 'The fact that Arco has done what they have done doesn't for ever insulate them.'

When asked: 'Then who *is* safe?' Pickens answered: 'Only Exxon.' So has he an eye on the next largest, IBM? We will have to wait and see. Meanwhile, following Arco's lead, all the major oil companies are paring their operations in an effort to shrink.[9]

102   Takeovers, Acquisitions and Mergers

Times have most certainly changed: the growth motto has gone with the wind. Notice that company policy is now being dictated from the outside. Companies are no longer doing what they believe to be best for the company in terms of efficiency, but doing what they believe to be best to ward off a takeover.

Even dynasties are vulnerable

Family-owned companies – some of them quite large, with assets and annual sales in the billions of dollars range – where control usually passes from father to son, used to be immune from takeover. Not any more. To fend off the raiders, they too are having to become slimmer and more efficient. This is sometimes achieved by calling in an outside professional manager to act as chief executive, a really revolutionary procedure with such companies.[10] But some major privately-owned companies, such as Seagram, are carrying on 'as usual'.[11]

Some of the huge publicly-owned American businesses are still family managed. We present a listing in Table 9.2. Their record is a mixed one. On the basis of return on equity for 1985, only four

Table 9.2 *Family fortunes*

Company	Market value (US$ billions)	Family Name	Stock controlled (%)	Return on equity 1985* (%)	(%)	Total return to investors 1975-85* (%)	(%)
Anheuser-Busch	6.0	Busch	20-24	20.6	8.8	17.1	17.0
Corning Glass Works	3.0	Houghton	ca. 20	11.2	10.6	14.1	14.6
Loews	5.5	Tisch	29	15.0	10.0	36.7	18.8
Marriott	3.4	Marriott	21	19.7	14.0	22.2	18.2
McDonnell Douglas	3.2	McDonnell	14	13.5	18.6	20.0	26.4
Motorola	5.4	Galvin	7	3.2	7.4	12.9	17.9
Seagram	4.9	Bronfman	39	9.0	16.5	21.1	24.8
Wang Laboratories	2.8	Wang	38	–5.0	10.9	44.5	18.0
Weyerhaeuser	4.5	Weyerhaeuser	10-12	5.8	9.5	1.2	13.4

* This is the industry average, which can then be compared with the company performance
Source: Fortune 17 March 1986, p 24

out of the nine listed have done better than the industry average, and on the basis of total return over a decade the record is similar, although in two cases (Loews and Wang), the return is nearly twice the industry average. Others are trailing behind their competitors, perhaps because of in-breeding or is the blood getting 'thinner'?

The raiders feel that many of the family-run companies are undervalued on the market because they are considered to be 'takeover-proof'. Not so, according to the raiders. For instance, Richardson-Vicks, which had been managed by the Richardson family for four generations, was taken over by Procter and Gamble when it offered a price nearly twice the market value: US$69 a share against US$37 a share. The family trusts which held a sizeable proportion of the shares could not turn down such an attractive offer: it would have been against their proper duty as trustees.

Getting to know the internal ownership pattern is not easy, but the raiders have their own intelligence sources and they can also exploit family squabbles. Normally, a 20 per cent family stake without extensive trusts would be a good safeguard against a takeover, but not if 'two cousins hate each other'. Such internecine strife affords the raider just the entry he is looking for. But the well-established long-term creed of the family-run business does afford protection against takeovers. It runs:

> This not for us or our children, but for our grandchildren ... We care about investors, not speculators.

But the prospect of a 'raid' may well cause family-run companies to concentrate more on the short-term prospect than the long-term future of the company. This may or may not be a sound approach; the firm and the family may or nor benefit; it all depends. But so long as the controlling family identifies their interests with those of the shareholders, they can be protected against the raiders.

William J Reik Jr, managing director of an asset management company seems to have the knack of spotting attractive investments in family-run businesses and as a result he has done well both for himself and for his clients. One of his star investments was in the New Yorker Magazine Incorporated, owned by the Fleischmann family. This was taken over by Advance Publications Incorporated in 1985. Reik has so much faith in family-run companies that his son is to join him as a researcher and account manager.

One sure way to keep raiders at a distance is to go outside the family for better talent. The forklift truck manufacturer, Raymond

Corporation, with a US$113 million turnover is headed by George Raymond Jr who, at 64 years of age talking about his two sons aged 39 and 36, is quite clear on his priorities:

> I'm not sure whether either really has his heart set on succeeding me, or even if they have the capability. What happens to more than 1,000 employees is important to me. I'd love to see one or both stay but not at the expense of the company.

So he brought in William R Weber, who had 28 years' experience at General Electric, to be his chief operating officer, holding out the possibility of taking over as chief executive officer.

In the case of the family-run company Seagram, the successor has come from within the family, but it is the younger son, Edgar Bronfman Jr, aged 30, rather than his elder brother Samuel, aged 32. We are told that the father had a heart-to-heart talk with Sam and told him bluntly:

> You're good, but an unfortunate fact of your life is that you'll always be compared with your brother. And as my successor he's better.

Jealous and chagrined, Sam nevertheless wished Edgar good luck, which is a good omen for both Edgar and Seagram. Edgar has already shown his qualities, and confirmed his father's judgement. Although not highly educated, with only a secondary school education, he had most of his work experience in show business. But he had only been in the family business for three years when his father made up his mind to have him as his successor. He has a good grip on the family business and has appreciated very clearly the problems facing the organisation in the international marketplace. He drew up a major reorganisation plan and asked his father what he thought of it. The plan scored 95 per cent with Edgar Sr. It seems that Edgar Jr can be quite abrupt when his decisions are questioned, and he is honest enough to admit:

> I suppose you always can find something better in the way you do things ... But any mistakes that I've made I think have been executional in nature, not fundamental.

He is surely on the right track and Seagram should be safe from raiders as long as he is in command. In the early 1980s Seagram had enough cash to attempt the acquisition of the giant oil company Conoco, which was ultimately acquired by DuPont, and this must have provided some substantial training in takeovers for Edgar Jr. This should hold him in good stead in keeping the raiders away from Seagram.

Weathering the storm

Based on their past experience, Standard & Poor of New York and the Practicing Law Institute, also of New York, have compiled a list of 12 ways to ward off takeover raiders and share sharks.[12] The more important among them are:

- A new class of stock.
- Supermajority rules.
- Increased ownership by insiders.
- Golden parachutes: a stock option for senior managers.
- Negotiated standstill agreements.
- Spin-off/disaggregation defence.

(The golden parachute ensures that the top managers are freed from any worry about their own financial position and can concentrate on corporate matters. They provide for substantial payments to senior managers if their services are terminated as a result of an acquisition, takeover or merger.)

An excellent book on hostile and friendly takeovers reviews the situation 10 years after the takeover in order to determine who was hurt and who benefited from these transactions.[13] The consequences of the spin-offs, the refinancing, any subsequent public share offers and even bankruptcies are analysed. The fortunes of some of the early winners in these transactions have been found to change with time. For example, some of the aggressive acquirers of the 1960s found themselves saddled with a lot of problems in the 70s. So one has to go far beyond the normal news media to ascertain the long-term effect of takeovers before one is in a position to pass judgement and say whether they can indeed help a company in decline. Friendly takeovers are more in number, but the hostile takeovers dominate the economic, financial and management media.

What is certain is that the speculation that goes on in relation to takeovers, the rumblings caused in the stock markets and the impact that they can have on a country's economy have got everyone worried. Sommers, of the *Business Roundtable*, which represents the 200 biggest US corporations presents the concern of his members thus:[14] 'The business of this country is fast becoming, if it is not already, in the words of Keynes [a noted economist] a "bubble on a whirlpool of speculation".'

The view of the corporate raiders, as expressed by their

self-styled leader Boone Pickens, is that corporate restructuring on a massive scale will continue so long as there are 'undervalued assets in the marketplace'. The noted economist, J K Galbraith, warns:

> ... [there is] nothing economically useful in this merger activity. It does not produce goods or increase efficiency ... or improve the operation of the system. If anything it is damaging to the system because it diverts attention from the hard tasks of producing goods and service efficiently.

It has been estimated that US companies have spent over US$7 billion since 1979 in buying back shares from corporate raiders at a premium, a process known as 'greenmail', doing this in return for a promise that they will be left alone. So such payments become the raiders' 'reward' for their activities, whether they be fair or foul.

What do we conclude from all this? Is a hostile takeover the answer when companies are in decline and need to get back on to the road to recovery? We think not. There are better ways, as we will see.

References

1. 'In defence of raiders. Takeovers, and the bonds that finance them, are helping make American business less flabby' *The Economist* **301**, 15 November 1986, pp 19-20.
2. 'Getting rough with the raiders – Companies will do almost anything to thwart takeover artists' *Business Week* 27 May 1985, pp 24-6.
3. 'The takeover game' *Financial Times* 24 December 1985.
4. 'You never know when a takeover attempt will strike your company' advertisement by the Continental Bank *Fortune* **105**, 28 June 1982, p 51.
5. 'An outcry against hostile takeovers' *Business Week* 27 August 1984, p 16.
6. Hector, G 'Is any company safe from takeover?' *Fortune* **109**, 2 April 1984, pp 18-20.
7. Ehrlich, E 'Twilight for the lone raider? Higher stock prices and Volcker's curbs make deals more difficult' *Business Week* 27 January 1986, pp 19-29.
8. Worthy, F S 'What's next for the raiders?' *Fortune* **112**, 11 November 1985, pp 20-8.
9. Norman, J R 'ARCO enters oil's new era – the majors are slimming down before the raiders do it for them' *Business Week* 13 May 1985, pp 16-7.
10. Leinster, C 'Business dynasties face the raiders' *Fortune* **113**, 17 March 1986, pp 20-5.

11. Leinster, C 'The second son is heir at Seagram' *Fortune* **113**, 17 March 1986, pp 26-9.
12. 'How chemical companies are fending off raiders' *Chemical Week* 11 July 1984, pp 34ff (6 pp).
13. Michael A and Shaked, I *Takeover Madness – Corporate America Fights Back* John Wiley, 1986. Reviewed in *Financial Management* **15**, 2, Summer 1986, pp 59-61 by Bradley M Bloom under the heading 'Putting takeover madness in perspective'.
14. Hall, W 'UK takeovers: the storm's last gust – for now' *Financial Times* 2 December 1986.

Chapter 10
Who Takes Over Whom?

When we examine takeovers in detail we see that sometimes there are no winners among the companies concerned: just losers. The only beneficiaries are likely to be the consultants, lawyers and the host of advisers, together with the investment bankers. In this chapter we consider, by way of illustration, the Pennzoil, Getty Oil and Texaco takeover triangle. But first, let us look briefly at the role played by the investment banker.

The bankers always win

The investment bankers' role in acquisitions, mergers and takeovers is to advise their clients on such deals and also to arrange the finance required. The finance is usually in the form of 'junk bonds', high-yielding bonds that are just pieces of paper (IOUs, which someone has to guarantee) until they are converted into cash. Of course, in some cases they may not be converted into cash, if the companies concerned in the deals are unable to pay.

We do not know, nor is it relevant to this present study, which of the investment bankers were involved in the series of triangular deals among the three oil companies whose experiences we will now review. It is the principle that we are concerned with.

The heading of a three-full-page advertisement of The First Boston Corporation & Credit Suisse First Boston Limited reads:[1] 'Leadership in Mergers, Acquisitions and Divestitures'. The copy reads in part:

> In 1986, First Boston's Merger & Acquisition Group acted as financial adviser on seven of the 10 largest deals announced, more than any other investment banker. First Boston advised on more than 240 mergers, acquisitions, divestitures and leveraged buyout transactions worth over $75b, including over 100 transactions over $100m each. Together with its affiliate ... the firm advised on more than 50 international transactions worth $20b.

It then discusses its 'unparalleled depth' of experience in its 160-person Merger & Acquisition Group with professionals in New York, London and Tokyo. This is followed by a list of the deals presumably put through by them. One page is devoted to international deals, another to domestic (that is, US) deals, where the values range from US$9 million to US$3.6 billion, but there are a number where the value is not disclosed.

This is quite a set-up, and it must cost a lot to keep it all in being. But of course it must be profitable: after all it is in the business purely for commercial purposes. What would the investment bankers involved in the triangular deal between our three oil companies have earned? A considerable amount of money, and this for merely providing a service, with no direct involvement.

A takeover triangle: Pennzoil, Getty Oil and Texaco

The background

This particular deal, or rather deals, since there were two of them, is a first of its kind. It is no wonder, therefore, that it has attracted a number of cover stories.[2,3,4,5] In addition, the drama has not only attracted a large number of write-ups in the economic and financial media all over the world, but has been the basis of several full-length books.

The oil industry has been shrinking since the 1973 oil crisis and for mere survival the oil companies have had to 'restructure' themselves. What is more, the value of the larger oil companies has been falling because both the reserves of oil and gas, together with the price of their products has been falling, particularly in the 1980s. As part of the restructuring process there had been 11 major deals valued at over US$1 billion each by 1983, with total property worth US$50 billion changing hands. The companies concerned included Conoco, Marathon Oil and Cities Service.[6] Soon thereafter Getty Oil was for sale and the possible suitors included Sun, Superior Oil and Pennzoil, each with its own credentials and offers.

Pennzoil had as chairman J Hugh Liedtke, while Getty Oil was run by Gordon Getty, the sole trustee for the Sarah C Getty Trust and the four son of J Paul Getty. These two got together round the negotiating table, and seem to have liked each other, so that the other suitors were pushed into the background. (We mention the names of the 'players' concerned, because what we are dealing with is essentially a human drama, where the personal egos, the likes and dislikes, played a crucial role.)

Pennzoil first offered US$100 per share; this was then raised to US$110. They finally settled in January 1984 at US$112.50, there being at the same time a complex financial deal. The Getty board had expected a better deal and although they did not favour the Liedtke offer, they approved it on the basis that a 'bird in the hand is worth two in the bush'. The market quotation was around US$65. However, one director, Chauncey J Medberry III, held out and refused to ratify the deal. Prompted by him Gordon's niece Claire Getty, a beneficiary of the trust which he was representing on the board, won a stay order pending full disclosure of the terms of the agreement.

Texaco, who had been watching what was going on, now stepped into the fray. Just a day after the Pennzoil deal was approved by the board McKinley, the chairman of Texaco, brought in First Boston to hammer out a deal which would be marginally more attractive than the Pennzoil offer. Texaco offered US$125 a share and final agreement was reached at US$128 a share. It was also a good deal for Texaco, since it worked out at around US$5/bbl, compared with Texaco's own cost of around US$12/bbl over the past five years. The deal would have increased Texaco's debt from 11 per cent to 39 per cent of the capital, which McKinley considered to be quite moderate as a short-term burden.

Happy with the deal, First Boston concluded that investors in Pennzoil had gained while the stocks of the buyer company (Texaco) declined. So who really won? It was too early to pronounce judgement at the time the deal with Texaco was struck, but the two investment bankers involved got away with big fat fees. First Boston received US$10 million from Texaco and Getty's investment bankers, Goldman Sachs, collected US$18.5 million. In addition, Kidder Peabody got US$15 million for representing the Getty Trust and for playing to the tune of Claire Getty. All these several parties are clearly winners at the point when the deal was struck, but we have to reserve judgement concerning the companies themselves because of the ensuing 'war'.

War between the Gettys

One of the star players in the above drama has been Gordon Getty, aged 53. His wife Ann, 45, who claims to be a housewife and a mother, is known to have played a major role behind the scenes. For one thing she helped her husband in recruiting new directors who would support him on the board. Busy overseeing the battle for the right suitor, he may have delegated this recruiting function to his wife. Also his main love is music, not business management; he composes and sings and is also a brilliant mathematician.

While young, Gordon spent short terms at Getty Oil but without making much of an impression on his father, J Paul, who ignored all his children and Gordon was no exception. Gordon was in fact not considered competent by his father. On his father's death in 1976, Gordon, as a trustee of the family trust, went on to the board. But he was not able to provide the type of leadership Getty Oil needed, with the result that the company was put up for sale. Gordon and Ann saw the chance of a lifetime when the Pennzoil offer was made, but Claire Getty saw it differently and moved the deal towards Texaco.

Gordon continued to turn to his first love, music, rather than to the US$4 billion family trust amassed as a consequence of the sale of Getty Oil. Even after the huge capital gains tax had taken its toll there would still be some US$3 billion left, almost as large a trust as the Ford Foundation, which has assets totalling US$3.3 billion. Gordon Getty was the sole trustee, but the family began to fight over the control of this huge trust and the way it was to be managed. A legal action was started in 1983 in the name of Tara Gabriel Galaxy Gramophone Getty, a boy then 16, who was in line to inherit part of the assets of the trust. The dispute has escalated to an all-out war between the three sisters who are entitled to a share of the income from the trust. They are pictured by the media as sweet, unassuming and non-materialistic, but there is such a lot of money at stake that almost anything can happen.

Before the sale to Texaco, each sister's income was about US$8.6 million per year, but after the sale of Gerry Oil in early 1984 for over US$10 billion, their income jumped practically four-fold overnight. That should have made them happy. They had their uncle to thank, who as the sole trustee had for himself three times the share of each of the three sisters. But the sisters are annoyed since, according to them, the sale violated the provisions of the trust. More than that, they do not want Gordon to be in charge of their money and destiny. To add fuel to the fire the sisters have charged that during the negotiations to sell the family oil company Gordon leaked some confidential information concerning the company to one of the bidders.

While this legal battle goes on the income from the family trust is being deposited in the Treasury. It seems that the battle could well go on for years and meanwhile they are losing millions in interest alone.[4] However, Gordon himself couldn't care less: he would rather keep on enjoying his first love, music. He does not want to be the keeper of his nieces. He, therefore, personally favours a solution where the money is partitioned out between them all. Meanwhile the lawyers and the money managers retained by the various members of the family are doing very nicely.

Let us now leave this family feud and return to our main theme, the three oil companies and their future.

Pennzoil goes to court

Pennzoil had a contract to buy Getty Oil and has charged that the Getty family breached this contract and that Texaco induced them to do so.[7] So far the facts; now for the fiction. The net worth of Pennzoil was about US$1.2 billion, but nevertheless the company claimed US$14 billion in damages thus: US$7 billion in compensatory damages; US$7 billion in punitive damages.

Such astronomical claims are quite normal but the plaintiffs are usually satisfied with only a small fraction of the original claim. Indeed, even a few hundred million dollars would have made Pennzoil a lot richer, and in anticipation of this Pennzoil's stock rose by 37 per cent during the latter half of 1984, at a time when most of the oil industry stocks were sluggish.

It seems – and this later became a crucial legal point – that Texaco indemnified the Gettys against any damages arising out of the Texaco-Getty merger. That alone, argued the Pennzoil lawyers, indicated that Getty had a contract with Pennzoil and had asked Texaco to cover them accordingly. Pennzoil's chairman, Liedtke, called the Texaco-Getty deal 'absolutely outrageous'.

Based on the agreement reached between Pennzoil and Getty on 3 January 1984, Getty had issued a press release saying that an agreement, in principle, had been reached for the deal. The Texaco lawyers argued that the price had been agreed upon and that the board would have had to approve any definitive agreement. Although Pennzoil were unable to stop the deal with Texaco coming into effect, the judge agreed that a transaction had been agreed upon between Pennzoil and Getty and that perhaps Pennzoil could establish that it had a contract to that effect.

Pennzoil were satisfied that the trend events were taking was in its favour and therefore on the basis of a legal technicality dropped its charges against Texaco in Delaware and brought up a new case against Texaco in Houston, Pennzoil's hometown. It was on the basis that Pennzoil opted for a jury trial which they could get in Texas but not in Delaware. Texaco, however, alleged that Pennzoil was looking for favourable hometown treatment in Texas.

Pennzoil won and the jury awarded it US$10.5 billion in November 1985 – the largest ever award. It seems that this was far more than even the most optimistic hopes of Pennzoil itself. So intensive negotiations started in order that the two companies might reach an out-of-court settlement. Texaco offered to buy Pennzoil for some US$3.5 billion in cash and debt against Pennzoil's net worth of about US$1.2 billion, the difference between these two figures representing the compensation payable against Pennzoil's claims for damages. The attitudes between the two companies had hardened and the main stumbling block was the personal animosity between Liedtke and McKinley, respectively the chairman of Pennzoil and Texaco. Texaco's offer was rejected outright.[8] However, the very fact that Texaco had accepted its liability in principle triggered off a lot of speculative action and Pennzoil stock soared.

Texaco's offer was rumoured to be US$100 a share and this added further fuel to the fire. Offers for the conclusion of an out-of-court settlement ranged from Texaco's figure of US$0.5 billion to Pennzoil's asking figure of perhaps US$2 billion. Meanwhile the legal battles continued.

Liedtke is know to be a stubborn and shrewd financier and is credited with a history of creative and even controversial deals, and it was thought that he could teach Texaco a thing or two.[3] Liedtke in fact preceded the present generation of raiders by nearly two decades. Pennzoil had been built on a hostile takeover back in the 1960s.

Born in 1922, the son of a lawyer who acted for Gulf Oil, Liedtke attended Amherst, the Harvard Business School and the Texas Law School. He started in practice in 1947, but six years later joined George Bush to form Zapata Petroleum. The two parted as friends and Liedtke spotted a reserve-rich but management-poor oil company, the South Penn Oil Co, controlled by – who else – the legendary J Paul Getty. After having been put off by an offer to manage it, Liedtke and his circle of investors bought up the shares, got Getty as an ally and won control.

Three years later Pennzoil was born as a merger with Zapata, and it then took over United Gas, 10 times its size. Growth continued slowly but steadily until that crucial deal was struck with Getty Oil in January 1984, which would have made Pennzoil an industry top ranker. Texaco stepped in and frustrated this ambition by walking off with Getty Oil, at which point Pennzoil sued Texaco for breach of contract and won a US$10.5 billion award.

Texaco under pressure

The attempts at an out-of-court settlement failed, so where will they go from here? Would the US number three oil company (Texaco) and fifth largest industrial corporation in the world seek protection under Chapter 11 of the bankruptcy law, while appealing against the verdict, meanwhile posting a bond with a value that would be almost one-third of the company's total assets of some US$38 billion?

Immediately after the court ruling in favour of Pennzoil its stock shot up from US$63 to US$91 and then fell back again following rumours that a settlement was being negotiated. Meanwhile, Texaco's stock nosedived from the year's high of US$41 down to US$27. Pennzoil went on a shopping spree and was busy drilling for reserves while Texaco was trying to sort out how to get out of trouble.

Texaco won a victory in January 1986 when a Federal Court of Appeals in New York upheld a lower court ruling reducing the Texaco bond from over US$12 billion (this was inclusive of interest and penalties) down to US$1 billion. But in April 1987 the Supreme Court in Washington ruled that only the Texas courts are competent in this matter, so the Federal Court had acted improperly.

McKinley, who was planning to retire in April 1985, stayed on, but it is said that the Pennzoil litigation takes up nearly three-quarters of his time. Will he be able to see his company through, and get it out of the 'web' he has woven round it? In the past McKinley has been known to thrive under pressure and he has almost always succeeded in his objectives.[5] But while he has very strong opinions and is quick to speak his mind, McKinley is said to humiliate executives in the presence of their peers. McKinley retorts: 'I may be interpreted as asking harsh questions, but I don't mean it that way. If people are afraid of me it's because of fear of their inadequacy.'

It is also believed that it was not any specific flaw in Texaco's legal position, but its arrogant deportment that led the jury to favour Pennzoil. This situation may have arisen because of the wrong personal equation between Liedtke and McKinley, but no-one dare tell McKinley about it or advise him that he is mismanaging the Pennzoil case.

The original jury award of US$10.5 billion was reduced to US$8.5 billion by a higher court. Seeing that such stakes were involved, Pennzoil and Texaco could have come to an amicable agreement in January 1986: Pennzoil had a big victory (the award was firmed at US$8.5 billion), while Texaco had a little victory (the value of bond that had to be posted had been reduced from some US$12 billion to US$1 billion). But with attitudes hardening and the personality clash continuing between the two chairmen they were getting nowhere.[9] It seemed that they were preparing for a winner-take-all situation, which for Pennzoil meant collecting the full award, while for Texaco it meant paying nothing. With such attitudes of mind the legal process could take years and meanwhile interest alone on the award was adding up at the rate of US$2,000 a minute!

With respect to the US$2 billion offer, Liedtke termed it one 'designed to be rejected'. The proposal had further convinced Liedtke that talks would serve no useful purpose. To quote him: 'So far Texaco's management has been totally unwilling to face up to the fact that they have got a problem here. In my opinion there is no chance of a settlement until they do.'

McKinley justifies his taking over of Getty Oil as follows: 'We did nothing wrong ... We were simply the high bidder.' But it most certainly was not as simple as that, as McKinley knows or should know, otherwise why did Texaco have to indemnify Getty Oil against the takeover? Prior to the jury award, Texaco thought that its liability from the suit was 'not expected to be materially important' and according to Liedtke this description fits in with McKinley's post-verdict negotiating stance.

Pennzoil probably wasn't willing to settle for less than US$4 billion before the talks broke off. The directors of Pennzoil and Texaco will have to consider several factors as they decide whether to settle or whether to fight on. The will to fight must be weighed against the enormous cost of operating a business in such a state of stress and uncertainty. There is also substantial pressure on the shareholders, especially those of Pennzoil, anxious to reap their 'windfall'.

The outcome?

At the moment nearly everyone is losing; meanwhile the lawyers are still receiving their fees. Texaco, Pennzoil, the two companies' suppliers, the shareholders and the employees are all suffering loss because of the dispute. America needs all the oil they can produce but at the moment their managements' efforts are mainly unproductive because of two stubborn men with strong egos, and a very peculiar US litigation system.

The US$8.5 billion award that Pennzoil won has now grown to some US$11 billion including interest and penalties. Texaco offered to pay some US$2 billion to satisfy all the Pennzoil claims, but it didn't take Liedtke much time to reply with an emphatic 'no'.[2] Immediately Texaco filed for bankruptcy for protection, the largest company ever to do so. The step is harmful to both the companies and to the country as well. Gerard Nirenberg, a lawyer and president of Manhattan's Negotiation Institute observes:

> This is a typical degenerating negotiating situation, each side seeking to be firmer than the other ... this is how we get into wars. This is how divorces occur. And it's simply how two giant corporations can go down the drain.

Liedtke was willing to settle for something between US$3 and 5 billion and sent an offer to this effect, but it was already too late. Texaco had filed for bankruptcy. The two men were adamant. If Texaco had agreed upon US$3 billion the market would have reacted so favourably as to up its market value by more than US$3 billion. Texaco doesn't think much of this argument and counters that with the statement: 'Whatever we offer now will be less than our last proposal.'

The two chairmen seem completely incompatible: they do not seem to understand or respect each other enough to be able to communicate effectively. Both talk, neither listens. Instead of filing for bankruptcy, Texaco could have posted a billion-dollar bond while the appeal process was going on, but it threatened to opt for bankruptcy and Liedtke didn't take the threat seriously, hence the stalemate.

Bankruptcy doesn't really help either of the two parties. It reduces Texaco's incentive to settle out of court, since it is protected and shielded from the execution of the US$11 billion judgement. Yet, as long as the jury verdict stands, Texaco has not great leverage over Pennzoil. Further, bankrupt companies need not pay the unmatured interest, since it has not yet come due. One asks whether recourse to Chapter 11 was a ploy or a negotiating stunt. Texaco says definitely not: 'It was done to stay alive' – but one feels that this is very much an overstatement. A reorganisation plan will have to be approved by a majority of the creditor groups (shareholders, secured debtors and unsecured debtors) under the watchful eye of a judge. This could take years, but meanwhile Texaco is protected and it may well emerge from bankruptcy a healthier company.[10]

What will Liedtke do with the windfall, if and when it comes? Perhaps conduct a spin-off, one of his favourite tricks, whereby the parent company takes some of its own assets and a new company is created by using them. The ownership does not change but in due course the shares of the two companies are traded separately. His long-term plans? To retire once the case is resolved. He has no heir apparent and he intends to break up

Pennzoil into four companies, but of course all this must await the final outcome of the historic battle royal raging with Texaco. In a way, both Texaco and Pennzoil are to be blamed for mismanaging this affair and letting it run into a stalemate.

The lessons

Before closing this chapter, let us draw some lessons:

- Even the best of lawyers and investment bankers can be wrong.
- Before agreeing to indemnify, find out why this is required.
- Try to avoid a jury trial. If that is not possible, then treat the jury trial with seriousness – a jury may do anything.
- It is often wiser to settle even if you are right.
- In negotiations, respect your opponent's position.

Of course, it is far too late now for Pennzoil and Texaco to learn these lessons. The damage has been done, but it could be prevented from getting worse by heeding them. Hopefully Liedtke and McKinley's successors will see sense and settle the affair, starting with the last lesson first.

References

1. Advertisement in *Financial Times* 20 January 1987, pp 19-21.
2. Sherman, S P 'Managing – The gambler who refused $2billion' *Fortune* 115, 11 May 1987, pp 50ff (6 pp).
3. Norman, J R 'The scrappy Mr Pennzoil – Hugh Liedtke didn't need the Texaco fight to learn how to play rough' *Business Week* 27 January 1986, pp 48-53.
4. Loomis, C J 'The war between the Gettys' *Fortune* 111, 21 January 1985, pp 20ff (9 pp).
5. Sherman, S P 'The man who got hit for $10.5 billion' *Fortune* 113, 17 March 1986, pp 70-3.
6. Nulty, P 'How Texaco outfoxed Gordon Getty' *Fortune* 109, 6 February 1984, pp 106-9.
7. Loomis, C J 'Pennzoil goes for gusher in court' *Fortune* 111, 21 January 1985, pp 29-30.
8. Norman, J R 'Pennzoil still has Texaco squirming' *Business Week* 20 January 1986.
9. Sherman, S P 'Inside the Texaco-Pennzoil poker game' *Fortune* 111, 3 February 1986, pp 90-2.
10. 'How Texaco lost sight of its star' *The Economist* 303, 18 April 1987, pp 59-60.

Chapter 11
UK Takeover Battles

The newspapers call him 'Lord Jim'. To his secretary he is simply 'Lord H'. To his enemies he is the 'predatory peer'. However he is described, James Hanson, chairman of Hanson Trust Plc and a member of the House of Lords, has become the undisputed leader in Britain's swelling takeover scene. He has now been in the takeover game for more than 20 years and the companies he has acquired produce a number of mundane, straightforward products such as bricks, batteries and shoes. But Hanson has managed to put together one of Britain's largest, fastest-growing groups. In the course of his leadership, Hanson Trust has increased its profits from £138,000 per annum (in 1965) to over £467 million in 1986 and now employs more than 90,000 people. Let us look at just one takeover bid involving Hanson Trust.

The fight for Imperial

It seems that with the battle to acquire Imperial, the hostile takeover bid, born in the USA, arrived in Europe with a vengeance. The contestants took full-page advertisements in all the dailies to sustain their case and some of this advertising was suspect.

Hanson Trust won the support of Paul Channon, the Trade and Industry Secretary, when in February 1986 he made his first contentious takeover judgement. He gave Hanson Trust full rein to pursue its bid for Imperial, thus effectively scuppering the agreed tie-in between Imperial and United Biscuits, which was being reviewed by the Monopolies and Mergers Commission.[1]

Within a week United Biscuits had moved in an attempt to thwart Hanson Trust by buying a 9 per cent stake in Imperial, while at the same time improving its offer: a shares-and-cash bid worth £2.5 billion (US$3.5 billion). The Hanson bid at that time stood at £2.3 billion.

United was trying to keep its bid alive while waiting for government approval. It was favoured by the Imperial board and had proposed the sale of Golden Wonder, who manufacture potato crisps, in order to avoid the problem of a snack market monopoly. On that basis, it was thought, the Office of Fair Trading would wave the bid through.[2] But this move was challenged by Lord Hanson, who said that Imperial was selling Golden Wonder 'at a discount' and 'over the heads of its own shareholders'. There were press reports that the sale of Golden Wonder was imminent at a figure between £50 and £60 million, while City analysts valued the company at around £70 million.

Hanson Trust issued two documents entitled 'Why you should vote *no* to United Biscuits' offer for Imperial' and 'The value of Hanson Trust's offers'.[3] Hanson claimed that the purchase of Imperial by United Biscuits was a breach of the Stock Exchange rules, which forced the Exchange into introducing a rule to prevent companies entering into similar arrangements without the shareholders' consent.

It seems that there was little between the bids in terms of value and the outcome at that point was expected to be decided on the two different concepts involved and the expectations concerning the after-bid performance of the shares.

Thus far phase one of the battle. Towards the end of March United Biscuits finally got permission from the Trade and Industry Secretary to go ahead with its bid. This was after a nail-biting 10-day wait.[4] It did not increase its offer, so what happened next depended to a large extent on the way in which the shares of both United Biscuits and Hanson performed up to

Figure 11.1 *Hanson Trust advertisement: Imperial takeover battle*

United Biscuits	Hanson Trust
United Biscuits' best and final bid values your Imperial shares at 355.7p.	Hanson Trust's best and final bid values your Imperial shares at 378.5p.
United Biscuits' earnings per share have grown by 9.2% pa over the last 5 years.	Hanson Trust's earnings per share have grown by 33.9% pa over the past 5 years.
United Biscuits' shareholders have, over the last 5 years, seen their dividends grow by 13.2% pa.	Hanson Trust shareholders have, over the last 5 years, seen their dividends grow by 28.7% pa.
United Biscuits gives you the option of taking well under half their offer in cash.	Hanson Trust gives you the option of a 100% cash alternative.
United Biscuits would be buying a company 2½ times its own size.	Hanson Trust would be buying a company smaller than itself.
£1,000 invested in United Biscuits in 1980 would now be worth £3,308.	£1,000 invested in Hanson Trust would now be worth £13,962.

the date their respective offers closed. At that point United Biscuits had 21 per cent of Imperial and Hanson 26.9 per cent.

Then came the full-page, bold advertisements in all the dailies. Hanson came out with an advertisement offering 'a few facts for every Imperial shareholder caught in the middle of the current takeover battle'.[5] The 'facts', of course, all favoured Hanson, as shown in Figure 11.1 (page 119). Two pages away from the advertisement (key text as Figure 11.1) was another full-page advertisement, placed not by United Biscuits, but by the target company, the Imperial Group. The text of that advertisement is shown in Figure 11.2.

Figure 11.2 *Imperial Group advertisement: Imperial takeover battle*

Imperial Shareholders: for direct advice telephone your Chairman, Mr Geoffrey Kent.

Mr Kent will tell you precisely why he and the Imperial Board unanimously recommend the United Biscuits offer.

Sir Hector Laing, Chairman of UB, will tell you why the agreed partnership between UB and Imperial makes such profitable sense – both immediately and in the future.

Please ask the operator for Freephone Imperial Group.

Hanson won, paying £2.7 billion in the end. Six months later we read that its two latest acquisitions, SCM in the USA and the Imperial Group in the UK, are being rapidly dismembered, enabling Hanson to recoup most of the original purchase price.[6] Imperial's brewing subsidiary was being sold to Elders IXL, the Australian group (see Chapter 13). This was in accord with Hanson policy, since when it buys up a conglomerate it does so with the clear intention of keeping only part of the business for its own portfolio and selling the rest to the highest bidder.

This could be a good approach: it is probable that Elders, with its brewing experience, could prove a more effective manager of Courage than Imperial. Thus Hanson's role in the redeployment of industrial assets could be very helpful. But it seems that the Hanson 'touch' is not liked in the City: apparently it doesn't allow large fees to be won by the City institutions. Indeed, although not directly relevant here, since it took place in the USA, perhaps Hanson's greatest coup was not the acquisition of Imperial, but of the US conglomerate SCM, best known in Britain for its typewriters. Purchased for US$930 million, Hanson Trust immediately began carving it up at immense profit. By selling the

SCM paint operation to ICI and other minor disposals, Hanson recouped the whole of the purchase price. In other words, in a matter of months Hanson had gained control of a major office equipment and chemicals company at practically no cost.

Let us bring the Hanson saga to a close by quoting from another of its full-page advertisements that appeared in the dailies at the end of that same year. It presented the Hanson Trust results for 1986, saying:

- Profit and dividend *up* for the twenty-third consecutive year.
- Profit *up* 83%.
- Earnings per share *up* 35%.
- 28% annual growth in EPS over last 10 years.
- Dividend *up* 33%.
- One for three scrip issue.
- Balance sheet shows £3.5 billion in cash.

The same advertisement also proclaims, in view of the large interests Hanson Trust now has in the USA: 'A company from over here that's also doing rather well over there.'

Elders bids for Courage

We mentioned that Elders IXL bought Courage, Imperial's subsidiary, from the Hanson Trust. It took this company a long time to break into the UK brewing industry, which has always been unfriendly to outsiders.

Elders IXL spent some two years stalking Allied-Lyons, eventually in September 1986 gaining the approval of the Monopolies Commission, which took nine months to consider the case, but found almost everyone else opposed to the idea, including the Bank of England, seven trade unions, the National Union of Licensed Victuallers and the Maltsters' Association of Great Britain.[7] Hence Elders IXL purchased Courage instead for £1.4 billion.[8]

Remember that Hanson had paid £2.7 billion for the complete Imperial package only six months earlier. The sale of Courage, together with SCM Paint and other companies, gave Lord Hanson some £3.5 billion cash in hand, to which he proudly refers in the advertisement quoted above. With so much cash in hand, he was in a position to make another sizeable acquisition without borrowing from the banks.

Having bought Courage, Elders IXL dropped its Allied bid in the face of the general opposition.[9] It opted for the simpler, safer but more expensive way of breaking into UK brewing. The decision was also a compliment to Allied-Lyons' management, who fought a classic takeover defence, driving its share price out of reach by dangling before the market the best part of another £100 million in acquired profits. To quote – and this is very clearly seen in the City as a 'game':[10]

> The £1.4bn purchase of the Courage brewery business by Elders IXL from Hanson Trust confirms the corporate reputation of both Lord Hanson and Mr John Elliott as supreme dealmakers. It leaves Sir Derrick Holden Brown, chairman of Allied-Lyons, as the delighted wallflower at a ball he never wanted to attend ... Hanson was a latecomer to the dance, but this deal leaves it in an even stronger position to pursue its own acquisitive ambitions.

The Guinness saga

No review of the takeover scene in the UK would be complete without a mention of the Guinness takeover of Distillers. In the space of five years, Guinness, the maker of the black beer born in Ireland, has transformed itself from an ailing brewer with a stockmarket capitalisation of under £100 million into an international drinks company worth more than £2.6 billion. To achieve this, the Guinness family had to give up the executive chairmanship of the company it founded and Ernest Saunders took over as managing director in 1981. Saunders' strategy for improvement concentrated on four main areas: drinks (still only beer when he took over); retailing; health products and services; and publishing. The latter is based almost wholly on the *Guinness Book of Records*, whose two million sales each year are exceeded only by the Bible.[11]

Guinness entered into the wine and spirits business with the takeover of Bells. Saunders had taken a look at Distillers, but felt that it was too big to swallow whole. But Arthur Bell, a whisky distiller and hotel group, was a better proposition, and Guinness succeeded in taking over the company in August 1985 for £410 million. It was a contested bid, and of particular interest were the whole-page advertisements placed by Guinness in support of its bid. For the first time graphs were used to make a point, as illustrated in Figure 11.3, with the caption: 'Bells has lost its way. Guinness is good for Bells'. This caption picked up the longstanding Guinness advertising motto 'Guinness is good for you'. This was the forerunner of a great flock of full-page advertisements in the same style when the battle for Distillers took place in the following year.

It was not until the end of 1985, when Mr James Gulliver, chairman of Argyll, the supermarket group, made his £1.9 billion

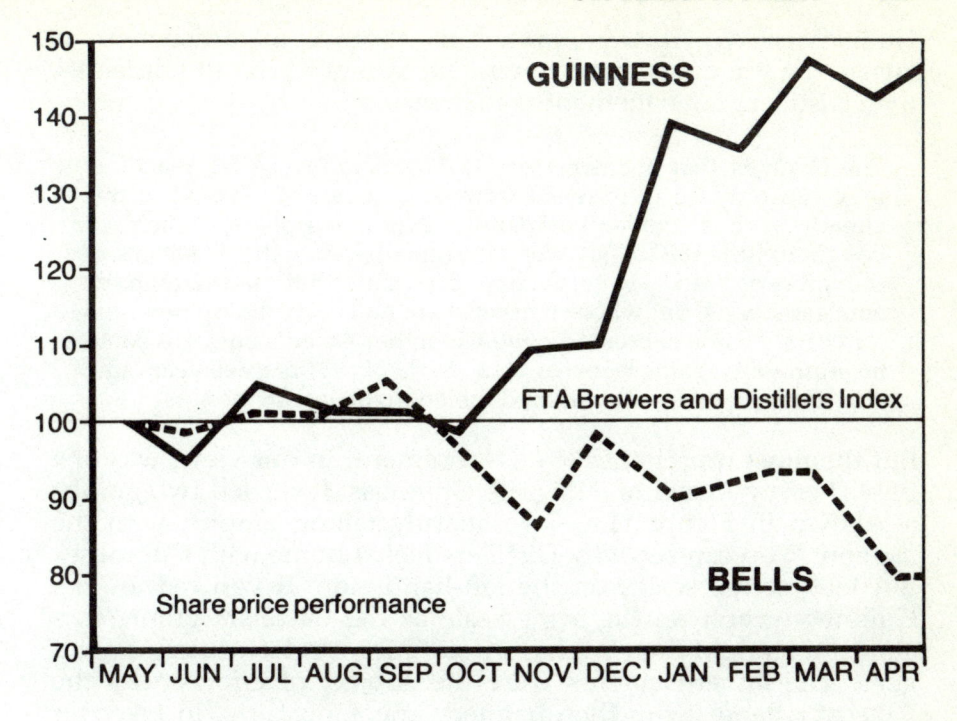

Figure 11.3 *Share price performance compared*

bid for Distillers, that Guinness took a second look at the company. Saunders and the Distillers chairman, John Connell, began talking about a rival but friendly bid from Guinness: the 'white knight' approach which we discussed earlier. It came in January 1986, valuing Distillers at £2 billion. Then battle commenced, with both Argyll and Guinness taking a series of full-page advertisements in the dailies, as were Hanson and Imperial. It must have been wonderful business for both the advertising agencies and the newspapers. One Argyll advertisement proclaimed:

> Distillers is one of the worst-run large companies in Britain. In its way it is a classic British failure. We can revive Distillers' spirits.

As we have said already, this series of advertisements was remarkable in the way graphs were used to make a point. Distillers responded a week later with a graph showing declining sales of Argyll scotch whisky in the USA with the slogan:

> Come, come Argyll. It's your spirits that need reviving.

124 Takeovers, Acquisitions and Mergers

Gulliver of Argyll was quoted in another advertisement as answering the question as to why he thought he could do better than Distillers' management as follows:

> The changes that are necessary at Distillers are so far reaching, they can only be introduced from the outside. We've done this already with a similar company – Allied Suppliers, which we bought in June 1982. They were, in some respects, the 'Distillers' of the grocery trade, a very large company that had grown by amalgamations, but whose market share had been sliding downhill for years. People expressed doubts whether Allied's business could be improved. Profits last year were 240% of profits three years ago. Our share price has more than doubled in the last 18 months.

But the most reprehensible advertisement, in our view, was one published by Argyll to denigrate Guinness. It carried two graphs as shown in Figure 11.4. Two sharply falling graphs, with the caption: 'You can see why Distillers feel at home with Guinness'. But look at the scales on the left-hand side. If you redraw the Guinness graph on the same scale as the Distillers graph, it is almost a straight line: we have dotted it in to let you see how it goes. The advertisements were the subject of criticism by the Takeover Panel, who then banned 'knocking copy' in takeover advertisements. To quote:[12]

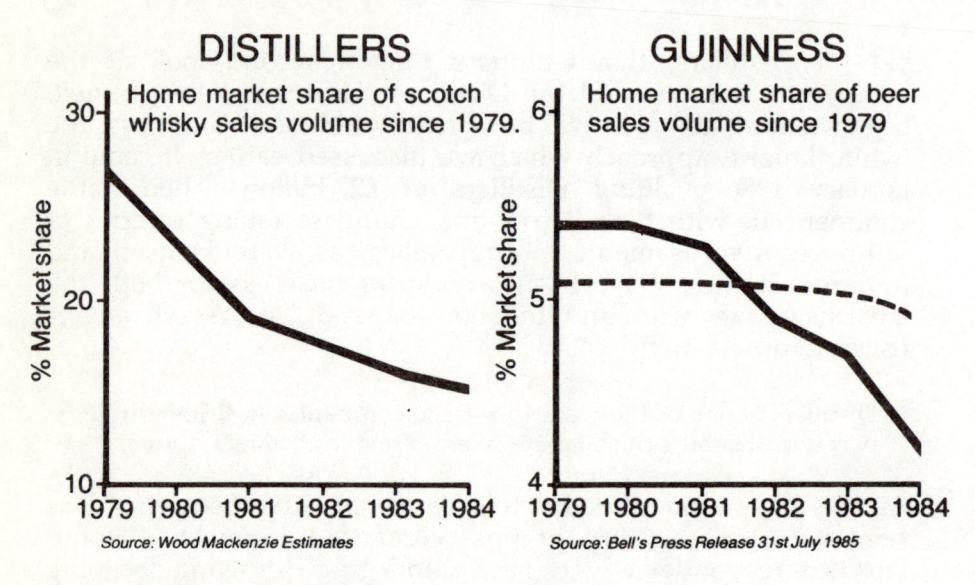

Figure 11.4 *A comparison of Distillers and Guinness*

It hasn't been a week for takeover ads. After the Takeover Panel clampdown comes a £200m lawsuit against Argyll for alleged libel filed by the Guinness-owned Bells distributor there.

Guinness won the takeover battle. It cost £2.5 billion (US$3.8 billion) and an article at the time lauded Ernest Saunders to the skies:[13]

> The unstoppable 50-year-old Guinness chief executive has just emerged as victor in Britain's fiercest and biggest ever takeover battle for Distillers ... The grey-haired, six-feet plus Saunders had his London headquarters swept for secret listening devices regularly. 'I have never been in a war', he told me over poached salmon and hollandaise sauce, 'but I imagine the takeover is as close as I have come to one. I felt like a general who has to be dynamic. People would bring recommendations and I had to make big decisions in minutes, like whether to buy shares involving millions of pounds.'

It was those share deals that were to attract a great deal of attention only six months later. We can tell the story in the headlines which appeared over some two months from December 1986 to January 1987:

- Guinness hit as inspectors start enquiry
- City wipes £315m off share value as Government moves in
- Guinness may be a Pandora's Box for the City
- Shares row goes on
- Chairman of Guinness [Ernest Saunders] steps down
- Oliver Roux [finance director] resigns from Guinness
- £200 million Guinness slush fund
- Guinness's second secret Boesky link
- Roux sparks crisis talks at Guinness
- Remarkable defence of Guinness fee
- Clear-out ordered by Guinness

The board of Guinness sacked Ernest Saunders, its chairman, on 14 January 1987. He was on an annual salary of around £350,000, with a contract running to at least 1990, so Guinness could well be faced with a demand for more than £1 million in compensation for loss of office. It all revolves round the worldwide wheeling and dealing to support the Guinness share price during the closing stages of the takeover of Distillers. The buying kept the Guinness share price strong during the key closing stages of the bid. The offer for Distillers was in Guinness shares, so the higher the Guinness share price, the better the chance of winning.

Notice as well the international link through who else but the notorious king of raiders, Ivan Boesky (see Chapter 12).

Guinness is now embroiled in a legal battle with Ernest Saunders who, it alleges, was responsible for a possibly illegal payment of £5.2 million, £3 million of which passed through his account. The legal battle continues, but meanwhile the Guinness trading record has emerged remarkably unscathed by the scandal, with pre-tax profits of £355 million for the 15 months to the new 31 December year-end. But the true cost of the Distillers débâcle emerges below the line, where £125 million has been written down, but not written off. Under its new chief executive Anthony Tennant and chairman Sir Norman Macfarlane, the group remains determined to get back every penny it can. Meanwhile experts are determining whether existing laws are adequate to regulate and police affairs of this type.[14]

The Westland victory

The year 1986 was outstanding in terms of takeovers that enjoyed a great deal of attention from the media: it opened with the Westland drama, crystallised in one of many headlines as 'Zero hour for Westland'.[15] The Westland affair was yet another takeover that resulted in full-page advertisements in the dailies, in an endeavour to persuade the shareholders. Indeed, Westland took a two-page spread in the *Daily Mail* to explain its point of view in great detail, and it is interesting that it did not see what was happening as a takeover. To quote from the advertisement:

> Some shareholders have asked why they can't vote on the two [sets of proposals] and make a decision as they do in a competitive takeover. There are two reasons why not. First, this is not a takeover. It's a capital reconstruction for a company in extreme financial difficulty. The Board's overriding duty is to assess, with its wide knowledge of the commercial background, what is best for Westland and to make clear recommendation to its shareholders. Second, because of the urgency of the situation, we need a quick and decisive solution. We simply can't risk falling between two stools.

Surely this is just a play on words. The choice lay between a Sikorsky-Fiat offer of £74 million and a European consortium offer of £75 million.[15] The Westland board favoured the Sikorsky-Fiat proposal. As it said in its advertisement, they had been working together successfully with Sikorsky for a long while, Westland building a wide range of helicopters under licence from Sikorsky. On the other hand, the European consortium was described as an *ad hoc* grouping of companies, some of which were state-owned and fierce competitors both of Westland and of each other.

Public interest was aroused when it appeared that there were political overtones, and that members of the Cabinet were taking sides. The political drama broke when Michael Heseltine, the Defence Secretary, walked out of a Cabinet meeting and resigned, promising a series of embarrassing disclosures.[16] Heseltine supported the European consortium, whereas Margaret Thatcher and other members of her Cabinet supported the Sikorsky-Fiat deal. The Trade and Industry Secretary, Leon Brittan, came out strongly in opposition to Heseltine, but finally had to resign because he released for publication a confidential letter with the intention of discrediting Heseltine. The outcome for Westland was that the shareholders voted 2 to 1 for the rescue package proposed by Sikorsky.[17]

Then followed an all-party House of Commons Defence Committee investigation into the Government's handling of the Westland affair. The Committee's report was published some six months later and was severely critical of Leon Brittan, the former Trade Secretary, and senior civil servants for their handling of the leak of the Solicitor General's letter. Although the 73-page report did not add substantially to the revelations that had already been made about the Westland affair, it was sternly critical of the professional ethics of the officials who decided that the letter should be leaked.[18]

How has Westland prospered since the reconstruction? Let us look at the situation a year later. Westland's chairman, Sir John Cuckney, who masterminded it all, declares:[18] 'A company which one year ago was facing insolvency is now adequately financed, has strong international connections and is now trading profitably.' (We have described Sir John elsewere as a company doctor with a wide experience in the healing of sick companies.)[19]

Let us conclude with the message from yet another full-page advertisement issued by the Westland Group:

Westland. You don't know the half of it.
From what you read in the papers, you'd think Westland only made helicopters. Wrong. The truth is, we're a broad based, high technology company with an enviable reputation for quality and innovation ... We supply corrosion resistant filters for air regeneration systems of nuclear submarines ... Every year hundreds of thousands of holidaymakers cross the English Channel in hovercraft built by British Hovercraft, a Westland company ... Make no mistake, though, we're proud of our helicopters. Westland. It's twice the company you've been led to believe.

References

1. 'Hanson cleared to pursue bid for Imperial' *Daily Telegraph* 13 February 1986, p 21.
2. Gribben, R 'United Biscuits moves in for 9 p.c. of Imperial' *Daily Telegraph* 18 February 1986, p 19.
3. Fleet, K 'Golden Wonder price attacked by Hanson' *The Times* 11 March 1986, p 17.
4. Gunn, Cathy 'UB set for a bite at Imps' *Today* 26 March 1986, p 29.
5. Advertisement published by N M Rothschild & Sons Limited on behalf of Hanson Trust Plc *Daily Telegraph* 3 April 1986.
6. 'Reshuffling of assets' *Financial Times* 19 September 1986, p 24.
7. Lambert, R and Wood, L 'The Allied-Elders contest: Ready for the next round' *Financial Times* 4 September 1986, p 23.
8. Clark, M and Leonard, C 'Elders emerges as favourite to bid for Courage brewery' *The Times* 18 September 1986, p 23.
9. Batchelor, C 'Elders buys Courage in £1.4bn deal and drops Allied bid' *Financial Times* 19 September 1986, p 1.
10. Batchelor, C and Wood, L 'Dealmakers confirm reputation' *Financial Times* 19 September 1986, p 8.
11. 'Guinness: stouter and stouter' *The Economist* **301**, 4 October 1986, p 72-3.
12. Jamieson, W 'Last rites in the Distiller-bunker' *Today* 28 March 1986, p 31.
13. Lithman, A 'The genius who put the head on Guinness' *Daily Express* 15 May 1986, p 32.
14. 'Rules for the City – The Guinness affair shows the need for tougher sleuths, not new law' *The Economist* **302**, 7 February 1987, pp 17-8.
15. Levi, J 'Zero hour for Westland' *Observer* 12 January 1986, p 21.
16. Raphael, A 'Heseltine warns: I'll tell all' *Observer* 12 January 1986, p 1.
17. Becket, M 'Westland victory for Sikorsky' *Daily Telegraph* 13 February 1986, p 1.
18. Bates, S 'MPs rebuke Brittan over Westland row' *Daily Telegraph*, 25 July 1986, p 8.
19. Kharbanda, O P and Stallworthy, E A 'One man can make the difference' in *Company Rescue* Heinemann, 1987, ch 4.

Chapter 12
The Raiders

Acquisitions, mergers and takeovers can be friendly, and usually are. This is normally achieved through negotiation. There are differences of opinion, of course, especially on the price and exactly how it is to be paid, but the two parties agree that they are dealing for their common advantage. A raider, however, tries to take over suddenly, unexpectedly, and against the target company's wishes. The strategy is planned behind the scenes and a *fait accompli* is presented to the concerned company. Such deals are usually full of high drama, tension and excitement, and involve large sums of money.

We considered some deals of this type both in Part 2 and Part 3, but looked at companies rather than personalities. It may be useful to take a look at the individuals involved, the raiders or 'respectable rogues'. First, let us bring you some definitions of words that have been coined in this field and are to be met in articles published on the subject.

Some definitions

The taking over of companies by hostile raiders against the consent of their management has given rise to a host of new words, some of which have not yet found a place in the English dictionary but will in due course, as they become common usage. The listing of words that we present below is by no means complete and the definitions have been collected from various sources, mainly the economic and financial newspapers and journals, and also books on the subject of acquisitions, mergers and takeovers.

Arbitrageur. Persons like Ivan Boesky (considered to be king of the arbitrageurs) who have turned hostile takeover speculation into a full-time profession and claim that it is a science covering such esoteric subjects as workout values and leveraged arbitrage position. The *Concise Oxford Dictionary* defines arbitrage as: 'traffic in bills of exchange or stocks to take advantage of different prices in other markets'.

Golden parachute. The guarantee of a fairly large sum (US$500,000 or more) to be paid to senior executives whose services may be terminated as a result of a raid or takeover of their employer.

Greenmail. To get rid of a raider, a target company buys shares back from the raider at a higher price than that which the shareholders can get on the open market.

Pac-man defence: A term borrowed from the popular video game, where a company tries to swallow its raider. Even if it does not succeed, the ploy may drive off the raider.

Poison pill. A defence strategy that makes the takeover so expensive that the raider gives up the raid. To give an example, the target company give its shareholders securities that can be turned into cash if the raid succeeds.

Scorched earth. The target company seeks to set up a self-destructive strategy which makes it less attractive, so discouraging the raider. For example, it could sell the very divisions and other assets that had attracted the raider. Alternatively, the company may take up huge loans which become due as soon as the company is taken over. The objective is made very clear when we look at the definition in the *Concise Oxford Dictionary*: 'burning crops, removing or destroying anything that might be of use to an enemy occupying the country'.

Shark repellent. Any measures that are adopted to repel the raider (or shark), such as a change in the company's by-laws making it virtually impossible for the unwanted raider to gain control. For instance, it could have a rule that any change of ownership must be approved by at least 75 per cent of the shareholders before it becomes effective.

White knight. A company that is invited to rescue the target company from the raider by arranging a friendly takeover on more favourable terms. These could include a higher purchase price, together with an assurance to senior executives that they will be retained and that there will be no need to use golden parachutes.

There are now a great number of raiders, a breed that originally started, it seems, in the USA, but more recently has spread across the Atlantic and lately across the Pacific as well. They claim to represent and look after the interests of the small shareholder but the results that they have achieved and other indicators point to the fact that they are mainly engaged in these activities for their own profit. They are *not* altruistic. One result of their activities may well be that the shareholders benefit, but this is only a secondary effect: it is not their prime objective. Some of the many terms used to describe raiders include:

Business celebrities. Those so described are in good company: Lee Iacocca is one such.

Junk bonders. An alternative description of a 'respectable rogue'.

Respectable rogues. Said to include personalities such as Belzberg, Edelman, Hurwitz, Icahn, Jacobs, Murdoch and Pickens in the USA, Sir James Goldsmith in the UK, and many others elsewhere.

Short-termers. Also includes some of the 'respectable rogues': their characteristic is that they are interested in short-term profits rather than long-term prospects.

Let us now look at some of the individuals who, it seems, have earned the title of raider, according to the financial press. It is difficult to decide who is the topmost raider – in any event, what standard of judgement should we use? – so we shall select those who have been most heard of and written about recently.

T Boone Pickens Jr

Pickens, chairman of the Mesa Petroleum Co, has been described as the 'king of the company raiders' and even as the 'scourge of the oil industry'. He loves to talk and preach about his gospel of company rebirth, rejuvenation and increased efficiency as a result of hostile takeovers by himself and those like him. In one packed Los Angeles conference room, he went straight to the heart of the matter and spelt out his mission as he saw it:[1]

> I am the champion of the small stockholder ... Many American companies are heavily undervalued, and I blame their management entirely. I get letters every day that start, 'Dear Mr Pickens, have you thought about our company'.

Wall Street lawyers, analysts and investment brokers, who thrive on raids and similar activities in the share market, speak the 'Pickens language' as well. On the other hand, an eminent Wall Street lawyer who helps to defend companies against raiders, tells a very different story: 'I get calls every day from some company president who says, "Help! We're being taken over".'

The activities of Pickens, as publicised in the media, would fill a volume but until that happens let's look at some of the headlines and captions of some of the news items, feature articles and even cover features that have been written about him. To quote just a few:

- Corporate fear and trembling[2]
- The Pickens plot that has Gulf gulping[3]
- Boone Pickens tries on a white hat[4]
- The legacy of Boone Pickens[5]
- High time for T Boone Pickens – A wily raider shakes up corporate America[6]

That last was a cover feature and it had a box item entitled 'Swimming with the sharks'. The captions given to the photographs and sketches presented in this particular article are revealing enough to be quoted here:

- Heading toward New York City aboard his Falcon 50 jet on the eve of the surprise announcement of his latest move, an investment of nearly $600m in Unocal: 'We're the biggest shareholders!'
- Plotting the Phillips deal at a 7.30 am meeting with Batcheler in a Helmsley Palace suite – he moves swiftly with cloak-and-dagger stealth once he decides which target to attack.
- Explaining and defending his tactics at a Manhattan conference of major institutional investors.
- Sharing the platform with Ford at the inauguration of a new president of West Texas State – A Republican fund raiser, he does not discourage rumours that he will run for Governor.
- With his second wife Beatrice at their Palm Springs retreat – To some critics he is a veritable rattlesnake in the woodpile.

Written as captions, the above present a vivid picture of the man and his lifestyle and tell us a great deal about him in a very few words.

Even if a Pickens raid does not succeed, he still makes millions of dollars: it seems that he has the perfect 'win-win' situation. It appears to be an unwritten law of the stock market that when there is a raid that becomes public knowledge, there are a lot more buyers for the shares than there are shares available. This is a consequence of the general public seeking to make a 'quick buck' along with Pickens, or sometimes because the directors seek to defend themselves by maintaining a majority shareholding and thereby control of the company. Whatever the cause, the end result is that the market price of the shares rises, so that Pickens can sell out at a substantial profit if he abandons the raid against greenmail or is otherwise unsuccessful as a result of strong defensive action by the target company.

Carl Icahn

Let us bring you a profile of Carl Icahn by once again quoting the titles to some recent articles, the captions to some of the photographs and biographical sketches that have appeared:

- Three who watch, wait and strike – a trio of gamblers sends shudders through executive corridors[7]
- Carl Icahn plays daredevil at TWA[8]
- Nail biting time at USX – some tough corporate raiders circle overhead[9]
- Carl Icahn: rolling steel[10]
- Is Carl Icahn's TWA flying as high as he claims? – to lure suitors he has to prove the turnaround is for real[11]
- An interview with Carl Icahn – Confessions of a raider[12]

USX, referred to above, does business in two industries, oil and steel. Icahn believes that he can improve its management and cut costs. On taking over TWA, Icahn won concessions from the pilot unions and the machinist union but had to face a flight attendants' strike. However, he did succeed in cutting the airline's annual costs by some US$600 million and claims to have saved the company from bankruptcy.

Icahn seems to specialise in oil companies. His raid on Phillips Petroleum led the people of Bartlesville, Oklahoma, to rally to the company, which had its headquarters there. So Icahn sold his stock and walked away with a profit of at least US$35 million. When called upon to testify at a Congressional hearing on takeovers Icahn confessed that profit was his prime motive, but maintained that his activities help to improve corporate America.

There seems to be quite a debate as to whether Icahn is a raider or manager.[13] He claims that he can fix broken companies, while his critics say that he's after a fast buck. Alfred D Kingsley, investment adviser to Carl Icahn, referring to Icahn's activities in relation to USX, says: 'We've a price at USX. We're willing to own it, but if somebody else wants to pay more, let them do it.' Seeing that he 'rescued' TWA, let us quote D Joseph Corr, its vice chairman and chief operating officer at TWA: 'Icahn is the perfect chairman ... He's not a meddler, but the direction of the companies is his.'

Irrespective of Icahn's intentions and achievements, there is no doubt that he has made a lot of money over the years through his multifarious activities. Under the caption: 'Dealmaker's winning streak', Chuck Hawkins gives details of the profits Icahn has made from a number of major deals over the years. To list but a few:[11]

		Profit US$ million
1979	Tappan	3
1981	Saxon & Simplicity Pattern	9
1982	Anchor Hocking, American Can and Marshall Field	28
1983	Gulf & Western, Dan River & ACF	29+
1984	Cheesbrough-Ponds, Uniroyal and Goodrich	29
1985	Phillips Petroleum and TWA	135
1986	Union Carbide, Viacom and USX	200

The last two items, at the time of reporting, were partly a 'paper profit', not yet realised.

Icahn's prescription

It seems that Carl Icahn is no ordinary raider. He is a harsh critic of American business and has a word of advice to managers. He says that they should be more accountable to their shareholders and that American industry is in crisis mainly because of bad management. This is not universally so, but there are far too many large companies that are mismanaged. He suggests that perhaps the managers are chosen by directors following the advice of a primer, which Carl Icahn titles 'In search of mediocracy'. He suggests that the successors to chief executives are often chosen on the basis of someone 'likeable'. The top managers, he believes, are more interested in expanding their power than in improving company performance. Thanks to bureaucracy there is an army of non-productive workers – the paper shufflers in the managers' suites – and these people are worse than courtiers in the halls of the aristocracy. Managers seem to have forgotten that people are happier doing something positive and purposeful.

Icahn found in the course of his restructuring of ACF, a major railcar manufacturer, and TWA, the international airline, that many executives who were redundant are now engaged in productive work. Carl Icahn was tough with the unions at TWA, but dealt with them directly instead of leaving it to the 'experts'. As a result the airline is smaller, leaner but much more efficient.

Two specific suggestions made by him that he thinks would make US industry competitive once more in the international markets are:

1. Cut out layers of bureaucrats reporting to other bureaucrats.
2. Senior management must be accountable to the owners (shareholders).

He also thinks that some of the rules governing takeovers that are already in operation in Britain should be introduced in the USA. For instance, whenever an outsider purchases 30 per cent of a company's stock, he should not be permitted to acquire any more stock unless he offers to buy it all. He adds that as a result of steps such as these, the golf scores of the chief executives might suffer and they might have to travel by commercial aircraft rather than in executive jets, but company performance would improve considerably and, perhaps to their delight: 'I will be unemployed.'

Irwin Jacobs

This raider-liquidator has the knack of succeeding in the midst of failure. A snowmobile and boat making company that he acquired in 1978 went bankrupt and yet he was able to salvage some of the pieces and form a new company, Minstar, which in 1983 bought Bekins, a removals company, and then had record earnings of US$23 million in 1984. Some chunks of real estate owned by Bekins are now being sold off and this is an indication that more takeovers are in the offing. Almost a loner, sometimes answering the telephone himself, he drives to work in his Rolls-Royce Silver Shadow II and makes no claim to be a long-range planner. A person of instinct and action, he observes:

> You can't predict what I'm going to do next because there is no track, no character to it. Our big asset is our flexibility, being able to move on a moment's notice.

Jacobs failed to acquire Kaiser Steel, Disney and Avco, but in the process made some US$90 million. AMF is his latest success and by far his largest deal.[14] AMF is an industrial and leisure products conglomerate with a turnover of US$1.1 billion a year. Its directors approved of the deal and even offered its 'crown jewel', the leisure division (bowling, boating, exercise equipment) for US$300 million, thus protecting a favoured buyer against a possible competing bidder. This was a major victory for Jacobs.

Perhaps one of his prize possessions is a letter he received from a 13-year-old, saying:

> When I am older I would like to become a 'corporate raider'. I think it would be a very exciting life. For the past 12 months I have been watching takeover targets, trying to guess ... the raider's next moves ... could you please tell me how you got started?

A courteous reply was sent but it did not reveal the raider's next target.

Ivan Boesky

The headlines tell it all, and so precisely:

- Ivan Boesky, money machine[15]
- Corporate raider – science of speculation[16]
- After the fall – How the insider-trading scandal will change Wall Street[17]

Then there is his book, *Merger Mania*.[18] Boesky has arisen out of practically nowhere and has become a most daring and controversial arbitrageur. His ambition: to build an empire. For this he needs capital. How does he get that capital? Through risk arbitrage, the secretive business of trading securities of companies involved in acquisitions, mergers and takeovers. Ivan Boesky now owns one of the largest arbitrage companies on Wall Street. Usually his stakes are so high that he has been nicknamed 'Piggy'. But this is unfair, according to him:

> I don't take any particular pride in being big. I do take a certain amount of pride in creating wealth ... We want to be wanted. Companies can use the advice of experienced banking mentalities ... It's a question of people getting to know, understand, and believe, and all these things take time. People kind of have to sniff you to know what you are about.

Ivan Boesky trades through numerous 'blinds' in order to keep his position secret, but word often leaks out that 'Ivan Boesky is buying such and such stock' and the price of the stock then shoots up. Ivan Boesky can afford to and does live well, using a limousine to go from his 200-acre estate outside New York City to his midtown office. Ivan Boesky calls his estate a farm, but a friend describes it thus:[15]

> It's definitely how people live in books: there are formal gardens and gardeners all over the place, indoor handball and racquetball courts, saunas, spas, pools, poolhouses, indoor tennis courts, outdoor tennis courts, art, antiques etc.

His book *Merger Mania* has disappointed readers, who were looking for a 'how to do it' manual, together with a racy rundown of dirty tricks. Instead, it deals with esoteric subjects such as workout values and leveraged arbitrage positions. Ivan Boesky is a part-time professor at two business schools, thus fulfilling another side of himself. He likes teaching young people who are really interested in learning about the skills of arbitrage. In effect he tries to lend his occupation an air of respectability. But if such advice is followed by companies generally, they will need to 'massage' their short-term results at the expense of long-term investment and performance. Justifying his own profession he says:[16]

> There's a lot of misinformation, a lot of misunderstanding about what arbitrage is ... It's important that the truth be known. The more that corporate America becomes familiar with what the arbitrageur's role is, the less concern managements have for what he does ... Rumours and leaks are things that the professional arbitrageurs don't have time to pay attention to. That is a disease that some stock market investors tend to contract.

Ivan Boesky works phenomenal hours, starting at dawn and going on till late at night, in order to keep in touch with markets all over the world. He is most certainly a good customer of the Bell Telephone Company.

In May 1986, however, there came a bombshell. David Levine, a mergers and acquisitions specialist at Drexel Burnham Lambert was accused by the Securities and Exchange Commission of insider trading through his contacts with the arbitrage fraternity, of which Ivan Boesky was reckoned to the biggest operator. Suddenly the whole of Wall Street was on trial.[19] Under an agreement reached with the Securities and Exchange Commission there will be no prosecution of Ivan Boesky in return for his revealing the 'inside story' and the names of other players of the 'game'. He has agreed to pay US$50 million in penalties and to withdraw permanently from the securities business. It seems that he has also implicated several other figures and the hidden side of a very unpleasant business has now become an open book.

The two 'Jims'

Having had an extensive look at some of the US raiders we now take you across the Atlantic to look at two raiders in the UK, although one of them operates worldwide – even in the shark-infested waters of the USA. James Hanson (also called Lord H and Lord Jim), chairman of Hanson Trust and a member of the House of Lords has already been mentioned in Chapter 11. Hanson calls himself a company resuscitator rather than a company raider, buying up sick companies, cleaning out the directors and letting the managers run the show. People see him as a raider, but he strongly contests this: 'That's not our line at all. We go into the game park and get the wounded animal with the tranquilliser, put it right and then set it free again.'

Although Hanson does not interfere in day-to-day matters he does keep a tight hold on the purse strings, ruthlessly cutting jobs and funds for investment when so required. Born in Yorkshire, Lord Jim started building his empire after World War II with the proceeds from the nationalisation of his family's transport business. Once engaged to the actress Audrey Hepburn, Hanson has a keen interest in fancy cars and fancy homes. One of his close associates, Sir Gordon White, looks after his high-flying American subsidiary, Hanson Industries in New Jersey. Lord Jim has had a long and enviable record of successes, as we saw in Chapter 11.

The other Jim is Sir James Goldsmith, who is quite outspoken about himself and his role:[20]

> You can divide the world into conservatives and revolutionaries. Lenin was a revolutionary. Stalin was a conservative. I like to think of myself as a revolutionary ... My role is that of an investor, to make money. Let me make it quite clear: I don't come charging in on a white horse with a halo around my head. That's not my purpose. But it is interesting to see the ripple effect, which I believe is quite good.

He is described as a gambler with two passports and two cultures. Goldsmith is an egotist: brilliant, obsessed, charming and a very complicated person. Explaining his *modus operandi*:

> I'm not a do gooder. If I see a share with potential values that are untapped, like there was in Colgate, like there is in Goodyear, we buy our position. If management is willing to do the job, we're going to make a lot of money. In my view, the company is infinitely better at the end if they do it. That will be the case with Goodyear, if they do it. Crown Zellerbach didn't want to do it, so we took a run at them and did it ourselves.

How candid and refreshing! The company can probably do a better job than he can, but either way he makes a profit. But the main point is that whichever way it goes, the company in decline is put on the road to recovery and the raider makes a handsome income.

References

1. 'T Boone Pickens Jr' *Newsweek* 4 March 1985.
2. Greenwald, J 'Corporate fear and trembling' *Time* 14 January 1985, p 34.
3. Williams, M J 'The Pickens plot that has Gulf gulping' *Fortune* **109** 4 March 1984, p 34.
4. Norman, J R 'Boone Pickens tries on a white hat' *Business Week* 24 March 1986, p 35.
5. Powell, W 'The legacy of Boone Pickens' *Newsweek* 5 May 1986, pp 40-1.
6. 'High time for T Boone Pickens – A wily raider shakes up corporate America' *Time* 4 March 1985, pp 52ff (7 pp).
7. DeMott, J S 'Three who watch, wait and strike – a trio of gamblers sends shudders through executive corridors' *Time* 4 March 1985, pp 65ff (2pp).
8. 'Carl Icahn plays daredevil at TWA' *Business Week* 27 January 1986, pp 22-3.
9. Pauly, D 'Nail biting time at USX – some tough corporate raiders circle overhead' *Newsweek* 6 October 1986, p 42.
10. 'Carl Icahn: rolling steel' *The Economist* **301**, 11 October 1986, pp 74-5.
11. Hawkins, C 'Is Carl Icahn's TWA flying as high as he claims? – to lure suitors he has to prove the turnaround is for real' *Business Week* 13 October 1986, p 32.
12. Editorial 'An interview with Carl Icahn – Confessions of a raider' *Newsweek* 20 October 1986, pp 43ff (4 pp).
13. Hawkins, C 'Carl Icahn – raider or manager?' *Business Week* 27 October 1986, pp 54-9.
14. Ross, I 'Irwin Jacobs lands a big one – finally' *Fortune* **112**, 8 July 1985, pp 130ff (5 pp).
15. Kinhead, G 'Ivan Boesky, money machine' *Fortune* **110**, 6 August 1984, pp 102ff (5 pp).
16. Riley, B 'Corporate raider – science of speculation' *Financial Times* 29 March 1986.
17. 'After the fall – How the insider-trading scandal will change Wall Street' *Business Week* 1 December 1986, pp 20-5.
18. Boesky, I P *Merger Mania* The Bodley Head (London), 1986.
19. Glaberson, W B 'Who'll be next to fall: as the scandal spreads, Boesky could have lots of company' *Business Week* 1 December 1986, pp 20-2.
20. Rossant, J 'The two worlds of Jimmy Goldsmith – His winnings as a raider help bankroll his right-wing crusade' *Business Week* 1 December 1986, pp 64-8.

Chapter 13
Takeovers Worldwide

In this chapter we extend our study of takeovers to countries other than the USA and UK, in order to bring you worldwide coverage of this aspect of our subject.

Japan

We now go to the 'land of rising sun' – Japan. Starting anew from the ashes of World War II, Japan has in the course of some 40 years achieved a miracle to become one of the most developed countries in the world. The Japanese are now very active in the takeover game, not only in their own land but also in the USA where it all started, and which has now become the scene of high drama.

In August 1986, when Arco Plaza in Los Angeles, owned jointly by the Bank America Corporation and the Atlantic Richfield Corporation, was put up for public sale there was keen interest and a lot of bidders. The highest bidder, surprisingly enough, was the Tokyo-based, privately owned Shuwa Corporation, a name unheard of until then in the USA. What is more, it paid hard cash: all US$625 million of it. The following month it negotiated the purchase of Capital City/ABC Incorporated's New York headquarters for US$165 million and since then more properties on the East coast have been taken over. In 1985 the Japanese bought US$1.5 billion worth of real estate in the USA and in 1986 this figure was perhaps doubled or even tripled.

All this activity started in the early 1980s when Japan relaxed the conditions for Japanese companies to invest overseas. With plenty of cash and a weak dollar, the attraction of US properties and businesses is obvious; they were really begging to be taken over. The return on such investments in the USA is 7 to 8 per cent compared with a mere 2 per cent in Japan itself. To finance the deals the Japanese companies borrow yen to dollars at the very advantageous rate of exchange now prevailing and go on a buying spree, paying cash.

It is clear that the Japanese will be even bigger buyers in the US market in the future. For example, just one Japanese company, the Shuwa Corporation, is planning to invest some US$2 billion in the next two years.[1] It is far too early to say what effect the new owners will have on the 'bottom line' of their acquisitions, but Japanese management has become the envy of the world and we are sure that such a change of ownership can only benefit these companies.

A move to hostile takeovers?

Takeovers in Japan are on a friendly basis, the target company either seeking to marry or submitting to seduction. There has been a taboo on hostile takeovers, but this may soon be a thing of the past. A ball bearing and electronic components manufacturer, Minebea, with a fast growth record, wanted to grow even faster. To this end it quietly bought a 19 per cent stake (US$80 million) in Sankyo Saiki, a manufacturer of computer peripherals, as a prelude to taking it over. Sankyo Saiki didn't like it, nor did its bankers, the Mitsubishi Bank, who threatened to cease dealing with Minebea, the bank's fourth largest customer, if Minebea proceeded with its intentions. Minebea had grown in the past largely by friendly acquisition and takeover and for this purpose had set up credit facilities abroad for US$200 million with a consortium of British and Japanese banks.

Sankyo Saiki buys parts from Minebea and the two factories are close together, hence the desire to take over Sankyo Saiki. Minibea started buying Sankyo Saiki stock quietly outside Japan and announced itself as the largest shareholder. But the owner, Rokuichi Yamada, doesn't want to be taken over and has threatened to cancel the 2 billion yen purchases per year that he makes from Minebea. Some 50 per cent of Sankyo Saiki stock is held by financial institutions who may well side with Rokuichi Yamada. The threat by Mitsubishi Bank, which holds shares of both companies, also supports Rokuichi Yamada. What can Minebea do? For one thing, as the largest shareholder, it might instal its people in Sankyo Saiki's top management: this can be done. Then these nominees might be able to convince Rokuichi Yamada and the other shareholders of the merits of this marriage. The two companies are of comparable size in terms of both turnover (US$500-700 million) and profits (US$10-30 million), and their operations are complementary.[2] The relative growth of Minebea and Sankyo Saiki can be seen from Figure 13.1.

What one has to realise is the strength of the taboo in Japan: unfriendly takeovers there are despised and are therefore rare. In fact the Japanese word for takeover, *nottori*, also means hijack,

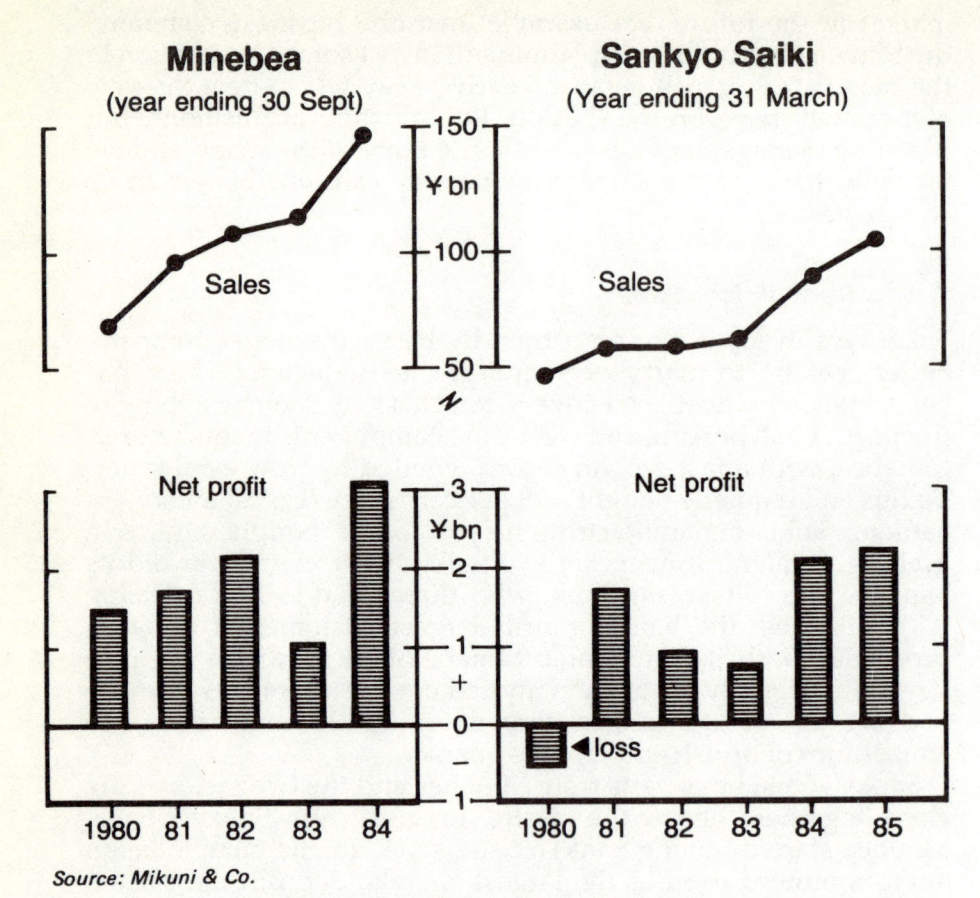

Figure 13.1 *Unfriendly neighbours*

while the word for acquisition, *baishu*, also signifies bribery. The flamboyant president of Minebea, Takami Takahashi, is known to the Japanese press as 'Mr Takeover', so presumably Japanese readers get a feeling that they are reading about 'Mr Hijacker'. Indeed, Takami Takahashi is renowned for hostile takeover bids, although mainly abroad. Since 1971 he has taken over 24 firms, eight of them in the USA, and the approach has not always been friendly. His takeovers in the USA in 1985 included New Hampshire Ball Bearings (US$110 million) and a power unit division of the Harris Corporation (US$12.5 million). But his use of the hostile takeover technique at home, as in the case of Sankyo Saiki, upset both the bank and Rokuichi Yamada. Even the Sankyo Saiki labour union, which had 3,500 members, resolved that the 'merger with Minebea is too risky'.[3] However, Takami

Takahashi is still optimistic: 'I will continued to pursue. It is a matter of timing, and I'm willing to wait for two or even three years.'

Takami Takahashi may be in good company: large Japanese companies with lots of cash want to accelerate their sluggish growth through acquisitions, mergers and takeovers because it is a lot cheaper than starting new projects. But a banker, Yok Kurosawa, deputy president of the Industrial Bank of Japan is not very hopeful:

> The number of big companies that are looking for friendly takeovers is increasing ... The problem is that there are not many companies for sale.

Isn't that exactly where a hostile takeover comes in? So we get the feeling that it won't be long before the disease spreads even into the conservative Japanese business society. Perhaps the infection needs to be carried by a Westerner, and this seems to be just what has happened. This time the tables are reversed: Takami Takahashi's Minebea is itself the target. Let us see how that came about.

A British raider comes to Japan

With Takami Takahashi's widespread activities in Europe and elsewhere receiving so much publicity, Minebea attracted the attention of a Briton, Terence P Ramsden, aged 33, and the owner of the Glenn International Financial Service Company of London. With his friend and partner Charles Knapp, formerly of the Financial Corporation of America, Ramsden seems so sure of taking over the US$1.4 billion Japanese company Minebea that he dares to say:[4] 'Japanese corporate management believe their little club cannot be broken into ... They're wrong.'

Ramsden claims to have collected an international team of backers including Arab, American, German, Swiss and even Japanese groups. Claiming to have gained control of 37 per cent of Minebea, he is sure of success despite what he is up against:

> There are forces in Japan that want the system [hostile takeovers] opened up and I'm quite close to them. They can't be seen to be opening the system for themselves, so they advise me. I'm a catalyst.

Terence Ramsden's sights seem to be set much higher than just Minebea. He may help to launch the first ever assault in the form of a shareholder suit against the consumer electronics and

144   Takeovers, Acquisitions and Mergers

appliances manufacturer, Tokyo Sanyo Electric, in which he has invested. Terence Ramsden's charge: Tokyo Sanyo Electric has unnecessarily taken on expensive debt and thus hurt the price of the share. He hopes to oust the management of the company. He claims to have mastered the intricacies of Japan's financial markets and learnt how to put together complex transactions in Japanese securities for issue in Europe. And he is not modest: 'It's pretty well accepted that I'm one of the foremost experts in the market, if not *the* foremost.' Much of his wheeling and dealing is done on the quiet, since Japanese securities, like those in the Euromarket, are traded anonymously. The Japanese issue warrants which add up to a much larger proportion of the total capital than is common in Europe.

Meanwhile, in order to defend itself against this raider, Minebea is out to dilute its foreign holdings with a private placement of convertible debentures as prelude to a merger with an apparel company. Takami Takahashi seems to expect that this will bring in more Japanese friends who will stand by him. Terence Ramsden, however, claims to be keeping himself a step ahead of the Minebea/Takami Takahashi moves by making allies of some of Minebea's supposed friends who are actually very unhappy with Takami Takahashi. He also plans to mop up enough shares in the market to gain control. So certain is he that he sets out the alternatives as: 'We win, or we win, or we win.'

The recent liberalisation of Japan's financial markets may well encourage many outsiders to enter the financial market of this hitherto over-protected country.[5]

Backdoor entry to the Japanese market

Having themselves been invaded commercially and financially over the years by the Japanese, Western companies are beginning to pay the Japanese back in their own coin. The buying up of Japanese companies is seen by Western companies as a very good way of entering a difficult culture and a difficult market.[6] We have given examples of this elsewhere, showing how the Americans, British, Italians and Swedes have scored successes in this way.[7] Some of the rules are:

- Attempt only a friendly takeover.
- For a meaningful dialogue you must have patience and time.
- Assure the target company about the well-being of its employees.
- Obtain full support from your senior management back home.

- Use an investment broker thoroughly familiar with the laws of the land.
- Maintain strict confidentiality until the deal is concluded.
- Ensure continuance of Japanese management practices.

The last point is most important, indeed crucial. One expert advises: 'If you buy a Japanese company, you'll want to keep it so.' The reason for this should be obvious: so much publicity has been given to the success that has been achieved by the use of Japanese management concepts. It is these same concepts which even Western industry is seeking to emulate in its own business environment.

Some recent examples of the foreign invasion of the Japanese industrial scene are:

1982 The British Oxygen Company (BOC) secured a minority (42.5 per cent) but controlling interest in Osaka Oxygen (OSK).
1982 Thomas Tilling acquired a 70 per cent interest in Snashin Enterprises.
1983 Hewlett-Packard increased its ownership in its 20-year-old joint venture with Yokogawa from 49 to 75 per cent.
1983 Merck & Co bought a controlling interest in two Japanese drug companies, the Banyu Pharmaceutical Corporation and Torii & Company.

These are likely to be only the beginning of a major movement, according to a London merchant banker with a long tenure in Tokyo:

> The tracks have now been laid and there are lots of people running around looking for deals to start happening ... takeovers won't be done mainly for financial reasons, as in the West.

But he cautions that sudden and hostile takeovers are out of the question. Let us also bring to you some words of advice from Kenichi Ohmae, managing director of the consulting firm McKinsey & Co, Tokyo:

> Instead of the word 'control', say 'strengthening our relationship' or 'if you are willing, we are prepared to hold some of your stocks'.

The emphasis in acquisitions, mergers and takeovers should be on the strengthening of joint developments in technology and international marketing for *mutual* benefit. Thanks to international pressure, Japanese companies and authorities are welcoming investments by foreign firms and this is helping to encourage the flow of technology and finance into Japan.

Now that we have some appreciation of the Japanese scene, let us update the progress of BOC's £30 million (US$45 million) investment in OSK. BOC took its time in explaining and implementing its rationalisation scheme, which had to include redundancies.[8] OSK was a medium sized (sales £163 million, US$250 million) but stagnating company, ranking a weak third in Japan's industrial gases industry. Now with fresh investment from BOC (£20 million, US$30 million) the company has got a new lease of life, with a modern and efficient air separation plant. The manning has been reduced from about 1,000 to just under 800.

Nottori and nottoru

We mentioned earlier that the word for an acquisition or takeover (and hijack) is *nottori*. Change the 'i' to 'u' and it can make all the difference, for *nottoru* means 'to be in accordance with custom'. Those entering the Japanese market must begin with *nottoru*, but perhaps as time passes *nottori* may become the name of the game. What is very certain is that things are indeed changing.[9]

Buying a company outright still poses a cultural problem and the solution to that is 'creeping' purchase: take a minority interest first with an understanding to increase it over a period of time until it becomes a majority interest. It seems that if the company concerned agrees, the Japanese government has no objection:

> We don't really want it to be seen as difficult, legally or culturally ... The Japanese authorities aren't a problem as long as the company being acquired is agreeable.

The target companies are often in decline or financial distress. They need cash, technology or sound management, or some mix of these. The company may be family-owned or family-influenced. The acquirer will have to learn the rules of business in Japan and it helps to have a third party, trusted by the target company in order to help to smooth the purchase. Often money alone may not be enough. It may have to be 'sweetened' with technology. This technique has to be mastered, and it calls for a lot of patience.

Corning Glass' first acquisition in Japan was a shattered glass laboratory. In the course of rebuilding it, Corning thought of expansion and diversification in Japan. Corning then acquired two medical equipment distributors. Next, it looked for a plant to do finishing work on imported American glass used in liquid crystal displays. One subcontractor, Tokina Optical Corporation, fitted the bill and used an intermediary who helped to 'sugarcoat' the proposal, Corning bought a 40 per cent interest in the company and later increased that to 80 per cent. The commitment must be a long-term one, and this has indeed been the case with Corning. It now has an established US$300 million business in Japan with a 15 to 20 per cent growth per year.[10]

Australia

Australian raiders

The Australian-born but now American media baron, Rupert Murdoch, has already made a name for himself as an international raider, who has built up perhaps the biggest empire in his field. There are, however, others not far behind. We bring you two among several.

John D Elliott

John D Elliott, chief executive of Elders IXL Ltd has built up a US$5.5 billion empire by acquiring and taking over many Australian companies which were even bigger but sleepier than his own. His activity is now spreading beyond his own country's shores. He had as target Allied-Lyons, a brewer and food giant, four times bigger than that his own company.[11] But the attempt failed and instead he bought the brewer Courage for US$2 billion from the Hanson Trust (see Chapter 11).

Elliott is described by an Australian business colleague as 'aggressive and ambitious ... his horizons stretch a long way'. It seems he may have his sights on the troubled British group Guinness and the US brewer Anheuser-Busch Cos Inc.[12] Market analysts describe Elders as having a 'good management and a very clever marketer of beer'. The company's revenue and net profit have nearly trebled in the four years since 1981-82 and Elliott's target is understood to be: 'one of the world's top three brewing groups within five years.' He may well achieve it.

Robert Holmes à Court
Another Australian raider, Robert Holmes à Court, has spent a considerable amount of his time in his Perth study thinking and planning moves in the takeover strategy game.[13] Already an expert in this game, Holmes à Court has raided many a company successfully at home and in Britain and is now looking for greener pastures in the USA.

Now 50, Holmes à Court is on the lookout for any kind of company that is undervalued, unlike his compatriot, Rupert Murdoch, who specialises in raids on publishing and broadcasting companies. Unlike Murdoch, Holmes à Court keeps himself completely aloof and doesn't even telephone people: they always have to contact him.

Pursuing a troubled US minerals company, Asarco, with a turnover of US$1.1 billion, he acquired an 11 per cent interest for US$76.7 million: a good start. Another big fish he is after is Australia's largest corporation, Broken Hill Proprietary (BHP), an industrial and natural resources giant with an annual turnover of over US$6 billion. He already owns 18.8 per cent of BHP and has offered to take a further 20 per cent through negotiations with the BHP chairman. But this proposal was rejected outright and there was even a court injunction against Holmes à Court's retaliatory offer. BHP then bought a US$70 million stake in Bell Resources, as a further preventive measure.[14]

Holmes à Court doesn't like the word 'hostile' and explains his philosophy thus:

> [hostile] introduces emotion ... it's a question of economic viability ... I don't see it as a game or an art form ... An acquisition must produce profits within 12 months, and the quest for it should have as close to zero risk as possible.

This makes sense, but the way he operates is difficult to understand. Most mornings he stays home, playing chess against a computer and planning his moves in the business world. All telephone calls are taken by a secretary, thus protecting his privacy. Holmes à Court knows what he is doing but is not loved as a boss. A former close friend who fell out because of differences says, 'the man hasn't got any soul'. His apprenticeship was in taking control of and turning around companies in distress. These included West Australian Worsted and Woollen Mills, and Bell Brothers (construction equipment supplier).

Holmes à Court now thinks he has spotted undervalued assets in Asarco. The company is losing money. It has part ownership (44 per cent) in Australia's MIM Holdings, which is also a company that is losing money, but it does have one jewel, the Mount Isa Mine. This is a highly efficient mine, with rich supplies of lead, zinc, copper and silver, and it is operating profitably. Holmes à Court is counting on making a good profit on his Asarco investment by spinning off the Australian mine on its own. Holmes à Court could buy, against the wishes of Asarco, many more Asarco shares but he seems to think he is comfortably placed, prepared to stay with some 11 per cent or so of the company for years, if necessary. That seems to be his strategy; judging from past experience it might just work.

Takeovers

As if to pay back the Australians in their own coin we read about a Malaysian corporate raider, Lee Ming Tee, successfully penetrating the prestigious Australian group Wormald International through the purchase of a major parcel of shares.[15] Wormald was the first blue-chip company in his strange Australian stable. Lee's company, Sunshine Australia, built up its stake to the 19.9 per cent threshold limit set by the regulations and then announced an offer of A$4 a share for the rest, thus valuing the company at A$324 million (US$219 million). The rival empire builder Adelaide Steamship promptly sold over 13 million shares, equivalent to 15 per cent of the equity, thus giving Lee effective control of Wormald. There was considerable controversy over the NCSC (National Companies & Securities Commission) ruling that there had been a violation of the takeover rules, but the Wormald board maintained that Lee's offer was 'fair and reasonable' and the deal has since been regularised. With this takeover, Lee gets control of a well-respected company ranking 88th among the Australian firms in profitability. In 1984-85 it had a net profit of US$15 million on sales of US$570 million.

The mystery and intrigue surrounding raids and takeovers can be assessed by considering the headlines of several articles that appeared just a month after the above transaction:[16]

- The Lee of the storm
- The Sunshine Group restructures worldwide operations
- Strategy and the law – Australian authorities look closely at Sunshine

Towards the end of one of these articles we are told: 'Sunshine's tentacles spread around the world.' It appears that the British authorities, as well as those of Australia, Malaysia and New Zealand, are taking a close look at Lee's wheeling and dealing.

France

Until recently, the French financial markets were primitive and complicated. But in the space of just two years they have been completely transformed, with the result that by the end of 1986 credit rationing by the Bank of France had been abandoned and most of the foreign exchange restrictions had gone.[17] This could bring about a sea change in the takeover situation for foreign companies in France and by French companies operating abroad.

Sir James Goldsmith, the Anglo-French financier, taking advantage of the changed climate in France, is seeking to diversify his US$2.9 billion group outside France. He has picked up hundreds of Grand Union Co supermarkets, making several raids right across the USA. He is now launching fierce takeover battles in France, taking advantage of deregulation and the privatisation programme. He seems, however, to have met his equal in the takeover battle in the person of Carl De Benedetti, who is building up a big multi-media group based in France. Should De Benedetti win in this contest for Presses de la Cité he would have created the largest European communications empire next to the West German's US$4.5 billion Bertelsmann group. Sir James likes to invest in countries with a political ideology similar to his own and the centre-right coalition in France is just what he likes. But the question now being asked is whether France is ready to tolerate the ruthlessness for which he is known.[18]

Takeover activity really gripped Paris towards the end of 1986 when there were a number of hostile bids, a comparatively recent phenomenon in France.[19] One such hostile takeover occurred in the construction field, when the leading French construction group Bouygues, with a very unwelcome bid, acquired a 34 per cent stake in Spie-Batignolles, a competing construction firm 57 per cent owned by the Schneider group, for FFr830 million. Major French groups have also been aggressively acquiring target companies in the USA. Thus, in 1986:

- L'Air Liquide acquired Big Three Industries of Houston for US$1.06 billion.
- Rhône-Poulenc bought up Union Carbide's agrochemical business for US$575 million.
- Yves Saint Laurent purchased Charles of the Ritz of London for US$630 million.
- Bull with NEC (Japan) as partner negotiated for 40 per cent of Honeywell Information Systems for US$600 million.
- CGE is joining up with ITT to take control of a new communications joint venture, contributing US$1.1 billion. The total assets are likely to be about US$4.6 billion. This joint venture will constitute the second largest telecommunication group after AT&T.

Takeover activity in France has picked up considerably, but it is still very small compared with the USA. Although France is the world's fourth largest industrial country, it has had very little international presence so far. To correct this French companies have recently been quite aggressive and hope to add to their collection of prized pickings. This is in contrast to earlier times, 'when they got the leftovers from the American table'. Opening French companies to foreign investors may still be controlled to some extent, judging by the fact that the government is keeping a close watch on the level of foreign investments. According to a keen observer of the French scene: 'The opening up to foreigners is likely to be one of the last stages of denationalisation.'

Although the US type of hostile takeover and raid is still rare in France, fear of its taking place is forcing French companies to be more dynamic, in order that they may protect themselves against an unwanted raider. This poses a dilemma: such companies want to be aggressive, taking over companies abroad, yet at the same time they want to protect their own companies at home against foreign raiders.

The Commonwealth

Raids and hostile takeovers, as we said earlier, know no national boundaries. We were therefore not surprised to read about a takeover attempt which shook up companies in three Commonwealth countries: Britain, Canada and Australia.[20] The three companies involved were Allied-Lyons of Britain, Hiram Walker Resources of Canada, and Broken Hill Proprietary of Australia.

This particular takeover drama reads like a Victorian novel with a modern scene and far-flung locales, with endless turns of plot and a bunch of scheming characters. However, it was no fiction, but very real. The characters who acted out the drama were: the Reichman family from Canada; Sir James Balderstone, the BHP chairman; Robert Holmes à Court, Australia's richest businessman; and John D Elliott, the aggressive chairman of Elders IXL, Melbourne.

Very briefly, the chronology of this particular Commonwealth takeover game went as follows:

Autumn 1985. Australia's John D Elliott makes a US$2.6 billion unfriendly bid for Allied-Lyons.

19 March 1986. Canada's Reichmann family tries to grab control of Hiram Walker through Gulf Canada.

1 April. Hiram Walker agrees to sell its liquor business to Allied-Lyons for US$1.9 billion in order to escape Reichmann's

152   Takeovers, Acquisitions and Mergers

bid. This would also help to block Elders' bid (discussed in Chapter 11).

7 April. Robert Holmes à Court renews his bid for an additional 20 per cent in Broken Hill Proprietary.

9 April. TransCanada Pipeline makes a US$2.9 billion offer to buy Hiram Walker, while letting it sell its liquor business to Allied-Lyons.

14 April. BHP and Elders join forces to block Robert Holmes à Court.

By September 1986 a truce, if not permanent peace had been declared.[21] Its main terms were:

1. Robert Holmes à Court is taken on the BHP board provided the two largest shareholders apart from BHP, namely Holmes à Court himself (28.5 per cent) and Elders (18.5 per cent), do not increase their shareholding except as specified below.
2. They will consult with BHP before selling BHP shares, and BHP will consult with Elders with respect to its 17 per cent holding in that company, before selling Elders shares.

Robert Holmes à Court has won a moral victory after three years of continual attack and argument. Elders has also gained: indeed everyone has now won except the Melbourne lawyers, whose services are no longer in such demand.

The end result? Wait and see – the truce could easily be broken and war resumed.

Takeovers elsewhere

To demonstrate that takeovers, friendly or hostile, are indeed worldwide, let us quote some headlines of 1986 and 1987. All the headlines have been taken from the journal *FEER* (Far Eastern Economic Review).

China	The takeover battle for a Zhengzhou lorry factory
Hong Kong	Defence in depth – Jardine Mathieson schemes to keep out predators
	Chips off an old block – another Hong Kong group restructures
India	Takeovers – the corporate raiders

Italy	Shake-ups in Italy's volatile corporate sector – angry Montedison ends takeover talks with Fermenta
	Italian steel – in the boardoom the heat is on
Malaysia	Tightening the rules – Malaysia sets a new code on takeovers and mergers
	Hard-days' knights
	All in the same boat – Malaysia's MBF Holdings adds three old friends to its stables

Notice the recurrence of words with which we have now become very familiar: battle, defence, predators, raiders. The friendly takeover seems a rarity, and yet is the only approach that is likely to have lasting success.

References

1. Armstrong, L 'The new wheeler-dealers in US real estate are Japanese' *Business Week* 27 October 1986, p 21.
2. 'Japanese takeovers – hostility to hostility' *The Economist* **296**, 24 August 1985, p 78.
3. 'Cold shoulder for Mr Takeover – a very unJapanese acquisition bid is repulsed' *Time* 16 September 1985, p 37.
4. Brown, A C 'A brash Briton plays shark in Japanese waters' *Fortune* **112**, 9 December 1985, pp 129-30.
5. 'Japan's rigid short-term money' *The Economist* **301**, 11 October 1986, p 77.
6. 'Takeovers: the new technique for cracking the Japanese market' *International management* June 1984, pp 27-9.
7. Kharbanda, O P and Stallworthy, E A 'Classics from Japan' In *Company Rescue: How to Manage a Business Turnaround* Heinemann, 1987.
8. Rodgers, I 'BOC and Osaka Oxygen – Giving the breath of life' *Financial Times* 13 April 1987.
9. Dobrzynski, J H 'If you can't beat 'em, buy 'em: takeovers arrive in Japan' *Business Week* 29 September 1986, p 22-4.
10. Treece, J B 'How one company mastered the gentle art of Japanese takeovers' *Business Week* 29 September 1986, p 23.
11. Debes, C 'An Aussie raider's heady bid to buy a British brewer' *Business Week* 23 September 1985, pp 32-4.
12. Richardson, M 'Elders is targetting beer drinkers abroad' *International Herald Tribune* 23-4 May 1987.
13. Kraar, L 'Australia's acquisitive recluse' *Fortune* **112**, 2 September 1985, pp 78ff (4 pp).
14. Johnson, M 'The battle for the "Big Australian" ' *Time* 31 March 1986, p 37.
15. McDonald, H 'Takeovers – early bird gets Wormald' *FEER* 21 November 1985, p 156.

16. Ellis, E 'The Lee of the storm' and McDonald, H 'The Sunshine Group restructures worldwide operations' *FEER* **134**, 25 December 1986, pp 46-7.
17. 'France's financial markets creep from their cell' *The Economist* **301**, 29 November 1986, pp 83-4.
18. Rossant, J 'Sir Jimmy charges back into France' *Business Week* 27 October 1986, p 58.
19. Betts, P 'French takeovers – the bandwagon gathers pace' *Financial Times* 26 November 1986.
20. Pearson, J 'Oh, what a tangled web these raiders wove' *Business Week* 28 April 1986, pp 20-1.
21. McDonald, H 'Peace at this time – an uneasy truce settles on the BHP boardroom' *FEER* **133**, 25 September 1986, p 96.

Part Four

Buyouts: a Stake in Success

Chapter 14
The Company Buyout

We have considered companies whose shares are sold on the open market, or who are family owned. Now we look at companies that were in decline but where, in an effort to revive them, they have been bought out by the people who work in them. The managers and employees work hard to make their company succeed, for after all it is theirs: their money and their reputation is at stake. This is one of the reasons why governments worldwide are doing all they can to encourage the 'small business': such businesses give the maximum return on the investment since there is so much personal involvement.

For instance, the Conservative government led by Margaret Thatcher, now in its third term, has always laid stress on the importance of small businesses to the economy and has done its very best to stimulate and encourage them. During the Conservative government's first five years in power it enacted some 760 measures specifically designed to support small firms. They enjoy generous loan guarantee schemes and since 1981 the individual, as well as the corporation, has been given tax relief on investment in a new or expanding business.

We have already mentioned the Japanese style of management, but some suggest that the 'Japanese miracle', as it is sometimes called, has its roots in something very different from management style. Teresa Gorman exhorts us rather to look at the small business in Japan.[1] She asserts that Japan's miracle ingredient is a mixture of low taxation and an apparently chaotic mass of tiny companies. It seems that Japan has the biggest self-employed and small-business sector of all 10 of the OECD nations.

The same principle lies behind another aspect of company takeover that we now wish to look at in detail: the company buyout. Whether a company is bought out by the management or by the workers, the theory is that the spirit of the company will be transformed. Those working in the company will be working for themselves, and there will be an increase in loyalty and devotion to duty, which is soon reflected in the profits being made by the company. It is therefore seen as an admirable way to rescue a company in decline.

A stake in the business

The buyout is a fairly widespread phenomenon: as witness the following typical headlines:

- A Silicon Valley wizard's life in five fast lanes[2]
- Management buyouts – the French don't have a word for it[3]
- Employee buyouts of troubled companies[4]
- Buyouts are the fashion, but there are still a few doubts[5]
- No more cosy management buyouts[6]
- Life beyond the buyout[7]
- Millionaires on the shop floor – US employees' stock ownership plans[8]

In modern business the bulk of the finance comes from the banks and other financial institutions, although the way this is handled will vary from country to country. With many governments committed to the encouragement of entrepreneurship, especially on the small scale and in the high technology industries, a financial institution can well be making the major investment. Nevertheless the entrepreneur, having perhaps invested a lifetime's savings, has very personal stake in the enterprise. For him, it *has* to succeed!

The situation is very different from that discussed in Parts 2 and 3. Those initiating takeovers, mergers and acquisitions do *not* have a real stake in the business. As we saw particularly in Chapter 12, a raider makes money whether he takes over a company, or puts it down again after he has taken it over. His concern is primarily financial gain: he has no sentimental attachment of any sort to any particular enterprise, product or persons. However, when we come to the management or employee buyout, there is invariably a very real sentimental attachment to everything concerned with the company, the product and the people.

The main motive in such takeovers is not so much to make quick money, but to get the company back on its feet, revive it and 'cure' it of all its ills. There is of course money to be made if they are successful, and that must be a powerful incentive: the management and employees all want to stay in work. But that particular reward will only come after months or even years of hard work. There are no 'instant profits', such as are won by the raider. Another difference is that with company takeovers there is a high success rate, at least when one looks at the first few years after the takeover. On the other hand, the employee buyout, whether it be by management or by the workers, has a rather low success rate. Indeed, such buyouts are notorious for failure: let us see why they succeed.

Leadership and cooperation

A French entrepreneur

Why does the employee buyout so often fail? We suggest that it is because of a lack of leadership. Everyone may be very anxious to do their best, but unless they have a leader they will get nowhere – and there can be no guarantee that they have a leader in their midst.

The career of Bernard Tapie is illustrative of this. He is exceptional among the takeover experts, in that he had very humble beginnings. The son of a poor pipefitter in a Paris suburb, he had to work his way through school by hauling sacks of coal.[9] He graduated from the Ecole d'Electricité Industrielle de Paris, a second-rate engineering school, in 1965. During his first professional job, with a management consulting firm, Tapie discovered that he could run a company better than his employer, but of course it wasn't that easy.

It seems that partly as a result of his humble beginnings and partly because of the experience he gained, Tapie became an expert in dealing with workers. His ability to win a union over, getting them to accept the necessary layoffs, and his success in motivating the remaining managers and workers were key elements in his phenomenal success: his group now employs some 10,000 workers and has an annual turnover of more than half a billion dollars. According to Gilbert Delhorbe, one of the advisers who are the nucleus of Tapie's staff:

> We must communicate a sense of challenge to all the personnel ... People in these companies feel like losers. We transform them into people who believe they are going to win, and do win.

It sounds simple enough, and it is of course the key to success in any enterprise. But someone has to be there to 'communicate' and inspire: a leader.

Academics rescue a doomed factory

The Rochester Product Division of General Motors set up a plant in 1977 at Tuscaloosa, Alabama, in the USA, to assemble replacement carburettors, emission control components and carburettor service kits. Demand for these particular products fell steeply in 1980 and nearly one-third of the employees had to be laid off.[10] But it was determined that the plant was still not viable and would not be unless costs were further cut by some US$2 million a year. With no improvement in sight, General Motors sent in an expert team in mid-1982 to analyse the problem.

The workers were found to be quite willing and cooperative, and prepared to do whatever the management called for in order to improve productivity and so cut costs. Together they devised a number of ways to improve matters, and these resulted in a further saving of some US$1.5 million a year. But although so close, the gap had *not* been closed: the plant was still losing US$500,000 a year and General Motors reluctantly announced in August 1982 that it had no choice but to phase it out.

The announcement came as a severe blow to the locality. Unemployment there was already some 17 per cent and now a major employer was to shut its gates. Tuscaloosa could ill afford the loss of another 200 jobs and the US$7 million they contributed to the local economy by spending their wages. Closure was not a preferred option so far as General Motors was concerned, and in a last bid to save the situation another team of GM experts was sent in, who sounded out the University of Alabama to see whether they had ideas as to the way in which this crisis could be resolved. The state university president, Joab Thomas, was very willing to do what he could, but he had problems of his own: he too had a financial crisis, since he was receiving a reduced allocation.

However, a team of management specialists from the university, together with engineering and energy specialists, reviewed the plant operations and systems. They managed to devise a scheme that would cut operating costs by the required half a million dollars a year. Their findings came at about the same time as the university received a sanction of US$75,000 from the local industrial development board to fund research at the university. These developments led to the drawing up of a three-year contract between the university and General Motors, whereby they would use the plant as an applied research facility against a payment to General Motors of US$470,000. This practically bridged the expected shortfall and any additional savings resulting from the suggestions made by the university personnel were to be deducted from that amount. So the university could finish up with nothing to pay if they did a good job.

Obviously, the arrangement had a number of qualifications. The savings had to be of a permanent and recurring nature, no 'one off' savings. As a token of *their* faith in these proposals and to demonstrate that they too had a stake in what was going on, the union employees agreed to accept a reduction of US$55.20 in their weekly wage. This was to be their contribution to the university research fund. However, General Motors not only agreed to return this money to the employees whether or not the project was a success, but also provided US$250,000 a year for three years to fund fellowships and scholarships at the university.

This was a unique arrangement, and all the parties concerned had a stake: General Motors, the university, the union and the town. The first three parties set up a task force, known as the 'Gang of Twelve', with four members from each of the three parties. Any cost-saving proposal had to have the unanimous approval of the task force. There were 'doubting Thomases' on all sides, but the University team, comprising members of the faculty and their students, and led by Professor J Barry Mason, chairman of the university's management and marketing department, 'brainstormed' in association with both the company management and workers and their colleagues in other departments of the university. All this led to a host of proposals and resultant savings as detailed in Table 14.1 (excluding 'one-off' savings).

Table 14.1 *Listing of proposed savings*

Item	Proposal	Saving per year (US$000)
Shipping parts from Rochester, New York, to Tuscaloosa	Reclassify auto parts for cheaper rates	88
	Lighter, less expensive containers for shipping	60
Teleprinters and photocopiers	Buy instead of leasing	23
Energy conservation – huge blowers, air movement too great	Change of pulleys	13
Air conditioning in a cavernous warehouse	Replace by fans – comfortable enough	30
Cooling water system	Series of wells to provide water	80
Inventory control system	Computerise and make five-year forecast	135

The first item was a one-time saving, so it did not count under the terms of the agreement. The five-year inventory forecasts required a one-time cost of US$165,000 for the purchase of a computerised inventory system, but it resulted in a one-time saving of US$414,000. Under the terms of the agreement, this was not to be counted.

Every time the task force approved a project the announcement was duly posted and cheered by the employees. What is more, they all *worked* to make sure that the forecast savings materialised. All departments, both clerical and production, were working at peak efficiency, because they had a direct stake in the outcome. The savings listed above total US$429,000, but in practice the initial target of US$470,000 was achieved in just eight months, the one-time saving helping almost to offset the one-time cost of the computer system and other hardware required. The employees' voluntary cut in wages was put into a trust fund, but in the event it was not needed and US$1,600 was returned to each employee well before Christmas 1983.

This was a remarkable turnaround and must be rare in that the turnaround was achieved with active participation from academics. It was of course very good experience for them: it brought them into direct and intimate contact with the 'real world'. All the parties concerned benefited very substantially and expressed their attitudes thus:

Union. The shop chairman Grady: 'We worked together as a team and we turned this plant around. The university people weren't outsiders. They were here with us, working to make things better.'

Cook University. President Joab Thomas: 'We have shown business and industry the practicality of using the talents and resource of a university.'

General Motors. Tom Gilligan: 'The success was the result of a concept that nobody else had ever tried. I believe what happened here will open a new way of thinking about doing business and being competitive.'

The primary lesson is that everyone, not only those who went to the factory every day, but all their families and friends, felt involved and wanted success. So everyone worked for it: encouragement at home is just as important as encouragement at work. It is the sense of involvement that is so important, as we shall see further demonstrated in the following case study.

Involvement

This is the story of a self-rescue of one of the three largest British brewers, the Ind Coope Burton brewery, a part of the

Allied-Lyons group, with an annual turnover of some £180 million (US$300 million). The first step was a communications exercise: management shared their apprehensions with the workers. Domestic beer consumption had been falling steadily over the years. Some 40 million barrels in 1979, by 1985 it was down to less than 36 million barrels.[11] Against this, the available production capacity of the breweries was around 50 million barrels a year, thus implying surplus capacity of some 25 per cent. So a quarter of the capacity was redundant and should be shut down.

How to ensure that Ind Coope at Burton was not one of those shut down? Its plant layout, staff structure and unionisation system were all about 100 years old. The skilled and unskilled workers and supervisors had rigid lines of demarcation in relation to their tasks. The layout was most inefficient, with the bottling plant some 2 km away from the production line.

The managing director was relatively new to the company, and he proposed a 'greenfield assessment at Burton Brewery', to which he gave the acronym GABB. He asked:[11]

> What would a newcomer recommend if his brief was to build the most efficient brewery in Europe on this site at Burton, starting from scratch without any of our existing plant or us, the existing people, being here?

One immediate answer that came up was that there would be 1,525 workers instead of the present 1,925. The company, while recognising this fact, promised that there would be no redundancy if the unions agreed to flexible working practices, dropping the restriction that no-one should do another's job. This is the demarcation restriction, common throughout British industry until recently. Two further steps were announced as part of the GABB package:

1. The hitherto hierarchical workforce to be split into a large number of tiny (usually less than 10) intrapreneurial teams.
2. The above to be preceded by the sending of a small team of Burton workers to various breweries in Britain, Western Europe and elsewhere and then to suggest any improvement they thought appropriate to GABB.

GABB envisaged a £30 million (US$50 million) capital expenditure over a period of five years for modernisation, which could well include sophisticated high-tech provisions such as on-line pasteurisation with computerised control. The feedback from the visits to the breweries at home and abroad was that many of these high-tech devices did not work. Some of their other findings were:

- An ultra-modern brewery in the USA had a brilliant plant layout, but miserable productivity. The reason: the workforce was the same and old habits die hard.
- An Australian brewery used superb computer graphics for effective and excellent process control. Where could Ind Coope purchase the necessary software? From a firm at Ilkeston in Derbyshire, only a few miles from Burton!
- A brewery in Japan had an automatic warehouse. A study on the introduction of this at Burton revealed a Discounted Cash Flow (DCF) return of 7 per cent against the current interest rate of 12 per cent. That pleased the unions!
- There was a slightly older plant than that proposed under GABB, with the same capacity, that had a workforce of 500.

Armed with this information they began to look at things back home. The intrapreneurial team exercise showed that the proposed workforce of 1,525 (originally 1,925) could be brought down to 1,400, but this was still a far cry from the 500 who coped with a brewer of similar size in California.

Perhaps 'intrapreneurial' needs some explanation, since it cannot as yet be found in the dictionary. It can be defined as follows:[12] 'Any of the "dreamers who do". Those who take a "hands-on" responsibility for creating innovation of any kind *within* an organisation.' The intrapreneur may be the creator or the investor of the idea, but is always a 'dreamer': the one who 'dreams up' how to turn an idea into a profitable reality.[13]

By contrast, we can define an entrepreneur as 'someone who fills the role of an intrapreneur *outside* the organisation'. The standard dictionary definition of an entrepreneur is:[14] 'Person in effective control of a commercial undertaking; one who undertakes a business or an enterprise, with chance of profit or loss; contractor acting as an intermediary.'

In all this we see what was expected of those small teams of workers set up at Burton. Above all, they each had to have a leader with ideas.

With management committed to a policy of no redundancy, it could not cut the workforce, so it formed a total of 170 intrapreneurial teams, the team leaders being selected on the basis of an in-house advertisement to which 350 workers respond. The prospective team leaders were taken in batches to a country house for a week at a time and tested for 14 qualities. One of these was 'achiever', which was explained to the applicants as follows:

The major driving force within every team should be task achievement. Therefore the team leader should assist his team to achieve or exceed its agreed output at the correct cost, time and quality. If the role is performed satisfactorily, then the team will be achievement-minded.

The company also introduced informality – addressing one another on a first-name basis; and operational equality – they all ate at the same canteen. The managing director changed his title and became known as the leader of the executive team, whose task was to monitor the performance of six other top teams: financial, marketing, personnel, production, distribution and management services.

But what was to happen to all that surplus manpower? Some of the intrapreneurial teams studied this problem in depth and came up with a number of suggestions, typical of which were:

- Do in-house some of the services which hitherto had been bought in, such as repairs to casks and kegs.
- Develop new products for sale to existing customers. Some 75 such products were identified.
- Develop totally new products for other than existing customers.

In order that these ends might be achieved an intensive training programme was initiated.

The results with GABB have been most encouraging. It has been demonstrated that because of the deep personal involvement, efficiency has been substantially improved. New investment has been very effectively deployed, since the teams were able to suggest the most attractive alternative from the various possibilities: they were *asked* what they thought, a novel approach. Then, when the scheme they have recommended is implemented, they have further personal, financial or other involvement, being committed to ensuring that their recommendations are a success, to the benefit of all.

The conclusion: once people have a stake in what is going on, they work with a will and find a solution to any problem.

References

1. Gorman, T 'The Japan giant's small beginnings' *Today* 17 July 1986, p 16.
2. 'A Silicon Valley wizard's life in five fast lanes' *Business Week* 10 October 1983, pp 54-6.

3. 'Management buyouts – the French don't have a word for it' *The Economist* **290**, 10 March 1984, pp 81-2.
4. Bradley, K and Gelb, A 'Employee buyouts of troubled companies' *Harvard Business Review* **63**, September/October 1985, pp 121-30.
5. Dawkins, W 'Buyouts are the fashion, but there are still a few doubts' *Financial Times* 11 November 1985.
6. Lowenstein, L 'No more cosy management buyouts' *Harvard Business Review* **64**, January/February 1986, pp 147-56.
7. Dawkins, W 'Life beyond the buyout' *Financial Times* 29 April 1986, p 21.
8. Dodsworth, T 'Millionaires on the shop floor – US employees' stock ownership plans' *Financial Times* 6 May 1986.
9. Sancton, TA 'France's high-flying fixer' *Time* 31 December 1984, p 56.
10. Blank, J P 'The University that saved a factory' *Readers' Digest* December 1984, pp 127-30.
11. 'By Gabb and by Gibb' *The Economist* **298**, 1 February 1986, pp 68-9.
12. Kharbanda, O P and Stallworthy, E A 'Intrapreneurship' In *Successful Projects With a Moral for Management* Gower, 1986.
13. Pinchot, Gifford III *Intrapreneuring – Why You Don't Have to Leave a Corporation to Become an Entrepreneur* Harper & Row, New York, 1985.
14. *Concise Oxford Dictionary* 7th ed, 1982.

Chapter 15
Management Buyouts

In many companies top management has some sort of profit sharing scheme, but this does not necessarily mean holding any shares in the company. When such profit sharing schemes exist, they are usually very restricted in scope: only directors and very senior managers can participate. The idea is that those receiving such benefits will be motivated and work harder, just as if it was their own company. To what degree such schemes are really effective is open to question. In any event their impact is limited, since the rest of the management do not enjoy such benefits and may well resent that fact.

The management buyout is a logical extension of profit sharing, extending the results of success to a much wider group: perhaps all the managers. Of course, the key difference compared with profit sharing is that management then has to bear a loss if it is incurred.

Background

Management buyouts in the USA came into vogue for two main reasons:

1. Over the years up to 1970, several states modified their earlier laws prohibiting share transactions with interested directors.
2. There was a slump in the stock market. The Dow Jones Industrial Average practically halved in a couple of years, dropping from 1036 in 1972 to 578 in 1974. In the ensuing 'panic' management opted for buyout in certain cases, seeking to ensure better growth and better prospects.

In the beginning most of the companies involved were quite small. But the size has grown over the years: from companies having an asset value of some US$1-3 million in the 1970s, to companies having an asset value of as high as a billion dollars in the 80s. The magazine *Forbes* often recommends potential candidates for management buyout so that its readers can be among, 'those lucky investors who happen to be in the right place'.[1] The implication is that a group of managers will pay a good price for a company with potential, but we shall have to look at that more closely.

Of course top management has no hope whatever of buying a controlling interest in a very large company and another problem is that a management buyout proposal can trigger an uninvited offer from a third party, leading to a 'Dutch auction'.

To take one example of this, a chief executive who had a substantial shareholding in his company, Stokely-Van Camp, wanted to increase his holding so that he had a controlling interest. He offered to buy additional shares at US$50 a share, compared with the prevailing price on the market of US$38. In the face of a competing offer from Esmark, he raised his price to US$55. But others came into the fray, and one company, Pillsbury, bid US$62. Finally, Quaker Oats won at a price of US$77 a share, more than double the market price prevailing when the management buyout was first mooted.

Of course, in the process the shareholders who sold had an immediate benefit, but they may well have lost out in the long term. To what extent the long-term benefits are realised will depend upon the way Quaker Oats manages the company it has acquired and the corporate strategy it adopts. It is not on record what the chief executive did: if he allowed his emotions to hold sway he probably sold out too, realised the profit and went elsewhere.

Unfortunately some management buyouts are accompanied by a great deal of intrigue, with the 'wheeling and dealing' that we saw earlier as typical of the takeover syndrome, particularly when a raider was involved. But it need not be and should not be like this.

In general, as we have just seen from the above example, the shareholders gain an immediate benefit, but they have to invest elsewhere and there is no guarantee that their next investment will be as sound as the one they have just sold. Management buyout tends to meet with general approval, and it is part of the new entrepreneurial wave all over the world, since it comes close to an entrepreneur taking charge of his own business and fulfilling the ambition to be 'one's own boss'.

The balance sheet of management buyout is the subject of much debate. Some aspects are desirable. It is good that those who run a company should own it: this should and often does result in better management. But it is alleged that in a management buyout, the management gains a financial advantage by virtue of its special inside knowledge about the company.

Typical of the adverse comment in this context is that of Lowenstein:[2] '... proponents of [management] buyouts are simply putting sociological icing on what is a very financial cake.' The shareholder is said to be at a disadvantage because he is unaware of what is going on, and it is felt that the buyout process should be much more open than it is now. The present secrecy makes the process somewhat suspect, and it is felt that complete openness would benefit both the process of management buyout and ultimately the company.

The situation in France

While management buyouts have become the craze in both Britain and the USA, they are so rare in France that there is no recognised French word for the procedure. However, this may change when the present tax and legal problems are removed, as is proposed by the Compagnie Financiers de Suez and the Paribas group. At present, if a group of managers sets up a separate company to buy out the company they are working for, the law does not permit tax write-offs to the new owners. However, the government has agreed to remove this anomaly.[3]

Meanwhile the two financial groups mentioned above, who have taken the initiative in this respect, are already gearing themselves up for management buyouts by setting up two new companies for this purpose. Compagnie Financiers de Suez is forming a FFr200 million (US$25 million) company in conjunction with the state financial institution, IDI, to finance promising new ventures, including management buyouts. Paribas is setting up a US$5 million fund specifically to help to finance companies with annual sales of the order of FFr50 million (US$6.5 million). It is doing this in collaboration with some banks and other financial institutions.

Both Compagnie Financiers de Suez and Paribas see management buyouts as a useful solution when family firms are faced with tax problems, such as the impact of the inheritance tax, or internal family squabbles. Subsidiaries of foreign companies are also seen as a fruitful field for management buyouts. Their move in this direction has been inspired by the encouragement that the French government is now giving to entrepreneurship, especially in relation to the small business. Of course, *their* interest is purely financial and commercial: they sense that they can make a profit out of management buyouts and in the process put companies in distress back on the road to recovery.

A new lease of life

Let us now take a typical example from the UK, to see how it works there. The Cornwall-based computer stationery group Roffs Print found itself, back in 1983, burdened with a debt of £650,000 (US$1 million), supported by an equity of the same amount. This is typical of many small firms, and conditions can only get worse, since with such a heavy debt burden the company cannot modernise. It usually spends most of its profits paying interest. The situation was so critical for Roffs that its managing director, Cliff Brown, just did not want to know. He expressed his feelings thus:[4] 'I do not like the spend too much time thinking about it.' Indeed, it is a subject a managing director should not be burdened with: he should be busy with a number of constructive ideas for the future of the company.

How did the company get into this position? It began in 1982 with a management buyout. The management acquired the company from its two founders for £1.3 million (US$2 million). By 1986 the company had repaid some of its debt, its gearing (debt/equity) had dropped from 1.00 to about 0.70 and the company had been able to effect some modernisation, having spent £774,000 on presses and others equipment to keep up with the fast-moving technology in this particular field. The competition is so intense in the printing trade that Roffs did not sell its old machines, since that would only strengthen a rival company, but broke them up to provide spare parts.

Sales increased from £3.4 million in the year 1983-84, when the buyout occurred, to £5.5 million in 1985-86, but profits dipped sharply, from £300,000 to £170,000 in 1984-85, only to climb back to £350,000 for the year 1985-86. The profit dip was mainly a result of the heavy debt burden arising not only from the initial purchase but also from the general modernisation programme. There was also a deliberate broadening of the customer base in an overcrowded market with cut-throat competition. Prior to the takeover just one customer, HM Stationery Office, accounted for more than half of its sales. This made Roffs very vulnerable in an industry that was only growing at the rate of 1 per cent a year: a broadening of its customer base was considered imperative.

As would be expected in a cut-throat market, the customer is very price conscious and there was practically no customer loyalty. Roffs' strategy therefore was to cut profit margins in order to gain new customers, and then try to increase its margins once it had established a reputation through satisfaction of a new customer. This is a long-term strategy and the results were slow in coming. Roffs also began to acquire some 'small fry' in the

Management Buyouts

printing business, in order to consolidate its position in the trade. This also helped diversification in that, for instance, it bought up Datachase, a small printer of computer stationery that had gone into receivership. This extended Roffs' customer base into the smaller end of the market, where runs of 10,000 are usual. Till then, its print runs had been several million a time.

Cash flow was improved by appointing a full-time credit controller shortly after the buyout, who by diligent watchfulness could help to ensure that customers paid up promptly. Because of over-capacity in the paper making industry Roffs was able to negotiate extended credit terms from its raw material suppliers (62 days instead of 40) and also to persuade them to hold stocks for it. This was significant, since paper cost represented more than half of its turnover. But for all this to bear fruit the plant must be used efficiently. Roffs therefore allowed its staff of 80 unlimited overtime in exchange for full holiday cover. Prior to this, one of its four presses used to be out of action for nearly three months in a year, causing a considerable loss of production.

What a struggle! But that is what management buyout means: long hours and much anxiety, with the shadow of debt ever present. However, not only are Cliff Brown and his partner working for themselves – and the bank – but they have kept another 80 people in work in an area when there is massive unemployment. In addition, the business has now proved to be quite profitable.

UK management buyouts

A management buyout makes both technical and commercial sense. It is good for the managers and workers, whose jobs might otherwise be in jeopardy. There is no doubt that the presence of those who have a substantial stake in the company increases efficiency, productivity and profits. It is the next best thing to owning your own little business – it must nearly always be 'little', because otherwise capital has to be found, and that brings in others whose only interest is the 'interest' they get. There is no doubt that despite all the difficulties, some of which we have sought to portray above, management buyouts are on the increase.

If we take the British scene as an example to illustrate this, management buyouts have grown in numbers over the years as shown in Table 15.1.[5,6,7] The value of management buyouts for 1985 is more than the combined value of all such deals in the previous five years, and 1985 also shows a marked increase in the average size of buyout. Bison, a civil engineering company, was bought out by its management for £10 million; Vosper Thorneycroft (shipbuilding) for £19 million; St Regis, a paper and packaging company, for £32 million; Haden (engineering) for £56 million; Mallinson-Denny (timber products) for £90 million; and Mardon Packaging for £173 million. The figures speak for themselves, and we have only named six out of some 150 such buyouts.

Table 15.1 UK management buyouts 1980-85

Year	Number	Total value (£ million)	Average value (£ million)
1980	100	36	0.36
1981	170	91	0.54
1982	180	205	1.20
1983	195	225	1.05
1984	180	160	1.52
1985	150	1200	8.00

In the case of Mallinson-Denny, Terence Mallinson is now the only family member on the board after the management buyout and we are told that 'he seems to like it'. To quote:

> It's a different atmosphere. The six of us directors are now a close knit club, whereas before we were all getting on with our jobs separately. Nobody now has any doubts about the effort being put in by anybody else. There is a great deal more communication between us. The feeling now is one of being proprietors rather than staff.

Funding management buyouts

The Mallinson-Denny buyout was at the time the biggest deal to date involving a wholly-owned British company. Mallinson-Denny was part of the Brooke Bond group and it was acquired for £90 million by its directors and staff with the help of 25 financial institutions. It is typical of the transactions that are now being put together for this purpose, whereby large sums are mobilised for the buyout. As one can see from Table 15.1, such deals have been growing in size very rapidly: in 1985 there were 13 buyouts worth more than £10 million each.

To cope with this burgeoning 'fashion', several specialist management buyout institutions and funds have come into being. Jon Moulton, managing partner at Schroder Ventures, who launched one such fund, sees them as a source of encouragement for British managers seeking to buy out their company. Moulton sums up the situation thus:

> The psychology is ahead of the business. If it is believed that these things can be done, then more managers will say to themselves: 'If the parent is going to sell our division, then maybe we should buy it'.

But once again we have a conflict of interest. Moulton and his like are not interested in the well-being of the managers: they are interested in making a profit by deploying the funds at their disposal to the best advantage. The creation of funds for management buyouts may well be in excess of the actual requirements, in which event the cost of such acquisitions will rise; too much money chasing something always puts the price up. The rate of return on the investment will then fall and the proposition may no longer be attractive either to the financier or the managers, burdened with the repayment of debt.

A very comprehensive report of management buyouts in the UK is available in a slim (180-page) but expensive (£1,095) publication giving the results of a three-year research project.[8] Sue Lloyd, managing director of *Venture Economics*, the consultancy who published the report, sees a danger:

> Large management buyouts are really becoming an exercise in corporate financing and are thus moving out of the venture capital world. If everybody moves up the scale, there is a danger that a gap will be left at the bottom of the venture capital market.

Management buyouts in the UK have grown to nearly one-third of all acquisitions, a dramatic rise from 1977, when they were a mere 3 per cent. In general, divestments have been the most common source of buyouts, but other factors giving rise to this buyout boom are:

- Managers' willingness to invest, to have a secure job.
- Receiverships, due to the economic recession.
- General encouragement of entrepreneurship by government.
- Favourable legislation.
- Growth of the venture capital market.

Management buyouts have now come of age, and the time between a management buyout and the floating of the revitalised company on the stock market has been getting shorter.

Bigger deals, higher debts

In general, management buyouts seem to begin with a heavy debt burden, giving them high gearing (debt/equity ratio). High gearing is both a danger and a threat to any company. It seems that in the USA this has reached dangerous levels (9:1) in contrast to the UK (2:1). For instance, the case is cited of a Californian maker of cleaning products, Purex Industries, which was successfully bought out by its management in 1982 for US$356 million in cash. But the debt burden proved too great for it to bear and it finished up in the arms of the transport and food giant, Greyhound, which bought it for US$264 million.

In the UK the value of management buyouts is currently between £1-2 billion a year, but the corresponding figure across the Atlantic is bound to be much higher, perhaps three or four times as much, although we have no statistics. The only data available in relation to the USA concerns *all* leveraged buyouts. Even this data presents only a partial picture. In 1985 over 250 leveraged buyouts were reported for the USA, but the value is known for only about half of that total: it comes to some US$20 billion. This type of activity was reported to be about 50 per cent higher in 1986 than in the previous year, so it is growing fast.[9]

Based on experience in the USA, management buyouts are found to be sound only under the following conditions:

- Strong, stable earnings history with a predictable cash flow.
- Growth not too fast – high technology companies are particularly bad in this respect.
- Must have a well-defined niche in the market.
- Not too capital intensive or requiring much capital in the near future.
- Must have a strong, proven management.

It seems that management buyouts have now developed their own jargon, with terms such as 'leveraged buyout', 'sponsored spin-out', 'second round financing', 'tranche funding' and 'bridge financing'.[10] Indeed, the subject is continually growing in importance, rating a 16-page supplement in the *Financial Times* and receiving regular coverage in journals such as the *Economist*, the *Wall Street Journal* and the *Mergers & Acquisitions Magazine*. The spirit imbuing the management buyout is, we feel, well captured by the caption to a full-page advertisement by a finance house specialising in funding such buyouts: 'We'd rather you became a captain of industry than stay the first mate.'

Caveat emptor

This is a basic principle in all business transactions: let the buyer beware. He alone is responsible if he is disappointed. We believe that a great many managers will be disappointed with their buyouts: it will be a lot of hard work for very little profit. A leading research authority on buyouts, John Coyne of Nottingham University, makes the following relevant comment in this context:

> It used to be a good negotiating ploy for management to say that they couldn't pay more because the funds were not available. Now that the funds *are* available vendors are going to get greedy. It will only take a few spectacular failures to bring the whole thing tumbling down.

It seems that once again the intervention of the financiers is doing more harm than good. Why is this? Primarily because their objectives are so very different. Their business is money and the return it brings. The business of the managers of industry is production, their own well-being and the well-being of their employees. However, good managers should be able to cope with financiers and ensure that their company thrives.

References

1. Kichen, S and Pittel, L 'Selling high' *Forbes* **21**, May 1984, p 248.
2. Lowenstein, L 'No more cosy management buyouts' *Harvard Business Review* January-February 1986, pp 147-56.
3. 'Management buyouts – The French don't have a word for it' *The Economist* **290**, 10 March 1984, pp 81-2.
4. Dawkins, W 'Life beyond a buyout' *Financial Times* 29 April 1986, p 21.
5. Dawkins, W 'Buyouts are the fashion, but there are still a few doubts' *Financial Times* 11 November 1985.
6. 'British buyouts – odd timing?' *The Economist* **278**, 15 March 1986, pp 81-2.
7. Hawthorn, A 'Compass poised for big management buyout' *Financial Times* 8 June 1987.
8. *UK Management Buyouts* Venture Economics (London), 1986.
9. Dunne, N 'The US scene – scramble for piece of the pie' *Financial Times* 10 October 1986, p 14.
10. Rawsthorn, A 'A guide to the jargon – venture speak made easy' *Financial Times* 10 October 1986, p 13.

Chapter 16
The Employee Buyout

The employee buyout is no passing phenomenon. It is of very long standing and is now beginning to proliferate throughout the world. There are very good reasons for this: chiefly that it has proved to be a viable answer for companies in decline, or companies in declining industries who are under threat of disappearing. In some cases even partial ownership has been found to be superior to other forms of reorganisation. This is because if both the management and the workforce own the company either partly or wholly, they have a personal stake and are therefore more likely:

- To see the results of their performance, in that company profitability has an immediate impact on their pay packet.
- To opt for long-term benefits, in sharp contrast to the short-term objective of the raider.
- To be able to repulse takeovers and government intervention effectively.
- To make efficient use of public funds.

A number of books have been written on the subject, which are well worth perusal by those who will be or are involved in an employee buyout situation.[1,2,3]

A real alternative?
Common sense tells us that managers and employees who have a stake in their company *can* do wonders, and there are a number of case histories to demonstrate that this is so. As we consider companies in distress or decline, there is no doubt that buyout by the employees (by which we mean both management and workers) should be a very effective means of achieving a successful turnaround. However, if we exclude the employee share ownership plans, which quite a few major companies operate in one form or another, the record of employee buyouts has been very mixed. This is contrary to expectations, and we

shall be considering the possible causes of failure (and reasons for success) in this chapter.

The justification for employee buyout in a free economy is, it seems, highly controversial. The informed public is very much against an employee takeover or buyout, particularly when it is government sponsored. Some form of support or sponsorship is of course necessary with almost any company of substance: the individual worker just has not got the resources to pay for his or her share. Thus, it is alleged, a small group of people – the employees and the shareholders of the company concerned – receive a special benefit for which the community at large has to pay, via the government. So it is argued that the law of the 'survival of the fittest' should prevail.

Based on the available data we estimate that since 1970 some half a million employees in the USA have tried to save their companies and their jobs by either partial or complete ownership.[4] Employee buyouts, it seems, are taking place not only in the USA, but also in Canada, the UK, France, Spain, Australia, India and elsewhere. They seem to have fared best in the USA and worst in the UK. Three categories can be identified:

1. The employees made a substantial sacrifice, such as by taking lower pay, but saved their jobs.
2. The employees lost both their stake and their jobs.
3. The company was not only saved but the employees went on to reap substantial reward in the capital appreciation of their shareholding.

In principle, properly structured employee buyouts should offer both managers and workers in troubled companies or declining industries excellent prospect in the long run. It is common enough for employees to have some sort of stake in their company, but an employee buyout in response to a need to rescue a failing company has not always led to the desired improved results.

There are three main areas of attack when the problem arises:

1. Employees make a sacrifice, such as taking lower wages.
2. The union makes a sacrifice, by accepting redundancies.
3. Efforts to achieve a substantial improvement in productivity.

Let us look at a few examples and see how it all works out in practice.

When the employees become aware of the gravity of the situation they are ready to accept lower wages and redundancies.

Workers at Tembec in Canada took a 26 per cent cut, while workers at Rath, also in Canada, were prepared to forego Can$2,000 annually in fringe benefits. In Britain there were three cases where the employees took a cut of one-third in their salaries.

When it comes to cutting down on staff, an equally realistic attitude can be adopted. There was the remarkable case at Peterborough in Ontario, Canada, where the employees displayed an outstanding sense of responsibility. The company had 450 employees and they were asked to determine the minimum number with which the company could carry on. Of course, to begin with, they hadn't a clue. As their new managing director and a major shareholder said: 'That question blew their minds out. No-one had ever asked them that before and they couldn't cope with it.' However, after three weeks of furious debate they came up with 135. This proved too low and it finally settled down at 150, but that was still a remarkable reduction: two-thirds of the original workforce. And of course the redundancies were accepted as inevitable.

When it comes to improvements in productivity any number of cases can be cited as to the dramatic change that can be achieved once the employees take a good look at what is going on and are determined to cooperate. To take but a few examples:

Saratoga Knitting Mill: Pilfering was eliminated once they realised they were stealing their own materials, and there was substantially more scrap salvage.

Pioneer Chain Saw Corporation. The number of quality control personnel was reduced from 57 to 10 without increasing the defective product rates, as a consequence of increased quality consciousness at all levels.

Tembec. The job classification was broadened so that the operators could repair and maintain their own equipment, thus reducing the total workforce. Then, despite the fact that the machinery was old, downtime was reduced to below that in any other Canadian pulp mill.

Scottish Daily News. Outside experts were confounded by the employees, who converted their production from broadsheet to tabloid in three weeks without interrupting production. Outside experts had said that the conversion would be extremely costly, involving at least a one-month shutdown.

The Employee Buyout

There is no doubt that no other form of ownership than employee ownership could have achieved such results as we have set out above: they are truly spectacular.

An early success

Just a few years ago employee buyouts were being written off in the USA, but now seem to have staged a remarkable comeback.[5] This has been largely due to:

- Legal changes and tax incentives.
- Economic trends: the desire to save jobs in areas of high unemployment.
- Improved management.
- Better profitability.

Puget Sound Plywood of Tacoma, Washington, is the first worker-owned company to be discussed in the *Harvard Business Review*. Founded in 1941, it is not an 'employee buyout' as such, since it started out as an employee cooperative. With 400 employees it sells its products worldwide. The worker-elected president, L J Bennett, interviewed by David W Ewing, said that everyone feels committed. Most of the top officers and the trustees are elected, but the general manager and a few other managers are appointed. To be a member of the cooperative, one has to own a unit of stock, worth about US$27,000. This has to be bought from someone who wants to retire. Newcomers have to work for about six weeks, under three foremen, before they are interviewed by the board of trustees and can become a member.

Each member owns the same number of shares, gets the same pay and has one vote. The majority of the workers (240) are owners, the rest hired employees, but this ratio fluctuates. There is a very small turnover among the owners: less than 3 per cent per year. There is no retirement age; that is a personal decision. However, a full day's work is demanded up to retirement – it is said that one worker carried on until he was 81. There are at the moment some 50 shareholders who don't work, but there is actually no advantage in holding on to the shares, since they yield nothing unless you are working. It is said that there is no difference between the owners and the hired in personnel workwise; they maintain an excellent rapport. Nor is there a union presence in the works.

Ownership and control

One of the companies that has made a succes of the employee buyout is Tembec, briefly mentioned above. On the eve of the Tembec employee buyout party, Charlie Carpenter, president of Local 233 of the Canadian Paperworkers' Union, predicted:

> It's a beautiful party but you know as well as I do that it won't last like this. The interests of management and our own interests are the two ends of the same stick.

Despite the results they achieved at this mill, we think this union boss knew his people very well. The initial euphoria did fade away – it usually does. This poses a vital challenge to the management in employee-owned companies. How to prolong the honeymoon, or at least settle down into a sound relationship?

Once again, it is the mistakes that are made that show us what should be done. South Bend Lathe improved productivity tremendously: rejects fell by some 70 per cent. They began very harmoniously, but disillusionment developed and labour relations deteriorated. The management failed to adapt to the new environment and the workers felt frustrated at their lack of influence and the management's refusal to agree to wage increases. The position was not helped by the worsening fortunes of the machine tool industry and in the end they became the first employees to strike against themselves.

In employee-owned companies it is important to understand the framework and relationship between employee ownership and control. There is a well-developed example available with the Mondragon Group cooperatives in Spain.[2] Here, worker ownership is complete and the management reports to a board which is then accountable to general worker assemblies: it goes full circle, as illustrated diagrammatically in Figure 16.1. We have set the normal straight-line shareholding arrangement against it to demonstrate the difference.

Other publicised cases of employee ownership have somewhat different arrangements. The arrangements depend to some extent upon the number of employees involved. Scottish News Enterprises, who ran the *Scottish Daily News*, mentioned above, had a small ownership but a high control. Such an arrangement seems to be unknown in the USA, where the community provides the funds while the employees (who are but a part of the community) are in some sort of control. In general, employee ownership in the USA has not led to significant worker control, since it is usually the managers who have the most significant stake in the company. Only where a large group of employees has

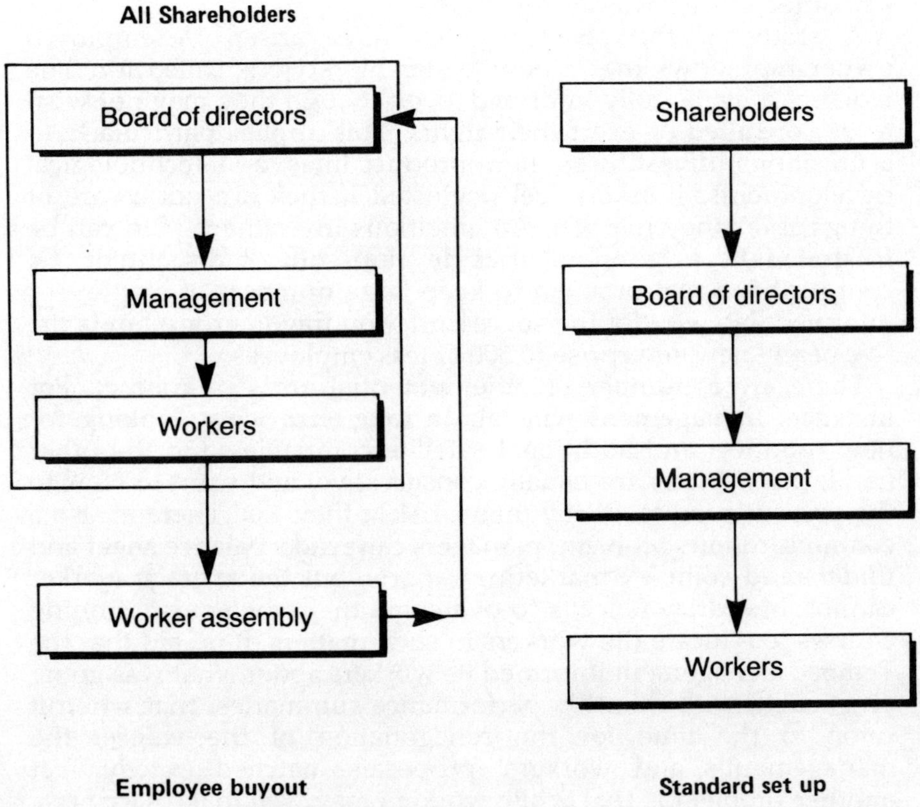

The Employee Buyout

All Shareholders

```
Employee buyout:
Board of directors → Management → Workers → Worker assembly → (back to Board of directors)
All Shareholders encompasses Board, Management, Workers, Worker assembly.

Standard set up:
Shareholders → Board of directors → Management → Workers
```

Employee buyout   **Standard set up**

Figure 16.1 *The employee buyout*

a substantial stake as well as the managers does control 'from the floor' begin to emerge.

Problems and conflicts

Part of the problem is that workers are workers and managers are managers. Workers can and usually do have very limited aspirations in connection with the running of their company; they are 'reluctant managers'. However, their part ownership confers certain rights upon them and the managers should recognise those rights even if the workers are not willing to exert them. While the workers may not be good at managerial decisions, they are very good in reaching and implementing task-related decisions. The reason is quite obvious: they know what they are talking about. Also, implementation will be smoother, since it was *their* decision.

A study of the problems that have arisen in employee ownership shows that a new leadership style is called for. The workers must be fully informed, even though they may not wish to be consulted or exert their rights. This applies particularly to acquisitions, divestitures, new product lines, and technological developments. Workers feel neglected if they are not aware of things *before* they happen. An ambitious investment plan can be frustrated by a 'go slow' that develops out of discontent. Of course, it is a real problem to keep large numbers of employees informed. No wonder the successful Mondragon group limits the size of any new enterprise to 500 or less employees.

There are a number of other potential areas of conflict. For instance, management will take a long-term view, looking for new products and additional satellite companies. On the other hand, the workers are usually conservative, and want to stick to the present product. 'Why take a risk?', they ask. There is also a communications problem: managers can read a balance sheet and understand complex marketing reports, but the average worker cannot. Mondragon seeks to overcome this problem by running courses to educate the workers in such matters. It is said that the Tembec management informed its workers about what was going on so well, with monthly performance summaries, that when it came to the time for the renegotiation of the wages, the management's and workers' proposals matched exactly. Yet another problem is that while workers may well make sacrifices, such as taking a pay cut, they do this in anticipation of being compensated when better times come and if that doesn't happen there will be a strong feeling of resentment.

The reaction of the unions to the employee buyout is also of importance. It is very mixed in the USA and decidedly hostile in Britain. Unions in the USA tend to support the employee buyout despite its adverse effect on jobs and wages, since they feel that is only an initial, one-off adverse circumstance. They may at times oppose the cost-effective reallocation of resources. But the British unions are very sensitive to the political risk involved. They see labour being fragmented and the development of decentralised negotiations as a consequence of employee buyouts. We believe this is a major reason why cooperatives have never really succeeded in Britain. In the political arena, Labour leaders do not support the employee buyout because they fear the loss of their leadership of the 'working class', while the Conservatives consider such buyouts too radical a departure from the norm to be really acceptable. The employee buyout concept seems to fall between these two stools.

The impact of government intervention

The 'bailing out' of companies in distress, together with protective measures designed to curb international competition has had some successes, but can be self-defeating. A free economy should accept the rule of the 'survival of the fittest'. A country's economy is not helped if inefficient management and a slack workforce are kept in being at any cost. It seems that when such things happen, they happen because of public opinion or as a measure of political expediency; never as the result of a systematic cost-benefit analysis. In any case, the government knows far less about the matter than those directly involved, although that fact is rarely admitted. We do, however, have one refreshingly frank admission by a British Prime Minister:[6]

> I never want to take on another BL. We shouldn't be in it at all, but now we're in it we have to choose the time and we have to back Michael Edwardes' judgement. He's the manager, I'm not the manager ...

The bail-out and protective measures, although supposed to be temporary expedients to correct an 'aberration' have a tendency to become permanent and in the long run this inevitably leads to complacency and inefficiency.

Employee buyouts have distinct advantages over government intervention and other conventional remedies; they almost invariably improve efficiency because there is such a strong incentive. An employee buyout supported by government funds seems to be sensible, in that what is of concern is the welfare of the local community and the prevention of mass unemployment in a particular area, but such support should be of limited duration.

It should be recognised that the employee buyout cannot solve the problem of declining markets, mature industries, or harmful economic policies. In the short term it tends to have a greater chance of success, because of the direct involvement of management and workers, but it does not have to be seen as a continuing policy, held to for its own sake. There is nothing wrong with the normal situation and the great mass of workers have no entrepreneurial spirit. So why not sell out once the company is back on its feet and reap the rewards of their effort? This has indeed happened in some cases.

Most employee buyouts have come about as a response to imminent disaster. They therefore begin under a cloud and perhaps this is one significant reason why so many of them fail. Britain seems to have many more failures than either the USA or

Canada, even when they have won government support. For instance, in 1974 the Labour government then in power encouraged three employee buyouts: Kirby Manufacturing and Engineering Co Limited; Meriden Motorcycle Cooperative, makers of the Triumph motorcycle; and Scottish News Enterprises, publishers of the *Scottish Daily News*.

In all these cases the employees lost both their investment and their jobs: none are in business today. They were all exceptionally weak firms and it seems the government support was a highly political move on the eve of an election. The last case was probably the weakest of the three. The government agreed to a one-time loan, half the capital cost of the purchase, if matched by an equal amount from the employees. The employees accepted large cuts in the workforce, contributed their redundancy pay and raised funds from local sources. But sales fell and advertising revenue declined: the paper closed down after six months under the new management. The government, as second creditor, recouped about half its investment, but the employees lost everything.

The John Lewis Partnership

All in all, we have a very variable picture when we look at the employee buyout. Some arrangements are of very long standing and are thriving. The John Lewis Partnership, a stores group in the UK, demonstrates another way in which it can be done. This is advertised as 'partnership on the scale of modern industry'. In 1986-87 the group's sales were £1,568 million, its net assets £401 million. The business belongs to those who work in it. All except those engaged temporarily are partners from the day they join, and all the ordinary share capital is held by trustees on their behalf. Under an irrevocable trust the partners get all the profits, after certain specific provisions have been made. The comparative sales figures for the group, compared with the national averages for the relevant industry for the past five years, as set out in Table 16.1, show its steady progress. Here we have another example of successful employee ownership, although once again it was not a buyout: it began that way.

Table 16.1 *Comparative sales figures*

Year	John Lewis Partnership Sales (£million)	Index	National non-food retailers Index
1982-83	500.1	100	100
1983-84	572.4	114	110
1984-85	638.1	128	118
1985-86	718.5	144	129
1986-87	822.6	164	140

Year	Waitrose food stores Sales (£million)	Index	National food retailers Index
1982-83	411.6	100	100
1983-84	487.6	118	108
1984-85	553.7	135	116
1985-86	634.1	154	125
1986-87	725.8	176	134

Source: Advertisement in *Financial Times* 13 April 1987, p 35

References

1. Bradley, K et al *Worker Capitalism – The New Industrial Relations* MIT Press (USA), 1983
2. Bradley, K *Cooperation at Work: The Mondragon Experience* Heinemann, 1983
3. Gunn, C E *Self-Management in the United States* Cornell University Press, 1985.
4. Bradley, K and Gelb, A 'Employee buyouts of troubled companies' *Harvard Business Review* **63**, September-October 1985, pp 121-30.
5. Ewing, D W 'When employees run the company' *Harvard Business Review* **57**, January/February 1979, pp 75-90.
6. Kharbanda, O P and Stallworthy, E A The Government 'bailout' In *Corporate Failure: Prediction, Panacea and Prevention* McGraw-Hill, London, 1985.

Part Five

Finding the Answers

Chapter 17
Lessons from Case Analysis

In the last but most crucial part of this book, we seek to find answers to the problems faced by companies in distress. In the earlier parts we studied case histories of companies in decline throughout the world and saw how they sought to arrest the decline, although this was not always successful. We now draw conclusions and lessons to be learned, so that the mistakes of the past are not repeated in the future. Let us look briefly once again at the basic routes to recovery: acquisitions, mergers, takeovers and management or employee buyout.

Acquisitions and mergers

Acquisitions and mergers are seen as *one* of the possible routes for recovery when companies are in financial distress. The motives for acquisition are briefly summarised in Chapter 5, and these can, of course, differ from case to case. But once a decision is taken, it is important that the right types of signal are sent to the company being acquired if success is to be achieved. Acquisition is easy and so is divestment, but making them work is not so easy. They are, of course, two sides of the same coin since acquisition by one company is divestment by another. The motives for the two parties are different but it does not really matter so long as they are clearly understood. Unfortunately there is so much excitement and tension when such deals take place, with each party having its own interests to serve, that there is usually an undue hurry to close the deal as soon as possible. This means that there is a failure to examine all the implications with care; when these then surface after signing the deal, conflicts arise.

Such transactions are subject to government approval in most countries and the policy relating to these changes from time to time in accordance with the experience gained in the marketplace and the changing business and economic environment. For example, we discussed how GEC's proposal to merge with Plessey was not approved by the Monopolies and Mergers Commission on the basis that it would lead to reduced competition in defence electronics equipment. In another case, BTR's bid for Pilkington, the government decided that it need not be referred to the Commission at all. The seeming inconsistency in government policy in the two cases came up for sharp criticism in financial circles, but the decision was right in retrospect. The government's objective is to ensure that the deal proposed is in the public interest in the long term.

The success rate

Acquisitions and mergers can sometimes help to prevent the decline of a company in distress, but not all such transactions are successful, especially those which are motivated by a desire to create an 'empire' without regard to strategic fit, rationality and other relevant factors. This has resulted in many such acquisitions turning sour, with subsequent divestment. Such large-scale failures turned out to be one of the reasons for the decline of many chemical companies in the 1970s. An analysis of nearly 400 such transactions relating to acquisitions by 33 large American companies from 1950 to 1980 indicates that over half of these acquisitions proved to be unwise and had to be undone,[1] as shown in Table 17.1.

Table 17.1 *Analysis of acquisitions by 33 US companies 1950-80*

	Later divested (%)
All acquisitions	53
Acquisitions in entirely new fields	61
Acquisitions in unrelated new fields	74
Start-ups	44
Joint ventures	50

Divestment does not usually get as much attention or media coverage as acquisition, since it is seen as an indicator of failure. The extent of divestment indicates an average failure rate of well over half, as high as three-quarters in the case of companies venturing into an unrelated field through acquisition. Despite this poor record, each case has to be considered on its own and it is very dangerous to make generalisations.

There is a craze for large-scale enterprise in the food industry and this is reflected in the number of supermarket giants, but there is a definite niche in the market which can best be filled by the small company. Consumer tastes are changing and this calls for a host of specialised and health foods, a need which can best be filled by small companies.[2] This concept has led to a host of promising and successful acquisitions of small food companies by USM. Typical of these is Hunter Saphir, acquired by USM in 1984 when its business was dominated by distribution and fresh produce, having earlier moved away from the mass market. The new Hunter is thriving, with a better performance every year, and it is now structured in four divisions: packaged food, distribution, fresh produce, and food manufacturing. Its original business should continue to grow at some 20 per cent per year and the new business should benefit with the changing trend in food habits. Its shares have already doubled since acquisition and are poised for further growth. Since 1984, USM has been on an acquisition spree for small food companies culminating in January 1987 with the group's acquisition of four food manufacturing companies from S & W Berisford.

An analyst observing the scene relating to small companies in the food business observes: 'There is lots of potential for small businesses in the food market. And if they put a foot wrong, someone will come along to take them over.'

Another survey of 600 acquisitions in the USA indicates that the chance of success is increased if the acquirer knows and understands the acquired company's business and how it fits in with his existing business. The chance of success is greater if the company is left to manage by itself unless there is a clear case of mismanagement. It was found that 'the bigger the better': surprising, but perhaps since with a large company the stake is high, the acquirer takes more care, investigates the situation carefully and so is forewarned and hence forearmed. It was also found that the chance of success is less if a premium is paid well above the market price for the acquisition. This happens quite often, since for each target company there is usually more than one suitor and the final acquirer is one who bids the highest.

An acquisition will always be attractive, both financially and time-wise, in comparison with initiating and executing a new project; but the haste with which some acquisitions are concluded can result in the asset acquired becoming a liability. The acquisitive should heed those wise words of an American university president, Richard Berenzden, 'Growth for its own sake is the ideology of the cancer cell.'

Merger and takeover fever

From megamergers to merger mania was just a short step, with everyone performing the merger 'tango'. Mergers have become a worldwide craze, with the ostensible purpose of putting companies in distress back on to the road to recovery. But the actual results have belied this expectation, as we indicated earlier by using a number of examples, statistics and the results of surveys. One wonders to what extent the activity is genuine and initiated by the companies concerned, and to what extent it is initiated by the middlemen who 'catalyse' such activity to meet their own ends.

In 1986 alone there were 38 billion-dollar deals (ranging from US£1 to 6.3 billion) in the USA alone, of which 23 related to acquisitions and mergers, the rest being leveraged buyouts, recapitalisation schemes and the like. No data is available worldwide, but it is clear that such activity is most dominant in the USA and other countries may contribute perhaps half as much again to that initial total.

A great egotist, Harold S Geneen, former chairman of ITT, tells us proudly in his autobiography that at one time ITT were acquiring a company a day.[3] Some deals, it appears, were signed after a mere 10- or 20-minute inspection of the books of the acquiree – the target company!

There can be no doubt that merger mania is spreading. The most recent craze is in the entertainment and information industries with such ridiculously high prices being paid that the chance of success is slim. That accords of course with the findings of the survey whose results we quoted above. The craze has also extended to the food and chemical industries as well. The scene is changing so fast that even experts such as George Bull, chairman of International Distillers and Vintners, a subsidiary of Grand Metropolitan and one of the major players in the wine and spirits field, hesitates to forecast:

> We have not seen the end of this cycle ... I would not like to forecast which of the major companies in the industry will be in the market, get bigger or sell their interests. But I do not regard it as impossible that changes could still occur among the major drinks companies ...

Major recent deals in this industry include:

- IDV acquired the US firm Heublin in January 1987 for US$1.2 billion.
- Allied-Lyons acquired a 51 per cent holding in Hiram Walker's liquor division with Gulf/Olympia & York retaining 49 per cent.
- Guinness took over Distillers Company in March 1986 for $2.5 billion.

But why is 'everybody after the same cocktail', as one article suggests?[4] It is found to be a part of a major restructuring process aimed at revitalising the image of major brands in an effort to make them more appealing to consumers worldwide. The process is proving to be a bloody battle, the results of which are still uncertain. According to Sir Derrick Holden-Brown, chairman of Allied-Lyons, who took over Hiram Walker's Canadian-based liquor business: 'We could be half way through the regrouping, but the results are yet to be seen and that could have an even greater effect on the competition in the marketplace.'

The spate of deals also seems to point to a pattern in the international drinks industry. For one thing, the UK-based companies, Guinness, Grand Metropolitan's IDV subsidiary and Allied-Lyons, have strengthened their position considerably and along with Seagram they now have nearly one-third of the international spirits business. Further, some of the deals are the result of aggressive moves taken as a means of defence.

The urgency and undue haste of some of the deals may prove expensive in retrospect, resulting in a host of divestments, if past statistics are any indication. In the process both parties, the acquirer and the acquired, will suffer more than just financial loss: their image, so important to companies trading directly with the public, will suffer as well.

A major merger that has worked extremely well is that of British Oxygen (BOC) with its competitor and counterpart on the other side of the Atlantic, Airco. This took place in the late 1970s, but it took a lot of hard work and some unconventional wisdom to achieve success. The BOC chairman, Sir Leslie Smith, 'made the merger work' and but for Dick Giordano, appointed chief executive of the US operations, 'it wouldn't have worked'. The corporate headquarters of BOC were moved to the USA and Sir Leslie himself took a back seat. BOC emerged as a multinational and its earnings doubled between 1979 and 1982, despite one of the deepest post-war recessions.[5]

It is also important to remember that some of the highly successful multinationals, such as General Motors, ICI and Royal Dutch Shell were created as a result of mergers. However, there have also been a number of ill-starred mergers of recent years in Europe, such as: Pirelli-Dunlop (tyres); Agfa-Gevaert (film); and VFW-Fokker (aircraft). These all ended in disaster and had to be undone. The main motive for these particular mergers was to get bigger in order to compete with their American counterparts.[6]

A recipe for disaster

All in all, the balance sheet for megamergers does not look good, with some half to two-thirds having been failures; yet they continue unabated. Undue haste seems to be the key to much of the trouble. An analysis of some 23,000 deals valued at about US$400 billion during the 10 years from 1975 to 1984 indicated that one-third of these were complete failures and another third had proved quite expensive.

Of course, each case is specific and all generalisations in this field, as in any other, usually prove to be inaccurate. Looking back over the cases we have reviewed it seems that sometimes even a mismatch, such as occurred when McDermott acquired Babcock & Wilcox, can work, while there are other cases where a company can change hands as many as seven times in 30 years, such as Avis, and be no better for it. Yet it can be that a succession of owners helps the growth and performance of a company, for example Pullman. The lessons may have proved expensive for the companies concerned, but we can learn from their mistakes at little cost.

Who wins?

It seems that it is possible to generalise to the extent of saying that the hostile takeover holds little for the companies involved. The only winners are the middlemen and the raiders. But friendly acquisitions, mergers and takeovers are in a very different category. Effected with the consent of both the parties, the chances of their success are better if sufficient thought and effort have gone into their making. A well thought-out deal has the seeds of success built into it.

Even stock exchanges have seen the merits of merging for the sake of economy and smooth business. There was a full-page advertisement by the Australian Stock Exchange in the *Financial Times* (22 April 1987) which proclaimed: 'Mergers and takeovers. Everybody's doing it, why not us?' It seems that the Adelaide, Brisbane, Hobart, Melbourne, Perth and Sydney Stock Exchanges have all merged into one, and the advertisement declares:

> It's a merger which makes a lot of sense ... a single, more efficient stock market means that Australia will continue to be a more attractive place for the investor.

We have described at length the fight over Getty Oil where Pennzoil was all set to complete a takeover until Texaco jumped into the fray; a battle which may not end for quite some time. As of now there is really no winner: Pennzoil may ultimately walk away with the 'prize'; on the other hand, events may yet take an unexpected turn and the final outcome must be anybody's guess. Meanwhile, the management of the three companies directly involved are fully occupied with this battle royal. But one should and must ask: what about the shareholders, the suppliers and the customers? Surely it was for them that it was all set in motion? One hopes so!

References

1. 'The state of strategic thinking' *The Economist* **303**, 23 May 1987, pp 19-22.
2. Rawsthorn, A 'Hungry for success and acquisitive too' *Financial Times* 7 June 1987.
3. Geneen, H S *Managing* Granada, 1985.
4. Wood, L 'Everybody is after the same cocktail' *Financial Times* 4 July 1987.
5. Foster, G 'BOC goes West' *Management Today* January 1984, pp 42ff (8 pp).
6. Heller, R 'Why mergers make mayhem' in *The New Naked Manager* Hodder & Stoughton, 1985.

Chapter 18
Man Management

We have sought the answer to the problem of companies in decline in a change of ownership, however that comes about, although in some cases the solution has been worse than the problem it was designed to overcome. The previous chapter drew some valuable lessons from the various case studies we reviewed earlier, but we are certain that the real answer to the problem is management, and particularly man management.

Management skills can and *must* be acquired if those who run the companies that supply goods and services are to achieve what should be the real mission of a corporate body: to serve the best interests of employees, shareholders, community and country. To quote:[1]

> The excellent companies were, above all, brilliant in the basics. These companies worked hard to keep things simple in a complex world. They persisted. They insisted on top quality. They fawned on their customers. They listened to their employees and treated them like adults. They permitted some chaos in return for quick action and regular experimentation.

Make the individual the focus of your attention and there is nothing that cannot be achieved. When people are treated like winners they strive to live up to their reputation.

If only this simple short message can be driven home to companies in decline and they then implement it, they will be well on the road to recovery. Better still of course, if they listen early enough and act, they will never go into decline in the first place.

The Japanese example

Learning from and adopting the Japanese management style is very popular at the moment, and not without reason. This may sound strange, in that the Japanese themselves rightly credit much of their own management style to the West. Perhaps where the Japanese have excelled is that they have taken the basics of management, including the fact that man is the key, to heart and have put them into practice. It seems to be a philosophy of life that fits neatly into the Japanese culture and business environment and this has made its acceptance much easier. There seems to be no doubt that the importance given to the individual has helped the Japanese to achieve the miracle they have, rising from the ashes of World War II to be near the head of the league of developed countries today. In addition they have shown that what they do at home can be transferred to their operations anywhere in the world.

To give you an example, we take you to a factory in Wales.[2] Yusawa Batteries (UK) Ltd have already expanded five-fold since production started in 1983. Yusawa is one of a dozen Japanese companies, including such world-famous names as Sony, Hitachi and Brother, who have set up factories not only in Wales but elsewhere in the world. Overall, there are nearly 50 such factories opened by Japanese companies in Britain, with a total investment of over US$3 billion. Yusawa has done so well, with productivity matching that of its Osaka works back in Japan, that it won the Queen Elizabeth award for export achievement in 1986. Yusawa's managing director, Kanzuo Murata, often walks through his battery factory carrying the simple message that every 10 minutes spent working should be taken as if it were the last 10 minutes of their lives. Today this no longer sounds strange to the 240 Welsh employees working there. Kanzua Murata comments:

> I tell my workers that if they don't enjoy their work, they are throwing away their lives ... If they do only what they are forced to do, the result is not good.

Yusawa encourages its workers to take initiatives, and deserving candidates are rewarded by quick promotion. In return, the company expects loyalty, total job commitment, flexibility and above all teamwork. Notice the continual emphasis on the man. There is no distinction whatever between the worker and the manager. Everyone, including the managing director, wears a similar uniform and hat and shares the same washing, toilet and canteen facilities. Deserving workers are sent to Japan for training and to imbibe something of the Japanese work ethic. A prominent sign on the factory floor proclaims: 'A little better every day.' The workers are encouraged to express their ideas, allowed to work on them and suitably rewarded if the ideas are finally implemented. This is in sharp contrast to the normal practice of British workers and their counterparts elsewhere, who work their hours out and keep their mouths shut.

The same story is being repeated at most of the Japanese

factories in the USA and elsewhere – and there are a host of them, mostly in the automotive, metal and high technology industries. Japanese labour practices and management are very distinctive, but they have been successfully transplanted outside Japan, including the USA.[3] As an example, we cite three Japanese car assembly plants: Toyota at Freemont, California; Honda at Marysville, Ohio; and Nissan at Smyrna, Tennessee. They are all turning out products of the same quality as made by the company in Japan, and at very nearly the same cost despite the higher cost and wage structure prevailing in the USA.

Strangely, one of these sites, at Freemont, is that of an old General Motors' plant which was in serious trouble and in sharp decline. The absentee rate was about 20 per cent, there were some 5,000 grievances outstanding, wildcat strikes were common and there was a constant tussle between labour and management. In 1982 General Motors shut the plant and turned it over to Toyota as part of a joint venture, appropriately called NUMMI (New United Motor Manufacturing Inc). Eighteen months later the situation has been transformed: yet they have the same workers and even their militant leaders. Total production is nearly the same as before but there are only half the number of workers now.

This same story is being repeated at many other plants and in many other industries all over the USA. The transformation has been achieved through three simple factors all revolving around the key message: treat people properly. This implies: mutual trust; efficient working practices; bigger bonuses.

To explain away the Japanese 'miracle' many observers in the West have tended to undermine the Japanese emphasis on the man and lay the stress on the role of the Japanese government and, more specifically, MITI (the Ministry of International Trade and Industry) as a major factor in achieving the 'miracle'. This is an over-simplification and even wrong, according to Abegglen and Stalk.[4] Both the authors have spent a considerable time in Japan as members of the Boston Consulting Group's Tokyo branch and have acquired as much of an insight into the working of Japanese business 'as anybody capable of writing a book in English'. Using Lubar's words, in his review of Abegglen and Stalk's book, to describe the way in which the Japanese 'miracle' has been accomplished:

> ... one of the government's most valuable contributions to the Japanese economy is something virtually never mentioned by Americans: it runs an excellent educational system. The authors state flatly that Japan's labour force is 'quite simply the best educated in the world'.

Notice once again that the emphasis is on the *man*. It is estimated that nearly 10 per cent of both the managers' and the workers' time in Japan is spent on continuing education: education is a continuing process, not a 'one-off' effort. This is the only way to keep up with new technology, new concepts and the changing environment in the international marketplace.

'Corporate fat'

Some recent books have lent considerable support to our thesis that corporate decline lies to a large degree in the failure of management to manage. To take but one example, Mark Green and John F Berry make a very valid point:[5]

> Corporate waste and bureaucracy is today a ball and chain around the ankle of the economy. How heavy is this ball and chain? The methodology here is necessarily primitive and imprecise. But the total of at least $862b annually is more than six times the size of the oft-cited Grace Commission estimate of government waste.

In most countries it is only governments that have been accused of bureaucracy and the related waste, but it seems that large companies everywhere are not much better. It is this enormous and avoidable waste that is one reason why many of the larger firms go into decline. The authors discuss this aspect in the first chapter of their book, 'Why the mighty stumble'. Despite the fact that the senior author, Mark Green, is Ralph Nader's best-known disciple, the book is all praise for corporate profits and it has been written with a view to making companies more profitable. Their plea to companies: track down and then eliminate 'waste, fraud and abuse'. The book is written in a useful 'how to do it' style and deals with such subjects as:

- Ten telltale traits of corporate bureaucracy.
- Seven deadly sins that drive corporations into decline.
- Waste of human talent and corporate resources in legal work.
- Maximising return on assets.
- Why a crisis is a good time to trim the bureaucratic waistline.

One review of the book decries what is said, asserting that many of the ideas are not new or original.[6] But we feel that they are basic and important enough to warrant restatement with real-life examples, which is what the authors have done.

Interviews with corporate executives are quite revealing. For example, the General Electric chief executive officer, John F Welch

Jr, is quoted as saying: 'We were hiring people to read reports of people who had been hired to write reports.' General Electric, it is pointed out, scrapped strategic planning as a distinct staff function and instead made it a line function. Of course that is where it should belong; not at the glass-cased central headquarters where the managers concerned may well have no 'feel' for what is going on at the various plants, which each have a specific environment.

Learning from the competition

Stiff competition is one of the factors contributing to the decline of companies. To meet the competition in the marketplace, it is not enough merely to collect data; that is only the starting point. The quality of data is obviously important and for this the prerequisite is high-calibre staff who get management support. It helps a great deal to put yourself in the competitor's shoes and even to try to predict their future moves, so that you can be ready to counter them.[7] Making a forecast of the competitor's plans and predicting their actions is like planning your move in a game of chess: you have to anticipate your competitor's next move and consider how you will be able to counter it effectively.

Competitor analysis cannot be limited just to the question: 'What *can* the competitor do?' There is another and even more important question: 'What *will* the competitor do?' The answer to the second question is crucial and requires additional data, such as:

- Competitor's past decisions – a chronology.
- Key personnel – their resumés, experience, etc.
- Organisation chart, also the ownership and control picture.
- Role of individual directors and of the board.
- Recent additions, deletions and promotions – often the sign of their future plans.

Equipped with such data, you can then attempt to answer the even more relevant question: 'What will the competitive move be in retaliation to my competitive move?' Other factors to be considered are cost, service and performance. Don't ignore the possibility of new competitors in the future, including barriers to entry to and exit from the market.

It is important also to know when you can profit from competitors, rather than attempt to destroy them.[8] The Japanese are particularly good at getting information about their competitors, whether at home or in the international marketplace. They compete fiercely and never rest on their laurels.

The story is told of Honda, already a formidable name in the motorcycle industry, diversifying into motorcars and generating more revenue from these than from motorcycles in 1975. It poured enormous resources into the new venture, draining away the profits it was making on motorcycles.

Enter Yamaha, seeking to take the motorcycle market share from Honda. By 1981 the two were nearly equal at home. Encouraged by this, Yamaha's stockholders were told in 1982: 'In one year we will be the domestic leader. And in two years we will be No 1 in the world.' Honda met the challenge head on by its president declaring: 'Yamaha has not only stepped on the tail of a tiger, it has ground it into the earth. We will crush Yamaha.'

No mincing of the words there! In Japan competitor information is considered so important that Mitsubishi, for example, has some 800 people in its New York office whose main task is to collect information about its American competitors and markets. Seiko, the world's biggest watchmaker, subscribes to and reads Swiss journals regularly to know what is going on in its field; such know-how is its major strength.

(An enormous storehouse of information exists just for the reading: while travelling abroad on business or consultancy we keep almost as much time for browsing through the libraries in the world capitals and elsewhere.)

As a long-term strategy, competition should be encouraged, for the following reason:[8]

> When a competitor is less pushy, a policy of live-and-let-live is often best ... the good competitor is strong enough to deter would-be entrants, but weak enough to realise that it would be self-defeating to get too ambitious. It will seek to expand the market by improving its products, not by cutting prices ...

We would draw your attention to the last part of this quotation. The cause of decline in many companies, large and small, has been their obsession for a major market share at any price. In pursuit of this they have cut their prices even below cost. That can never be good business.

A profile for success

Another important and stimulating book provides an extensive look at the causes of success and failure in business and government institutions.[9] The book deals with topics such as motivation, managing change, management development, education and training. The claim made by the publishers for this book is a bold one:

> Once in every ten or twenty years a book is published which makes a break with the past and pushes forward to new frontiers of understanding. *Success* is such a book.

This may sound rather brash but, as one reviewer of the book points out, the publisher, the Institute of Personnel Management, is not known for making extravagant claims, so it should be taken seriously.[10] Such a judgement will have to be reserved for the future when we can see whether this book, among others, has stood the test of time or whether it was just a passing fad.

The author visualises a 'managerial society' wherein the manager and the entrepreneur are given the recognition they deserve. There are two immediate indicators of this society already in view: the personal computer and the new style manager, called the 'ferryman', who is capable of linking the past, the present and the future of his organisation and leads by example; points the way forward; is a guide, counsellor and mentor to his staff; and maintains a fine balance between intellect, intuition and feelings. The central values of the managerial society are: achieving and caring, change, continuous critical reappraisal, effectiveness, emphasis on the individual, flexibility, innovation, numeracy, openness, a sense of history and a sense of wholeness. Quite a catalogue, but all vital factors. Beyond the managerial society is Utopia, where spiritual and human values converge and man will live 'in harmony and balance within himself and be externally at one with the environment'.

Many of the lessons of the book *Excellence*[1] are echoed here, but some more are added. The author is clearly an optimist, as witness his fascinating forecasts. He even envisages a major European cultural revival based on a Franco-British partnership. The book has three distinct but logical parts: vision, diagnosis of the present ills, and how to convert the vision into a reality. But enough of dreams: it is today that we have to live in, not tomorrow.

Company culture

In the field of management, as elsewhere, management concepts keep changing and that is how it should be: the business environment is highly dynamic and the strategy to deal with it has to be appropriate to the situation. The latest 'fad' is the company culture and a change of culture, among other factors, is supposed to perform miracles. It is alleged that a change in the company culture is all that is needed in order to get a company in decline back on the road to recovery.

What exactly is a company culture? One definition runs: 'The values, goals, rituals, and heroes that ... characterise a company style.' Company culture can be recognised and is easier to experience than to describe. It is the 'way things are done' in a company and two broad types of culture are known to exist:

Type A This creates anxiety: them *versus* us.
Type B This creates a positive environment: them *plus* us.

Type B encourages people to be effective leaders, allows people to work at their best and grow in the process. It offers fair payment, reward, participation and promotion. Type A is just the reverse.[11] As a consequence of the acquisition and takeover mania, companies with radically different cultures are often brought together and this inevitably leads to conflict. Some tips designed to resolve such conflicts are:[12]

- Initiate a communication strategy.
- Meet the managers and tell them the whole truth.
- Adopt integration as part of the corporate planning and management process.
- Balance autonomy and integration.
- Find a flagship for change.
- Look to the long run.

The company culture concept is so much in fashion at the moment that a 90-minute pep talk on the subject by Allan A Kennedy, a former McKinsey & Co consultant and co-author of a book on the subject, *Corporate Cultures*, draws a full house. He has put on this act some 200 times at US$5,000 a time and, with the experience gained, the show could play on Broadway. At a dinner following one of his talks the chairman of a company was heard to remark: 'This corporate culture is great.' He then said to his president, 'I want a culture by Monday'!

It is true that the culture of a company is significant enough to determine a company's success or failure, but it cannot be ordered overnight. It has to develop over time through a process of evolution. Because this is so it is also true that it cannot be changed overnight; an issue that we have dealt with elsewhere.[13] It seems, however, that a culture can be changed by a new leader who can dramatically get things done, and never mind the past.[14]

Personnel selection

We started this chapter by stressing the importance of the individual in a company and we wish to conclude by reemphasising the point. If people are the key, selecting the right people should be the most important task confronting management. This means that personnel selection plays a crucial and continuing role. But how to select people? We take recourse to that management guru Peter Drucker and commend to your attention an article of his in *Span*.[15] He maintains that making the right decisions about people is the ultimate test of a successful organisation. Such decisions are the most difficult to make and they should not be hurried through, if for no other reason than that undoing such decisions is a most expensive exercise. Let all managers take due note.

References

1. Ziegler, E Editorial review in the *Readers' Digest* September 1984 of Peters, T J and Waterman, R H *In Search of Excellence: Lessons from America's Best Run Companies* Harper & Row, 1982.
2. Elsner, A 'Japanese work ethic spoken here – Factory in Wales reflects wave of foreign investment' *International Herald Tribune* 30 October 1986.
3. Bernstein, A 'The difference Japanese management makes' *Business Week* 14 July 1986, pp 47-50.
4. Abegglen, J C and Stalk, G Jr *Kaisha – The Japanese corporation* Basic Books, 1985. Reviewed by Lubar, R 'Japan's business jungle' *Fortune* **113**, 3 February 1986, pp 131-2.
5. Green, M and Berry, J F *Challenging of Hidden Profits – Reducing Corporate Bureaucracy and Waste* Morrow, 1985. Reviewed by Kinsley, M 'A new kind of Naderism' *Fortune* **112**, 16 September 1985, pp 193ff (3 pp).
6. Weiss, S 'Corporate fat – a big helping hand of refried ideas' *Business Week* 16 September 1985, pp 10-11.
7. Copulsky, W 'Scoping the competition' *Chemtech* **15**, February 1985, pp 76-9.
8. 'Love thy competitor' *The Economist* **291**, 23 June 1984, pp 63-4.
9. Marlow, H *Success – Individual, Corporate and National* IPM Management Publications, 1984.
10. Sadler, P 'Diagnosis for our time' *Long Range Planning* **18**, January 1985, pp 114-6.
11. de Bard, R 'Bridging the culture chasm' *Management Today* March 1985, pp 89-92.
12. Price, C 'Life after merger' *Management Today* February 1987, pp 82-4.
13. Kharbanda, O P and Stallworthy, E A 'Every good company has a culture' In *Corporate Failure* McGraw-Hill, 1985.
14. Thackray, J 'The corporate culture rage' *Management Today* February 1986, pp 66ff (5 pp).
15. Drucker, P 'How to choose managers' *Span* (New Delhi), March 1987, pp 16-18.

Chapter 19

Is Change of Ownership the Answer?

We have seen companies in distress and decline, we have witnessed the recovery of some and the ultimate collapse of many. The time has now come to pose the question: 'Is change of ownership the answer?' The answer is: 'Not really.' What is actually wanted is not a change of ownership, but a change of management. Often, just a change of chief executive is enough.[1] This is what an acquisition or merger should bring about. Unfortunately, in many cases it does not.

At the beginning of this book we likened the corporate body to the human body, and just as one's life is a series of ups and downs, so is that of a company. One characteristic of people, enunciated by the famous author of *The Peter Principle* is that:[2] 'In a hierarchy individuals tend to rise to their levels of incompetence.' Dr Laurence J Peter declared this rule to be of universal application in the business world: people tend to be promoted until they reach a level beyond their competence. The concept has found acceptance among business analysts and has since become popularly known as the 'Peter Principle'.

A noted economist, Robert J Samuelson, has sought to apply the Peter Principle not to individual people in the company, but to the company as a whole.[3] Following the analogy, he feels that large companies expand to their level of incompetence. When they reach this point they go into decline, become distressed and can be put back on the road to recovery only through drastic measures. This ascent, decline and the possible reascent, he suggests, are inherent in the life cycle of every company, and perhaps the very success of a company is sowing the seeds for its future failure. Could it be that in striving to do more, in seeking to get bigger and better, the company becomes unwieldy and even enters into areas that it knows nothing about? The spate of failures that has followed unplanned and unwise diversification is surely evidence of this. Thereafter some change becomes necessary, whether that be in the form of restructuring, change of management or change of ownership. This seems to be the only way in which such companies can be given a new lease of life.

Restructuring

Restructuring is a very broad term and can of course include acquisitions, mergers and takeovers; or being acquired or taken over. The objective of such restructuring is to arrest decline, increase efficiency and improve profits. But that may not necessarily happen as planned.

The Peter Principle could explain the productivity slump in the USA in the 1970s. Managers are, in effect, what their company becomes: their desire for change is reflected in changes in their company, change brought about by diversification through acquisitions and mergers. Being human, managers make mistakes and while to some extent these can be tolerated because of the profits generated through their wiser moves, there comes a time when, in line with its managers, the company as a whole reaches its own particular level of incompetence. When that point is reached, trouble starts.

However, change of ownership as an answer to a company's problems when in decline, has been seen to be of doubtful value. A company acquires or takes over another – what for? Merely for the purpose of growing bigger? That is not a very healthy purpose and the final result may prove disappointing. The objectives are wrong. Had the company been acquired to create additional jobs and wealth, the sole objective its revitalisation and restoration, that would be a laudable motive. But acquisitions are rarely made for that specific purpose. Rather, it is the desire to build an empire – the bigger, the better.

However, there are groups and conglomerates which may embrace the noble and wider motive. We have looked at one such, Hanson Trust. The company attitude has been displayed in full-page advertisements in the British press. One such advertisement is captioned: 'It could teach you more than 3 months at the Harvard Business School.' The advertisement goes on to discuss Butterley, a company that has been part of the Hanson Trust for nearly 20 years. It says that when Butterley was acquired its profits were modest (some £300,000) but its headquarters were huge and its management somewhat under strength. Now Butterley's profits, it says, have risen to over £20 million and its managers are achieving profit margins well in excess of 25 per cent (remember that we are still reading the advertisement). Then come the closing comment: 'And, to the best of our knowledge, not one of them has attended Harvard.'

Where, then, did they learn their management skills? The advertisement tells us that as well. To quote yet again:

We plucked the brightest employees from the ranks and gave them something they had never had: responsibility ... Now if you're wondering what part Hanson Trust can claim in Butterley's revival the honest answer is very little. True, we impose strict financial controls. True, we vet every item of capital expenditure. And true, we make sure that bonuses are not payable to the management unless shareholders receive high returns. But, above all, we believe that managers should be left to run their own businesses.

Motivation

However, despite the achievements of the Hanson Trust, success with change of ownership through acquisition, merger and takeover has been seen to be somewhat limited. The term 'success' is being used here in relation to the health of the company. Has the decline been arrested and has the company been put on the road to recovery? Not if certain shareholders or a raider made a killing. Certainly some companies have benefited, as we have just seen, but not often enough for us to be able to assert decisively that a change of ownership is a sound answer to the problems of companies in distress. So much depends on the motivation for the change of ownership. A well thought-out acquisition, designed for the good of both the companies concerned, with due consideration of the pros and cons, has a better chance of success than one effected in haste, to pip someone else at the post, or just for the purpose of growing bigger.

On the other hand if the main motivation has been, as is usually the case, to enrich some of the individual players in the game, the chance of success, as defined above, is slim. Then the raiders and their like will have done a great disservice to their country's economy, focusing their and the shareholders' attention on the short-term gains at the cost of long-term growth and the general welfare of the company. That is why we like the Hanson Trust advertisement so much: it looks at Butterley over a 20-year period.

The evils of seeking a short-term profit have become abundantly clear in the USA, the UK and many other countries and legislation may well begin to restrict the activities of these short-termers. To that extent they may well have done a service to the community.

A quotation from one of the raiders, Ivan Boesky, once unknown to the general public, but now familiar to many, illustrates this point very well. He was quoted by the paper *Indian Express* (29 June 1987) thus:

My life will be forever changed, but I hope that something positive will ultimately come out of this situation. I know that in the wake of today's events, many will call for reforms. If my mistakes launch a process of re-examination of the rules and practices of our financial marketplace, then perhaps some good will result. After many years as an active participant in the financial market, I have enormous respect for its institutions and its people. To them, I offer sincere apologies.

Notice the confession, even though a somewhat concealed one. Boesky has, under a deal negotiated with the Securities & Exchange Commission (SEC), pleaded guilty, agreed to pay US$100 million in fines and to cooperate with the SEC in exposing and prosecuting others involved in insider trading and allied offences. In return, Boesky's sentence has been deferred.[4]

The Boesky affair in the USA has a counterpart in the UK in the Guinness affair, with which indeed it was linked. No wonder then, that legislators on both sides of the Atlantic are busy devising such laws as may make the raiders' job difficult if not impossible. The Supreme Court in the USA has upheld an Indiana law passed in March 1986 under which an equity holder with a holding of 20 per cent or more can only vote with the approval of a majority of 'disinterested shareholders', that is, shareholders who are not 'insiders', such as directors or officers. This could well lead to drying up of some liquidity which is usually the basis of junk bonds, and bring about a sharp increase in interest rates.[5] In Britain, a tougher policy relating to this field has become very necessary, as made obvious by the Guinness affair.[6]

It is clear that many of those involved in acquisition and merger are concerned primarily with their empire building ambitions, creating a personal fortune and the satisfaction of their own ego. Company welfare is secondary. In the process they have failed in both areas. With their diverse and expanding business activities, there may well have been a lot of acquisitions, mergers and takeovers, but the bottom line is eventually a sorry one; not only for the company, but more particularly for its shareholders and employees. In these and many other cases, change of ownership has *not* been the answer to a company's problems.

Strategic fit

Christopher J Clarke, Director of Strategic Finance and Planning, Wallace Smith & Trust Co Ltd of London, in an interesting article on acquisitions, has examined some of the reasons for the general disenchantment in the current acquisition boom.[7] An important factor for success is a good strategic fit between the target company and the acquiring company. This calls for the measuring of the synergies in financial terms, and the assessment of the benefits that will accrue to the acquiring firm. Clarke has described the methods of analysis in this respect, which can help to improve the success rate. This is by the use of resource portfolios, value chains, culture web and cash flows. The last item is, of course, the most important for this has a direct bearing on the bottom line.

The three key messages conveyed by the author are:

1. Synergy is crucial to ensure that the acquisition is one of the minority that benefit the shareholders of the acquirer.
2. This synergy can be analysed and also quantified to reveal cost and differentiation impacts on cash flow.
3. Cultural fit between the target and the acquirer company must be measured to ensure that there is no cultural incompatibility.

Is Japan better?

We have held Japanese management up as an example, so one is bound to ask whether the Wall Street scandal of insider trading and its parallel in London exemplified by the Guinness affair could occur in Japan. It seems unlikely, but can one be sure?[8] Although, as we write, there is an acquisition and merger boom in Japan, it is still a modest and very polite affair compared with American standards. One reason is the basic difference between the two countries. Unlike America, the shareholders' interests rank behind those of company directors and employees. But a Japanese counterpart of the consumerist Ralph Nader could change all that.

In 1986 there were about 2,000 acquisition and merger deals worth some US$3 billion in Japan, whereas in the USA the corresponding numbers were 3,000 and US$180 billion. Among the investment bankers in Japan, the largest firm started with just two employees in 1973 and now has some 25. In addition, the Japanese banks have set up small acquisition and merger teams since 1984, but as part of their international finance departments. Much of the activity in Japan in this field has been in the form of intra-group rationalisation. They seem to be aggressive abroad rather than at home. For instance, in 1986 Japanese companies acquired 44 American firms for some US$1.6 billion. Of course, this is an easier and quicker way of entering the American market than by starting from scratch. It is also cheaper, thanks to the strength of the yen in relation to the dollar. But by the same token, the restructuring of Japanese sunset industries such as steel and shipbuilding has assumed urgency, and acquisitions and mergers offer a short cut to diversification.

Conclusion

It is difficult to estimate how much of the acquisition and merger activity worldwide is for the purpose of arresting the decline of these companies, and how much is to make a quick profit. But the fact that it is usually companies that are grossly undervalued on the stock exchange which attract raiders and the like, is an indication that something is wrong. Undervaluation is, of course, in relation to the potential of the company. This does mean that with the right strategy and sound management the company could probably do much better in the matter of realising its full potential. Unfortunately, the existing management hardly ever seems to wake up to the position and do something about it and to that extent acquisition, merger and takeover serve a valuable purpose if the new owner can diagnose the malady and provide the right remedy.

References

1. Kharbanda, O P and Stallworthy, E A *Company Rescue: How to Manage a Business Turnaround* Heinemann, 1987.
2. Peter, L J *Why things Go Wrong or the Peter Principle Revisited* George Allen & Unwin, 1985.
3. Samuelson, R J 'How companies grow stale' *Newsweek* 8 September 1986, p 45.
4. 'Fiddler on the mat' *Times of India* 2 August 1987.
5. 'American takeovers – judged against' *The Economist* **303**, 25 April 1987, pp 79-80.
6. Dickson, M 'The takeover battleground comes under close scrutiny' *Financial Times* 13 May 1987.
7. 'Acquisitions – Techniques for measuring strategic fit' *Long Range Planning* June 1987, pp 12-18.
8. 'Japanese managers – a better class of raider' *The Economist* **302**, 21 March 1987, p 82.

Indexes

Author Index

Abegglen, J C, 204
Ansoff, I, 56
Armstrong, L, 153

Batchelor, C, 128
Bates, S, 128
Becket, M, 128
Bernstein, A, 204
Berry, J F, 204
Betts, P, 154
Bibeault, D, 33
Blank, J P, 166
Boesky, I P, 139
Boone Pickens, T Jr, 56
Bradley, K, 166, 185
Brown, A C, 153

Cameron-Jones, C, 79
Campbell, A, 33
Cavanagh, R E, 13
Cavedon, J Sr, 43
Clark, M, 79, 128
Clifford, D K, 13
Cooke, S, 43
Copulsky, W, 56, 204

Daily, J E, 67, 94
Davidson, K M, 78
Dawkins, W, 166, 175
Debes, C, 153
DeMott, J S, 139
Dickson, M, 94, 210
Dobrzynski, J H, 94, 153
Dodsworth, T, 166
Drucker, P, 204
Dunne, N, 175

Ehrlich, E, 106
Ellis, E, 154
Elsner, A, 204
Ewing, D W, 185

Fisher, A B, 94
Fleet, K, 128
Fogg, J G III, 43

Foster, G, 195

Gelb, A, 166, 185
Geneen, H S, 195
Ginzberg, E, 12
Glaberson, W B, 139
Goldberg, W H, 56
Goldsmith, W, 43
Gorman, T, 165
Gould, M, 33
Green, M, 204
Greenwald, J, 79, 139
Gribben, R, 79, 128
Gunn, C E, 185
Gunn, Cathy, 128

Hall, W, 79, 107
Hawkins, C, 139
Hawthorn, A, 175
Hector, G, 106
Heller, R, 195
Hodgson, C, 94

Jamieson, W, 128
Jamison, D B, 56
Jensen, M, 56
Jensen, M C, 43
Johnson, M, 153
Johnston, M, 24, 33

Katzenberg, D, 43
Kharbanda, O P, 12, 13, 33, 78, 94, 128, 153, 166, 185, 204, 210
Kiam, V, 13, 43
Kibel, H R, 33
Kichen, S, 175
Kinhead, G, 139
Kraar, L, 153

Lambert, R, 128
Laurance, B, 43
Law, W A, 13, 24
Leinster, C, 106, 107
Leonard, C, 128
Levi, J, 128

Lithman, A, 128
Loomis, C J, 117
Lorenz, C, 33
Lowenstein, L, 166, 175
Lucking, A J, 56
Lueck, T J, 43

Main, J, 94
Marlow, H, 204
McDonald, H, 153, 154
Merrell, V D, 56
Merwin, J, 79
Michael, A, 107
Mills, G, 13
Moore, T, 67

Nordhoy, F, 67
Norman, J R, 106, 117, 139
Nulty, P, 117
Nussbaum, B, 67

Parkinson, C N, 33
Pauly, D, 139
Pearson, J, 154
Perry, L T, 56
Peter, L J, 210
Petre, P, 79
Pickens, T B, Jr, 24
Pinchot, Gifford III, 166
Pittel, L, 175
Platt, H D, 12
Porter, M G, 67, 94
Powell, W, 139
Preminger, H, 43
Price, C, 204

Raphael, A, 128
Rawsthorn, A, 175, 195
Richardson, M, 153
Riley, B, 139

Ritchie, B, 43
Rodgers, I, 153
Rosenbloom, A H, 43
Ross, I, 139
Rossant, J, 139, 154
Rowe, N, 33
Russell, G, 79

Sadler, P, 204
Samuelson, R J, 210
Sancton, T A, 166
Saul, R S, 43
Shaked, I, 107
Sherman, S P, 67, 117
Sitkin, S B, 56
Slatter, S, 33
Sloma, R S, 33
Stalk, G Jr, 204
Stallworthy, E A, 12, 13, 33, 78, 94, 128,
    153, 166, 185, 204, 210
Stancill, J M, 24

Taffler, R J, 24, 94
Thackray, J, 204
Treece, J B, 153
Tseung, M, 24
Tully, S, 94

Vamos, M N, 67
Van de Vliet, A, 67
Vojta, G, 12

Weiss, S, 204
Williams, C M, 13
Williams, M J, 139
Wilson, J W, 12, 24
Wood, L, 128, 195
Worthy, F S, 106

Ziegler, E, 204

Subject Index

acquisitions
  and UK government policy, 52
  reasons for failure, 31
  rules for success, 59
  the lessons from case studies, 93
  the need for synergy, 65
  the success rate, 190
advertisements, their use in takeover bids, 119-20
advertising
  acquisitions by UK companies in the US, 78
  use of graphs, 122
advertising industry, and the Saatchi brothers, 76
airline industry, its acquisitions and mergers, 75
Allied-Lyons
  sought by Elders IXL, 121
antitrust laws, effective in the USA, 71
arbitrageur
  definition, 129
  see also Boesky, Ivan
Argyll, seeks to takeover Distillers, 123-5
Atlantic Richfield, its acquisition of Anaconda, 83
Australia, and the raiders, 147-9
Avis, acquired eight times, 88-91

Babcock & Wilcox, acquired by McDermott, 88-9
bankers, their role in mergers and acquisitions, 106
banks
  their fees, 70
  their role in takeovers, 99
Banks, R, and acquisitions, 36
Beatrice, their acquisition of Esmark, 62-3
Berenzden, R
  comments on company growth, 67
Boesky, Ivan
  a profile, 136-7
  linked to Guinness takeover of Distillers, 126

British Airways, and the British Caledonian takeover, 75
Brittan, L, role in the Westland affair, 127
Broken Hill Proprietary, pursued by Holmes à Court, 147
BTR, the merger with Pilkington, 53
BTR Plc, takes over Dunlop Holdings, 85-7
bureaucracy, in management, 199
Business Roundtable (US), concern over takeovers, 105
buyouts, a common phenomenon, 158

Cain, G, and acquisitions in the chemical industry, 65
Capital City, acquires ABC, 61
Cavedon, J, and Cavedon Chemical Company, 38
chemical industry, and mergers, 64
Colgate Palmolive, takes over Helena Rubenstein, 66
companies
  arresting decline, 8
  family owned, and takeovers, 102
  growth, the dangers, 67
  options for resisting takeover, 98
  predicting decline, 5
  the medical analogy, 26
company culture, its importance, 202
company management
  strategies for survival, 28
  see also management
company reconstruction, as seen by Icahn, 133
company reports, role of, 20
company turnarounds, notable failures, 66
Compton Partners, taken over by Saatchi & Saatchi, 76
Connell, J, chairman of Distillers, 123
Conoco, consequences of DuPont takeover, 70
Cookson, growing by acquisition, 37
Corning Glass, acquires Tokina Optical Corporation, 146

216 Takeovers, Acquisitions and Mergers

Cuckney, Sir John, chairman of Westland, 127

Distillers, taken over by Guinness, 122-6
Dixons, attempted takeover of Woolworth, 74
Drucker, P
  importance of communication, 32
  on takeovers, 42
Dunlop Holdings
  taken over by BTR Plc, 85
  work of Sir Michael Edwardes, 86
Dupont
  its acquisition of Conoco, 64
  its takeover of Conoco, 69

education, its importance to management, 198
Edwardes, Sir Michael, and Dunlop Holdings, 86
Elders IXL, its pursuit of Allied-Lyons, 121
Elliott, J D, activities in Australia, 147
employee buyouts, a doubtful alternative, 176-85
entrepreneur, the, qualities for success, 11
Exxon, and Reliance Electric, 66, 82-3

family owned companies, US listing, 102
food industry, and mergers, 62
France
  and management buyouts, 169
  Bernard Tapie, a French entrepreneur, 159
  takeover activity, 149-51

Galbraith, J K, dangers of mergers, 106
GEC, proposed merger with Plessey, 52
General Electric (USA), new ventures, 14
General Motors, cooperating with the workers, 159-62
Getty Oil, the Texaco takeover, 109-17
golden parachute, definition, 105, 130
Goldsmith, Sir James
  activities in France, 150
  and Crown Zellerbach, 101
  profile, 138
greenmail, definition, 130

Grow Chemicals, growing by acquisition, 37
Guinness, the Distillers takeover, 122-6
Gulliver, J, chairman of Argyll, bids for Distillers, 122
Gunn, J, and his takeover of Exco, 74

Halpern, Sir Ralph, chief executive of Burton group, 35
Hanson, Lord James
  a profile, 138
  chairman of Hanson Trust Plc, 118
Hanson Trust, the fight for Imperial, 118-21
Heseltine, M, role in the Westland affair, 127
Holmes à Court, R, active in Australia, 147-9

Icahn, Carl
  and companies in decline, 10
  a profile, 133-5
Imperial Group, subject of a takeover battle, 119-21
Ind Coope Brewery, rescue plan, 162-5
intrapreneur, definition, 164
investment bankers, see bankers

Jacobs, I, a profile, 135-6
Japan
  an example in management, 196-9
  and takeovers, 140-7
John Lewis Partnership, example of employee participation, 184-5
junk bonders, definition, 131

Kiam, V, the rescue of Remington, 34
Kingsley, A D, Icahn's investment adviser, 133

Lee, Ming Tee, raids in Australia, 149
Liedtke, J H, his battle with Texaco, 109-17
Lipton, M, and takeover legislation, 42
listening, significance of, 32
LTV, acquires Lykes, 84

management
  buyouts, a feasible alternative, 167-75
  dangers of bureaucracy, 199
  funding, 172
  Japanese example, 196-9

Subject Index 217

personnel selection, 203
road to success, 201
the company culture, 202
value of competition, 200-1
McDermott, acquires Babcock & Wilcox, 88-9
Mellon National Corporation, and their bank acquisitions, 50
mergers
 and the media industry, 60
 a warning by J K Galbraith, 106
 definition of the megamerger, 68
 some rules for success, 80-2
 the debt problem, 73
 the motivation, 38
Mesa Petroleum Co, chaired by T Boone Pickens Jr, 131
Minebea, seeks takeover of Sankyo Saiki, 141
Mondragon Group, example of employee participation, 180-2
Monopolies and Mergers Commission, its policy, 52
monopoly regulations, and acquisitions and mergers, 48
Murdoch, Rupert, and media mergers, 61

new ventures, funding, 18

Pac-man defence, definition, 130
Pennzoil, its battle with Texaco, 109-17
Philip Morris
 and 7UP, 81
 its takeover of 7UP, 66
Phillips Petroleum, resists Icahn bid, 133
Pickens, T Boone Jr
 and companies in trouble, 10
 a profile, 131-3
 chairman Mesa Petroleum Co, 131
 credentials, 23
Pilkington, the merger with BTR, 53
Plessey, proposed merger with GEC, 52
poison pill, definition, 100, 130
Porter, M, his analysis of takeovers, 31
Puget Sound Plywood, worker-owned company, 179
Pullman, revitalised by acquisition, 88

raiders
 and the 'poison pill', 101
 size of company no deterrent, 100

ways to ward off, 104
Ramsden, TP, seeks takeovers in Japan, 141
Raymond, George Jr, brings in William R Weber, 104
Remington, rescued by Victor Kiam, 34
Roffs Print, a management buyout, 170-1

Saatchi & Saatchi, its meteoric progress, 76
Sankyo Saiki, Minebea seeks takeover, 141
Saunders, E, role in takeover of Distillers, 122-6
Schwartz, B, advice on acquisitions, 52
scorched earth policy, definition, 130
Seagram, run by the younger son, 104
shareholders, their role, 55
shark repellent, definition, 130
Shell, its acquisition of Billiton, 81
Shuwa Corporation, activities in the USA, 140
Sikorsky-Fiat, its deal with Westland, 126
Spain, the Mondragon Group, 180
steel industry, LTV acquires Lykes, 84
steel manufacture, the impact of mergers, 49
strategic planning, its role, 28
Sweden, and steel manufacture, 49

Takahashi, Takami, a hostile raider, 141
takeovers
 growing role of raiders, 100-1
 growth in size, 100
 hostile, 98
 Japanese style, 140-7
 proposals for reform, 42
 the hostile takeover justified, 40-2
 typical takeover battles, 30
Tapie, B, a French entrepreneur, 159
Tembec, Canada, an employee buyout, 178
Texaco, its battle with Pennzoil, 109-17
Tribune Co, acquires Los Angeles TV station, 61
Turrell, M, builds up his WPP Group, 77

Union Carbide, its defence against takeover, 64
United Biscuits, fights for Imperial, 118-21

United Kingdom, management buyouts, 171-3
United States, and management buyouts, 167
USX, was US Steel; its transformation, 68

venture capital
  for management buyouts, 172-3
  how much, 16

Wall Street, its role, 58
Westland, the Sikorsky-Fiat takeover, 126-7
white knight, definition, 130
Woolworth Holdings, fends off Dixon bid, 74
worker participation, at Ind Coope, 162-5

Yusawa Batteries (UK) Ltd, example of good management, 197